Psych and Philosophy

Popular Culture and Philosophy® Series Editor: George A. Reisch

For full details of all Popular Culture and Philosophy® books, visit www.opencourtbooks.com.

Popular Culture and Philosophy®

Psych and Philosophy

Some Dark Juju-Magumbo

Edited by

ROBERT ARP

OPEN COURT
Chicago

Volume 75 in the series, Popular Culture and Philosophy ®, edited by George A. Reisch

To order books from Open Court, call toll-free 1-800-815-2280, or visit our website at www.opencourtbooks.com.

Open Court Publishing Company is a division of Carus Publishing Company, dba ePals Media.

Copyright © 2013 by Carus Publishing Company, dba ePals Media.

First printing 2013

Printed and bound in the United States of America.

ISBN: 978-0-8126-9825-1

Library of Congress Control Number 201393090

Contents

This Is the Introduction . . . But I Knew that You Knew That Already

ROBERT ARP

I know what you're thinking. No, I'm not *psychic*—but I still know what you're thinking. Why mix *Psych* with philosophy? Well, first off, philosophers are always honing their "powers" of observation, inference, and deduction in the same way Henry Spencer helps Shawn do this with his obnoxious challenges and games at the beginning of every episode. In fact, these critical thinking skills are essential to the philosophical life, and philosophers—like any good thinker—have hunches and hypotheses that they test out to see if they're true or not. Unlike "Lassie" Lassiter, who's always skeptical of "Spencer's stupid hunches," philosophers welcome such splendidly speculative suppositions (you like my alliteration?).

A big difference between Shawn and your typical philosopher is that philosophers aren't (generally) charlatans! I don't understand how people can be so naive and downright stupid enough to believe in psychic abilities, or in any kind of paranormal BS. I lump ghosts, the afterlife, and gods in there, too. That stuff's all either magic, sleight of hand, smoke and mirrors, or wishful thinking. Since the dawn of humanity, clever people have been *abusing* powers of observation and deduction to get other not-so-clever people to believe something that's false or crazy, or act in horrible and heinous ways, or do their self-serving bidding. As the original *consigliere*, Niccolò Machiavelli (1469–1527), put it in his famous work, *The Prince* (1532):

Men are so simple and so ready to obey present necessities, that one who deceives will always find those who allow themselves to be deceived.

Another reason to mix *Psych* with philosophy is the fact that lots of episodes touch upon many of the basic areas of Western philosophy. In this book you'll see chapters dealing with logic, metaphysics, epistemology, ethics, political philosophy—even some feminism and ideas from that dead German philosopher who's famous for claiming that "God is dead," Friedrich Nietzsche (1844–1900).

One ethical issue that comes up in numerous *Psych* episodes is whether it's really immoral to lie. When you tell a typical lie, you intend to deceive someone else, usually so that you—the liar—can gain profit, pleasure, or advantage (or to avoid hassles, pain, or disadvantage) as a result of the lie and deception. The whole premise of *Psych* is that Shawn's psychic detective agency is built on the lie that he's really psychic, so that he can avoid having to go to jail. Here, Shawn's lying to avoid the hassles of having to explain and prove to the cops that he's just really observant.

But, you can also lie to someone to avoid a perceived negative, detrimental, or painful physical or psychological consequence—or to promote a perceived positive, healthy, or pleasurable consequence—*for the person to whom one is lying*. In other words, you can lie to them for their own good. For example, let's say Shawn's mother dies in a horrible accident and Henry witnessed it, and he literally knows "all of the gory details." And one day, a young seven-year-old Shawn asks his dad point blank, "Dad, I know you were there when mom died, can you tell me exactly what you saw?" No one would think Henry did anything wrong if he simply lied to seven-year-old Shawn by saying something like, "I honestly don't know, son, I blacked out . . ." or made up some other baloney story.

You can also lie to promote a positive, healthy, or pleasurable consequence *for the sake of a whole bunch of people*. So, if you lied to a terrorist by telling him that you'll let him go free if he reveals where he hid the bomb, and after he reveals where it's located, you still throw his arse in jail, hardly anyone would say, "Tsk, tsk . . . shame on you! How *dare* you lie to that terrorist?" Your lie just saved several lives, so most would say you were right to lie!

Given that Shawn's lies always seem to have the benefit of solving the case—and helping to save lives, bringing criminals to justice, restoring order, and other good things—they might not be such a bad thing, in the end. Still, it seems that Shawn could get the same positive results without telling lies, and there's a part of us that wishes he would just "come clean" and do his job as a talented detective, rather than as a lying hack.

I could go on and on explaining all of the various ways that *Psych* is a perfect match for philosophy, but I *still* know what you're thinking. Enough of this intro stuff! Let's get to it!

I

In Between the Lines

1
I've Heard It Both Ways

Nicolas Michaud

Shawn Spencer lies . . . a lot. For a man who solves crimes, he spends an awful lot of time deceiving law enforcement and, well, just about everyone else. For the most part, Shawn seems to enjoy his deceptions, and it almost seems as if coming to the truth of a crime is just part of the game. However, in Shawn's defense, some might argue that Shawn isn't so much lying as he is indulging in logical fallacy—misdirecting others with bad logic.

In other words, Shawn simply throws people off the trail and plays with logic to get what he wants. What he's doing isn't really deceptive, because he uses these irrelevancies of his in order to lead people to the truth instead of away from the truth.

Gus, Don't Be a Fallacy

The first thing we need to consider is what logical fallacies are, and in order to do that we need to understand what logic is. Most people assume that they have a pretty good grasp of logic. However, consider how easily Shawn is able to deceive those around him. He has no magical psychic abilities, and logic seems to demand that those around Shawn accept that fact, but many people are quite content to believe in Shawn's "powers."

It's a rare case indeed where someone takes the time to consider how Shawn manages to solve his crimes without magic—like the student at the school for the gifted who points out that Shawn may just be hyper-observant, and they need not assume that he is a psychic ("If You're So Smart, Then Why Are You

Dead?"). As a matter of fact there's a great deal of evidence against the existence of psychics, but many people are not willing to push hard enough on Shawn's lies to get to the truth. Most people may not be as logical as they think!

Logic is really just a way of describing reasoning. Not all logic is good logic. It really isn't that difficult to see that there are examples of bad logic. If Shawn were to tell us that a mummy walked out of a tomb and strangled a man to death, we would be a bit skeptical. Imagine that you asked Shawn why you should believe his outrageous claim. He would reply, "Because I'm psychic." When you think about it, that really isn't great reasoning. We probably shouldn't believe that claim—not without good evidence. But logic isn't just about the quality of the evidence; it's about *the way we use the evidence.*

The primary concern of logicians is *how* we use evidence to substantiate our claims. Good logic means that our evidence connects directly to our claims. And while it seems obvious that our evidence should connect to our claims; it isn't always easy to catch—hence the problem of logical fallacies. Consider an easy example: If I were to say that I know that the murderer was wearing black, and my *evidence* for it was, "Because the sky is blue and the grass is green," you would think I had given bad evidence to my claim. Consider, however, the fact that "The sky is blue and the grass is green," is *true* (at least, it usually is).

So is the problem that my evidence was bad? Not really; the problem with my argument isn't the falsity of my evidence, but that *the evidence doesn't connect to the conclusion.* In other words not only should my evidence be true, . . . it must also be directly connected to my conclusion!

Consider another example about the connection of evidence to conclusions. Imagine I make the following argument:

1. If Shawn and Gus see a ghost, they will run away

2. Shawn and Gus are running away

3. Therefore, Shawn and Gus have seen a ghost

Take a look at the argument for a moment. Can you see where the problem is? Can we conclude, from the argument above, that, *if Shawn and Gus are running they must have seen a ghost*? No! There is nothing in that argument that tells us that they can only run away from a ghost. All we know from the argument is that *IF* Shawn and Gus see a ghost they will run, but there is nothing about *IF* they are running! They could have been running for many reasons—from murderers, mummies, or Shawn's father!

Notice that, once again, all of the evidence in an argument can be true, yet the conclusion can be false! That is a very powerful realization—it is possible to have an argument with all true evidence and yet the conclusion can be completely false! So you might think to yourself, "Yeah, but even Lassiter could find those flaws," but with some bad logic—some logical fallacies—it gets a little more tricky. Logical fallacies often *seem* like good reasoning, when in fact they are really poor reasoning.

Gus, Don't Be an Ad Hominem

So, to understand what it is that Shawn does that is a logical fallacy, we now need to consider one of the most common fallacy types—fallacies of relevance. Fallacies of relevance are cases in which the conclusion seems to connect to the evidence when, in fact, it does not. Shawn loves to use fallacies of relevance, and really his whole Psych career is based on a fallacy of relevance called "The Red Herring." We will consider Shawn's Red Herring in a bit. Let's first consider an even more obvious—and beloved by Shawn—fallacy of relevance, the Ad Hominem.

An *Ad Hominem* (translated "to the man") is a fallacy in which we attack the person instead of the claim that the person makes. Lassiter is a favorite victim of Shawn's Ad Hominem. Lassiter, especially early on in the series, would attempt to point out that Shawn is a fraud and, generally, Shawn refused to even engage Lassiter's claims. He would simply call Lassiter a name of some kind or make fun of some neurotic quality of his, and move on. Lassiter is often taken aback and dumbfounded by these comments, and before he can recover, Shawn has already moved on. When we think about it, though, we realize that Shawn has never really addressed Lassiter's claim—he has avoided it by making fun of "Lassie."

Most of us engage in Ad Hominem often. Politicians are especially fond of Ad Hominem—Why answer a question when you can simply attack your opponent, instead? Think of the criminals caught by Shawn: how do they generally respond when accused of their crimes? In many cases, they respond to the charges with an insult of some kind that doesn't answer Shawn's powerful (though usually florid and overly dramatic) accusation. Calling someone a name instead of addressing his or her point prevents us from getting to the truth of the matter. An Ad Hominem may not even be a case of a name calling; when we attack someone's motive, character, or fashion sense, instead of answering their question or addressing their conclusions, we engage in bad logic—we have introduced something irrelevant into the case.

Gus, Don't Be a Red Herring

When it comes to introducing an irrelevancy into an argument, Shawn is the king. And now that we have a better understanding of how important relevance is to logic, we can consider Shawn's own biggest fallacy—his Red Herring.

A Red Herring can be thought of as a distraction from the argument at hand. Shawn knows that he will get into trouble if he tries to stick with the truth because his talent for solving crimes can get him in trouble: it seems like he knows too much for an ordinary citizen. So, when the show first begins, he must come up with a lie that will convince others that he is not, in fact, a criminal himself. So he tells the police that he's psychic. Notice, though, this isn't just a lie. This claim of Shawn's is a distraction; it leads people away from the truth specifically in order to avoid having to deal with it.

The term "Red Herring" originates from foxhunting. Back in the day it was often too easy for the hunting dogs to catch the fox's scent and then follow its trail. So in order to make the hunt last longer, the hunters would have someone drag a dead fish, a red herring, on the ground to distract the hounds, and so the hunt would be more interesting and go on longer. We can see now how this relates to logic: when we introduce an irrelevancy or a deception into an argument in order to distract people, we're using a metaphorical dead fish to lead them off the scent.

Politicians are very adept at this kind of fallacy. When someone asks them questions to which they don't know the answers or don't want to give the answers, they will often reply with something like, "The American people will know what to think about that. I respect the intelligence of the American people!" As a result, the audiences will often stand up, clap and cheer, because they agree with the sentiment, and what they never notice is that the politicians haven't answered the questions about war, or policy, or their shady pasts.

Gus, Don't Be a Hypocrates!

Shawn uses a pretty huge Red Herring to avoid being arrested. By pretending to be psychic the hounds are thrown off his scent. While the cops and press are amazed, astounded, and intrigued by Shawn's psychic powers, he is able to go about solving crimes under their radar using old-fashioned logic and observation. So there's a real irony in Shawn's career: he uses logic and observation to connect the dots to solve crimes, but in order to do so he must distract others with bad logic! So, we can't help wondering, "Is Shawn doing what's right or is he doing wrong?" Is it okay for Shawn to use bad logic to accomplish his aims?

At first, it's hard to justify Shawn's actions outside of selfishness. He uses his Red Herring largely to keep himself out of trouble and because it's fun! Neither his father nor Gus trust Shawn because they believe that Shawn's unlikely to really work on something diligently and is likely just playing a game at the police's expense. But, as time goes on, Shawn comes to really love his work and the good that he does. And, so, the question of whether or not Shawn's use of bad logic is right becomes a bit more complex.

What are some of the arguments against bad logic? One philosopher who immediately comes to mind is Socrates (around 469–399 B.C.E.). Socrates's student Plato wrote a whole lot about Socrates and paints a picture of a man who was very concerned about bad reasoning and the misuse of logic. Socrates lived at a time when philosophy and logic were being used as a means by which people could gain power and prestige. Rhetoricians called "Sophists" who had training in argumentation and persuasion could be convinced to argue any side of a case, and train anyone in argumentation, for the right sum of money.

Socrates, though, was very disturbed by these Sophists. He was a big believer in the Truth with a capital T. Socrates thought that we should all seek the truth as the highest end, and that seeking—what we now consider philosophy—would lead to wisdom, beauty, and justice. Socrates has little patience with the use of a fallacy that we call "inconsistency," and it is for this reason that I think he wouldn't approve of Shawn's "harmless" deceptions. In fact, Socrates made a career out of finding and exposing the inconsistencies of people like Shawn.

An inconsistency is a case wherein our beliefs or actions contradict each other—it's a way of proving our own beliefs wrong. In other words, we're inconsistent when we say we believe in one thing, yet act in the opposite way. Inconsistencies can be very dangerous. Think of cases like Thomas Jefferson who wrote about slavery being wrong, and, yet, never freed his own slaves because it would cost him too much money. Shawn is similarly inconsistent; he seems to love coming to the truth, and finding out what really is the case (he himself would not want to be deceived; his observational skills, and the way he uses them, indicate that he has a keen eye and taste for what is true), however, Shawn is willing to deceive others in order to convenience and amuse himself.

In a very famous dialogue written by Plato, called the *Crito*, we see Socrates tempted by an inconsistency not so dissimilar from Shawn's. Socrates is condemned to death by the judicial system (largely for telling people the truth, which they *really* don't want to hear) and is offered the chance of escape by his friend Crito. Crito tells Socrates that he can bribe the guards—a common practice in Athens at the time—and Socrates can escape before justice is served. Socrates refuses, though. He argues that he would be inconsistent and do justice itself a disservice.

We must be consistent even when it's inconvenient, argues Socrates. He doesn't want to be the person who tells *everyone else* that they should seek the truth and be consistent, and then himself break the law and use bribery to save his own life. And, so, Socrates is willing to sacrifice his life to preserve the truth. Shawn, on the other hand, seems to take great pleasure in misdirecting the police. Could Socrates be right? Could Shawn actually be helping to make the world a worse place through his deceptions?

Gus, Don't Be One of Those Little Flies that Buzzes Around Your Head and No Matter How Much You Swat at It You Can Never Get Rid of It and Eventually You Just Give Up and Run Away

In Shawn's defense, there is good reason to think that his deceptions really aren't that bad. The best argument in his favor is that by stopping murderers, he is likely saving lives. Yes, perhaps he is deceiving the police, the press, and the public at large, but how many people are saved through his actions? So what if he enjoys it too and makes a living of it?— That's irrelevant. What matters is that Shawn is helping to clean the streets and save lives, and bring justice to others through his actions.

And we really should be as fair to Shawn as we can. He is selfish, childish, and thoughtless. But he also cares about people and wants to help them. Shawn is far more likely to take a case when someone desperately needs his help, money aside. Yes, we have seen Shawn clearly use his observational gifts to benefit himself, but it can't reasonably be argued that he shouldn't also benefit from helping others. Generally, it's a good thing when helping others also benefits us—it makes us more likely to do it again, not to mention that it raises the total amount of happiness in the world, for everyone!

But I don't want to move past Socrates's point too quickly. Granted, if we give Shawn the benefit of the doubt, he is doing real good, and only at the expense of a small evil. Let's imagine, though, a Platonic-style dialogue between Shawn and Socrates. Can Shawn really get out of his own inconsistency?

> *Shawn and Gus enter their Psych office; it is dimly lit. There is a woman lying dead on the ground clothed in white. Standing over her is a grizzly-looking, ugly old man with a beard. He has a pug face, red-rimmed eyes, and is clearly distraught.*

SHAWN: Okay, I'm impressed, Gus. I never thought you'd manage a surprise party without me psychically fortelling it.

GUS: You're not psychic, Shawn.

SHAWN: So who's Doc Brown over there? [*points at Socrates*]

Socrates: I am Socrates. I do not know this Doc Brown, of whom you speak.

Shawn: Really? Old guy, white hair . . . from the future?

Gus: The past. And Doc Brown didn't have a beard, Shawn.

Shawn: I've heard it both ways.

Socrates: [*Points sadly at the corpse*] Look what you've done.

Shawn and Gus look down at the body.

Shawn: [*Points back towards Gus with his thumb*] I'm sensing he did it. I'm Shawn Spenser, psychic with the SBPD, and this is my assistant, Sophie Magilicutty.

Socrates: You've killed Truth!

Shawn: [*Scans the room*] No I didn't. I wasn't here. Not to mention that there are no abrasions on her or any sign of struggle. I've never seen her before. Looking at her, I'd say she is more into the aging rocker kind of a guy than me, anyway.

Socrates: You killed her through your deception.

Shawn: What do you mean?

Socrates: Why is it that you claim to be a Psychic?

Shawn: Well mostly for the free mints at the police station, but also because it helps people.

Socrates: And how does deceiving them, help them?

Shawn: I solve crimes, using my psychic powers.

Gus: You aren't psychic.

Socrates: You aren't psychic, Shawn. You are deceiving hundreds of people, maybe thousands. What reason can you give that lying to them like this is right?

Shawn: Well, because it benefits them. I help solve crimes and catch murderers, and it does no harm.

Socrates: Would you say that you help bring criminals to justice?

Shawn: Exactly! Now that we are done, who wants a Toblerone?

Gus: Really, Shawn? There's a body here: we should do something about her!

Shawn: Why? She's not going to want a Toblerone; she's dead. Don't be silly, Gus!

Socrates: You are avoiding the question, Shawn. Why do you bring criminals to justice? Not all of them are cases in which they would kill again. Some of them are even cases in which the criminal is already dead. . . . Why do you still solve them?

Shawn: It doesn't matter if everyone in the case is already dead. We all want to know the truth.

Socrates: Why do we want to know the truth?

Shawn: Well, in this case, because it helps save lives.

Socrates: And in the cases in which no life is in danger?

Shawn: I don't know. I suppose just because I want to know what really happened. I'm good at finding the truth. It's a gift, really, . . . almost a curse.

Socrates: And you don't think those people trusting you with their jobs and lives deserve to know what really happens when you solve a crime?

Shawn: My lies are fun and harmless! At worst, they make me mysterious and alluring.

Socrates: But wouldn't you agree that you don't want to be lied to?

Shawn: Well that depends on the lie. If it's about my father's date last night, please do lie.

Gus: [*looks nauseous*]

Socrates: Wouldn't you agree that lying causes more lying?

Shawn: Well yes, often a criminal will have to lie more to cover up his other lies.

Gus: Sounds like someone I know. . . .

Shawn: Not now, Sophia!

SOCRATES: And is it bad if there are more and more lies in the world?

SHAWN: Possibly.

SOCRATES: Why?

SHAWN: Lies sometimes . . . may . . . in some cases, do harm.

SOCRATES: So you agree that the point of your job is to help save people from harm, and you agree that harm is a bad thing. You also agree that lying often causes harm, and that lying often causes more lying. So then you have to agree that by lying, you yourself are helping to create a world in which there is more lying, and, therefore, at least more potential for harm. Through your hypocrisy you have killed this poor woman here on the floor . . . her name is Truth!

SHAWN: Maybe. [*Observes the lipstick on Socrates's collar, and the redness of Socrates's eyes and touches his own temple with two fingers*] And I can see that you have been having an affair with the Truth for many years, Socrates! Shame on you! You are a married man!

While Socrates, caught, stumbles for a retort, Shawn and Gus quickly exit the office. . . . Shawn never has to face Socrates's accusation.

Gus, Don't Be a Conclusion

Shawn's use of fallacies is largely just amusing. He seems to do little, if any, harm when he uses them. In fact, he seems to do a whole lot of good. The fact is also, though, that Shawn never really has to answer a question. And there's something that Shawn is always going to have trouble with, . . . trust. As Socrates pointed out, there are people who are trusting Shawn with their careers and lives, and it's awfully hard to trust someone who lies.

Looking at the problem of using bad logic to help people, we can now see the two sides of the argument. On the one hand, Shawn is helping people, but on the other, he is deceiving them. The real question is: Does the deception really do harm? I can see at least four general ways that deceiving people with bad logic will do harm:

1. It helps reinforce people's bad logic, thereby reducing the chance that they will be able to come to the truth without our help.

2. They are more likely to be easily deceived in the future by others with less harmless motives.

3. They won't understand *why* something is the truth.

4. The deception helps increase the overall level of poor reasoning in the world.

More specifically, when Shawn uses bad logic:

1. He helps reinforce his co-workers' and clients' own ignorance of logic, reducing the chance that they will use good crime-fighting techniques themselves, and thereby making them more dependent on him.

2. He makes it so that they now believe they have good evidence that psychics really do exist and now they will be more willing to believe other "psychics" who may be con-artists and criminals!

3. Those who observe his techniques won't benefit from learning the real ways the crimes are solved, and therefore won't benefit from learning his techniques.

4. As his success hits the newspapers, more and more people in the world will believe that crimes should be solved by psychics rather than by hard-working detectives who keep their noses to the ground and their eyes peeled!

So I'll leave the verdict to you. Is Shawn just being cheeky and cute, helping make the world better?

Or is he really just helping make it easier for criminals to get away with deception in the long run?

I've heard it both ways.[1]

---

[1] I would like to dedicate this chapter to my grandmother, Nelkis Cobas. Keep writing, Grandma!

2
What's the Story?

MICHAEL J. MUNIZ

Imagine being confined in a room in which all four walls, the floor, and the ceiling are completely sealed. There is no way in, nor a way out. And, to top it all off, it's pitch black. This could be a rather frightening reality for most people, if not all. Of course, this reality is highly unlikely as it raises a series of very important metaphysical questions such as: How did I get here? Who built this room? Will I ever be able to get out? Why am I here? Where's the TV remote? Did I miss *Psych*?

Perhaps these last two questions might give some clue as to where I'm going with this. The dark room of reality isn't so unreal as we sit in front of our TVs. Consider the ideal environment: you're sitting alone (or between friends and family) on your comfortable living-room couch. The lights are off while a floor and a ceiling surround you. Although you know how you got there, the truth is you don't know what's going to happen next. When the bright light of the TV begins displaying images of a young boy and his police officer of a father, in color (no this isn't *The Andy Griffith Show* circa 1965), you're experiencing the illumination of the fourth wall.

Typically, the fourth wall is a term mostly associated with theater, or other live performance shows. It's where stage performers pretend the audience doesn't exist. However, the breaking of the fourth wall is when those performers become aware of the audience and include them into the performed story. Thus, this begs the question: is it possible for TV characters to break the fourth wall and interact with us, the viewers?

When Shawn and Gus are snooping around the office of wildlife television host, Randy Labayda, in the Season Three episode "Six Feet Under the Sea" you can see that the "window" is nothing more than a thick pane of glass separating the office from several dolphins swimming in a large aquarium. Soon after, Gus is seen in the background waving and speaking to the dolphins as if they could actually hear him or as if Gus had the super power to actually communicate with the graceful sea mammals. Perhaps if the dolphins were given lines to talk back to Gus, then the scene would be a bit more interesting.

Given our circumstances and our reality, how are we different from Gus trying to talk to the dolphins? Haven't we sat at the edge of our seat in our living rooms, yelling at the screen to tell the character in peril to "Get out" or "Don't go upstairs"? Perhaps there's a slight chance that they might hear us . . . or at least we hope they do.

The makers of most sitcoms try to incorporate the breaking of the fourth wall by allowing the laughter of a live studio audience to be heard throughout each episode. The issue of whether or not *Psych* is a sitcom isn't important. However there are a lot of moments, in each episode, where the characters seem to pause after some sort of comedic action, to allow us to laugh or chuckle without missing the actions that follow it. Is it me, or is it possible that Shawn, Gus, and the other characters are aware of their comedic effect and that they pause to allow some outside viewer to laugh at them (or with them), even though there is no sound of a laughing studio audience? If so, this would mean that they know that I exist and they're actually acknowledging my presence.

Unfortunately, (or fortunately . . . it depends on how you look at it) the level of obscurity that separates our reality from that of *Psych* is so much that there is no way this could actually occur. But what if it were true? How could it be done? Perhaps we need to look at how the stories (the episodes) are told.

Fake Philosopher or Real Narratologist

If Shawn and Gus can have an office in Santa Barbara that provides the services of Psychic Detectives, then why can't there be a place (like Hialeah, Florida) where someone can provide the services of Narrative Investigator? The cheesy slogan would read: "Having problems with a story? Then I'm your guy!"

Perhaps this service may not ever exist, but the reality is that narratologists do exist. Think of a narratologist as a philosopher of stories. He'll sit back on his big comfy couch and study how a story is told—as opposed what the story is telling. Every story has small connecting elements that make up the whole. The fun part is when they examine why every element is so important.

Narratologists aren't there to explain symbolism or uncover hidden meanings. That's for underpaid high-school English teachers. Narratologists reveal the structure—the form—of the story and explain how it works.

The purpose of all fictional stories, no matter how serious or lighthearted, is to entertain. Whether that entertainment includes a moral message or some hidden agenda is not the issue. The way the story is structured determines its effect. So, if a *Psych* episode is structured poorly, then the episode won't be as entertaining as those that were structured properly. For *Psych* to have the appeal that it does, it's inclined to meet audience expectations by having particular plot elements present in every episode.

Every episode of *Psych* has one or more of the following plot elements:

A. A prologue (opening sequence) usually set in the 1980s featuring a young Shawn and his father giving a clue as to what the theme of the episode might be.

B. An instance where Shawn gives either himself or Gus a funny pseudonym to disguise their real identities.

C. A pineapple (though not necessarily a plot element, it's a recurring visual element).

D. Shawn and Lassie disputing over details in a case, usually resulting in some insult where Lassie resigns to Shawn's level of maturity.

E. Gus providing a random piece of information that the average person may not know (usually involving pharmaceuticals).

F. Shawn performing a fake spiritual possession that reveals clues about the case in front of the Chief, Jules, and/or Lassie.

G. Shawn and Gus solving the case.

All of the above elements don't necessarily make up the show *Psych*. They are all secondary. That's why you'll never see all of them at once in every single episode. However, there is one necessary element that I didn't put on the above list. What is the one element to every episode that if it were not there, *Psych* itself would absolutely fail?

X Marks the Spot

If I were to add seventeen more elements to the above list, and save the most important for last, then letter X would be Shawn's hypersensitive photographic memory—his eidetic memory. His ability to see and remember the tiniest details is essential for both the plot and function of the whole series. It's also pretty cool! I think our memories would be more than just all right if we all had this special gift. Then you could say, "you're an adult disguising himself as a teenager" from twenty feet away, just like the episode "If You're So Smart, then Why Are You Dead?" from Season Two. Or you could see all of the blemishes and disturbing marks or dirt on everyone's faces, including your own. Now, that just sounds wrong.

Like Shawn, I digress. I'm not here to provide a medical or scientific explanation of what eidetic memory is or how it could be used in real life. However, I would like to show how it's important for the *Psych* series. But if it gets too confusing, just wait till the end, this mystery will get solved.

Have you noticed how Shawn's eidetic memory sequences are presented? It usually involves a close up shot of Shawn's face, first. His eyebrow raises and eyes squint. Then, it cuts to an extreme close up shot of some specific object that the average eye would not be capable of spotting. Depending on the reasons why this object is important, it is usually shown in some pale coloring (black and white, sepia, or some other faded colors). Then, specific elements of the object itself are highlighted rather quickly. A slight chime-like sound can be heard every time something is highlighted. Afterwards, Shawn will usually bounce his head around to indicate that he has thought of something.

The above sequence is mandatory for *Psych* to be properly functioning. Shawn must focus for brief moments, observe, and deduce. He must do the same thing every single time, though it never bores us, does it? In fact, it's quite likely that we sit and wait for these eidetic memory sequences to take place, to see what Shawn sees, to be able to experience what Shawn experiences, to focus on the details, to make some bizarre explanation, to show Lassie that Shawn gets it right in the end every damn time!

Doodles Are the Window to the Soul

In the episode "65 Million Years Off," Shawn and Gus are inside the shed of a paleontologist who's been trying to dig up a large collection of dinosaur bones. Inside the shed, Gus points out that there's nothing but a bunch of drawings and doodles. Shawn picks up what looks like the world's worst tic-tac-toe board and says: "Doodles are the window to the soul."

X			X		X
			X	X	
		O		X	X
X			X		X
	X	X		X	

Taking Shawn's point to a more philosophical level, watch how the following doodle shows the structure of *Psych*. Not including the show's theme song.

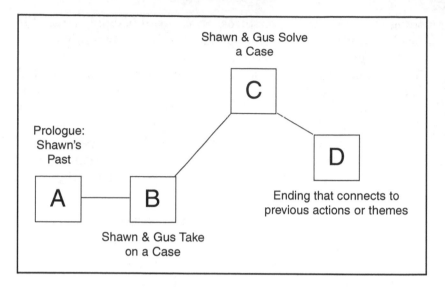

If there's any change with the above doodle, then the show's structure changes. The majority of a typical episode occurs between B and C. This area is called the conflict, or rising action. Typically, this is where you'd experience a majority of the humor with some minor eidetic memory sequences. However, at section C is where we get the most important eidetic memory sequence that allows Shawn to make a deduction that ultimately solves the case. The shortest time in every episode is the section between C and D. This is called the falling action, or denouement, and is usually about a minute or so long.

Although this might seem rather elementary, there is a reason why the story is structured this way. Storytellers need to form their stories in a way that allows for the audience to experience it properly. However, we need to understand, just like a narratologist would, that it is not the story that matters: it's the storyteller, or how the story's told.

Here's another example: we all know the story of the *Three Little Pigs*. Without changing the basic idea of the *Three Little Pigs*, ask yourself: what would happen if Stephen King or Alfred Hitchcock told that story? Or what would happen if the makers of *Glee* told it? We would get an entirely new experience with the same story! Therefore, we should consider the storytellers and their structuring of the stories whenever we're about to experience it.

So what does this have to do with *Psych*? Haven't you noticed that the whole of *Psych* is nothing more than a re-telling of old Sherlock Holmes mysteries? Shawn and Gus are alternate forms of Holmes and Watson. I won't get into the details; I'll let you run with it.

The Climax of This Chapter

What if I told you that this whole chapter is written in the same format as a typical *Psych* episode? No, this isn't a fictional story, but there is a prologue: the section on the dark room; the rising action: the previous three sections; and now the climax. Afterwards, I'll bring this chapter to a close. When you sit and watch a *Psych* episode, or any other TV show, or movie, consider the storyteller (who made the show) and why they made it that way.

Well, for *Psych*, the storytellers wanted to include you in the story. They don't have to acknowledge this statement as a fact. They may even deny it. However, the truth is that in every episode we get to become Shawn and see the world through his eyes, literally.

Remember that part on the breaking of the fourth wall? Well, every time that Shawn has an eidetic memory sequence, it's at that precise moment that we become Shawn. We literally see what he sees. Hopefully, we're able to draw the same conclusions that he does. However, there is a downside: you can't actually stay as Shawn, nor exist in the fictional reality. However exciting or boring your life might be, you can never exist in the world of *Psych*. That's like diving into the aquarium and swimming with dolphins as a dolphin. Maybe, as we crawl into our beds and dream about it, we can get closer to that reality, but then there is still that part of waking up. So was the wall ever broken?

What we've been experiencing throughout the forty-two-plus-minute episodes (not including commercials) is called *projective illusion of cinematic image*. There are three other kinds of illusions (Reproductive, Müller-Lyer, and Trompe l'Oeil), but they aren't relevant to the show. According to the above doodle, we're only watching what the show projects: X marks the spot. The show actually psychs us into believing that we're a part of it. In other words, the illusion of *Psych*'s reality is so good, that we believe we're there, or that it is here.

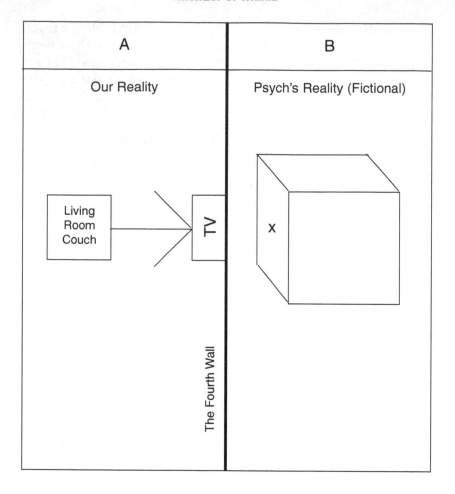

Psyched Out

The mystery is now solved. The fourth wall was never broken. It only feels like it's broken, but it never really is. Like I said before, the only proper instance of the wall being broken is if it were a live setting. The structure of *Psych*, as designed by the narratologist, is also its function, which means that you're supposed be psyched out in the end, just like the show's theme song says.

Have you noticed that I've been writing directly to you, the reader? Does that mean that I've been breaking the fourth wall? Perhaps you should use your inner narratological skills and determine if I have deceived you into thinking that I've been talking directly to you.

That voice in your head that you hear when you read this chapter could actually be mine! That conscious experience (or awareness) that is occurring right now is like you swimming with the dolphins. By allowing it to happen means that you gave in to the structure and function of this paper . . . the same way you give in to *Psych*. Hopefully, you'll be a bit sharper now, as well as narratologically stronger, to be aware of what it is you're watching or reading.

3
Why Phsysics Beats Science

Cynthia Jones

Like his fictional detective predecessors (for example, Sherlock Holmes, Hercule Poirot, Adrian Monk), Shawn Spencer has several skills that allow him to solve cases that baffle the police. Most notably, he discerns significant, albeit seemingly minor details, he has really good inductive skills, and he has a really good memory for minute details.

Shawn notices numerous details that most people either don't perceive or don't process. This is hypersensory perception, or HSP for short. For example, he notices cat fur on shoes, fine print on ID badges, how a body is positioned and whether it fits with nearby blood spatter, and relevant addresses or phone numbers from a long list.

HSP is a key component that allows Shawn to pass as psychic. His perception of mundane details that go unnoticed by most observers is the first key step in his pseudo-psychic talent. The second step is a version of induction known as inference to the best explanation (or IBE, for short). When he draws conclusions while utilizing the typically unnoticed mundane details as evidence, he is using IBE.

Shawn constantly employs IBE to draw conclusions about whether someone was actually murdered or to figure out who committed a crime or to infer how a crime was committed. (And sometimes, his use of IBE does not work in his favor, like when he figures out from the clues that the boyfriend of the pretty woman who just picked him up in a store was planning to propose to her, rather than cheating on her, as she had assumed ("From the Earth to the Starbucks").

Shawn often doesn't bother to read case files, nor does he always notice some of the most obvious clues, and he even sometimes lacks the basic knowledge of a subject that is necessary to solve a mystery, but then he has Gus, Juliet, and his dad for those things. And sometimes, a priest who knows Latin is needed as well ("Dual Spires").

HSP Versus ESP

Besides his wonderful hair, one of the other great things about Shawn is his savant-like ability to detect and process minute details of crime scenes, his surroundings, and other people's appearances.

At the same time, however, Shawn holds mistaken beliefs about tons of things the average person knows without much thought, like simple geography, the meanings of fairly common words, and sometimes what year it is. Fortunately for Shawn, his best friend Gus is always there to support him and fill in the details (despite Gus's aversion to blood, gore, and dead bodies, along with his belief in pretty much all things supernatural). Gus has a superior vocabulary as well as an amazing amount of knowledge on a variety of different topics, from comic books to paleontology to the spelling bee. And Henry Spencer is also invaluable to Shawn's amazing "psychic" sleuthing as Henry maintains connections to the "normal" crime-fighting circles and resources and possesses an uncanny ability to point Shawn in the right direction with a little advice.

But what is HSP, you might ask, and how can you get it? HSP is not a paranormal or supernatural ability like ESP (extra-sensory perception). Instead, an individual with HSP is utilizing the same perceptive faculties as the rest of us: he or she is just really good at it. There's some question regarding the source of HSP and whether you're born with it or whether it's learned. Like many abilities, it's likely a combination of both nature and nurture. Think of a world-class athlete for comparison. Those who win Olympic medals were likely born with some natural talent for their sport, but probably could not be at the top of their field without lots of practice. Henry Spencer obviously spent countless hours "training up" Shawn to hone his perceptive abilities, but Shawn was probably born with some innate talent for noticing details as well.

It's important that HSP, unlike ESP, doesn't involve some sixth sense or perceptive ability beyond the explanation of the natural sciences. Just as some people have better hearing or better eyesight than the average person, Shawn has superior perceptive abilities. And these abilities can be explained by science. ESP, on the other hand, requires postulating abilities that lie outside of scientific explanation, hence the designation as "supernatural" (beyond the natural world or unearthly) or "paranormal" (beyond the explanations of the natural world that we get from science).

Research from cognitive psychology suggests that very subtle clues can be perceived by many people without their even realizing they are perceiving the clues. This human ability to perceive behavioral cues from people looks like "intuition" or something beyond scientific explanation, but really is just our ability to notice cues without knowing that we notice these cues. Things that we perceive but don't realize we perceive are often written off as intuition. Even Shawn encourages Lassiter to "follow his guts" in the Season Four episode "The Head, the Tail, the Whole Damn Episode" after Lassiter notices what seems to be a knife wound and jumps to the crazy-sounding conclusion that a shark attack victim was actually murdered. But really Shawn is encouraging Lassiter to notice the easy-to-overlook details that might not fit well with the other clues.

Psychologists have demonstrated that experimenters can sway experimental subjects, judges can sway jurors, and teachers can sway students by nonverbal cues, often without either party knowing what's happening. This is a phenomenon beyond asking leading questions or inflicting bias consciously and, as mentioned, typically involves nonverbal signaling. There are even examples from the animal kingdom, like the case of "Clever Hans," a really perceptive horse who was believed to possess amazing intellectual ability (for a horse) like the ability to spell and do math. While Clever Hans was certainly a very gifted animal, as it turned out, his talents were in perceiving cues from the people asking the questions and not from great intellectual abilities.

Human examples can also be found, such as Ilga Kirks, a mentally-challenged Latvian girl who was believed to have telepathic powers. As it turned out, she did have amazing abilities, but her abilities were in detecting subvocal cues and reading lips. Both Ilga and Clever Hans are examples of HSP.

And so HSP is a rather remarkable ability, but unlike ESP or psychic abilities, it is not beyond scientific explanation or based upon supernatural abilities. And many of us probably have a little bit of ability in this area, if cognitive psychologists are correct, but we just aren't psychic enough to realize it.

IBE . . . not IBS!

When you have eliminated all which is impossible, then whatever remains, however improbable, must be the truth.

—SHERLOCK HOLMES, "The Adventure of the Blanched Soldier"

Variations of this oft-quoted line from Sir Arthur Conan Doyle's famous detective appear in numerous Sherlock Holmes stories. Sherlock Holmes might seem rather different from Shawn Spencer (Shawn isn't a cocaine addict, for example) but they employ similar tactics. And contrary to the claim made by Holmes when he says he employs "deduction," he's actually using a method of *induction*, or what some have called *abduction*, and what we are labeling *inference to the best explanation*, to draw his conclusions. In fitting with Holmes's claim that his methods are "elementary," it's indeed the case that IBE is a common way humans reason, even though some people (Shawn and Sherlock) are much better at it than others.

IBE is amazingly simple and, like HSP, many people have some ability in this area, even if they've never heard of it. IBE involves choosing the hypothesis that best fits the evidence and offers the greatest explanatory power and scope. Most of us employ IBE on a regular basis, although we are likely not aware we are doing it. Let's look at a few examples.

When my son believes that a winged supernatural creature has taken his tooth and replaced it with cash, he isn't employing IBE (because he's twelve and he should know better.) When I speculate that the cause of my dog barking at the front door is that he hears or smells something I don't, I am employing IBE. When my neighbor assumes that local hoodlums have trampled her garden gnome in a fit of destructive mischief, even though there is a dirt and grass trail running from her lawn to my car, she isn't employing IBE. When Lassiter claims that a body that just washed up from the ocean was the result of a boating accident and a whale maiming, he is not employing IBE ("Sixty Five Million Years Off").

Believe it or not, Lassiter's pretty darned good at IBE, as any decent detective must be. He just often lacks the extra information that Shawn gets from HSP and so he frequently draws the wrong conclusions or chooses the wrong hypothesis from lack of information. However, when Shawn tells Chief Vick that an apparent suicide is really a murder because he noticed relevant evidence that the police didn't, he *is* employing IBE ("9 Lives").

Using IBE correctly and effectively requires that we have as much evidence as we can reasonably gather (HSP comes in handy for Shawn here) and that we pick the explanation that best explains this evidence. When choosing the best explanation for a given phenomenon or for a given set of evidence, the best explanation is the one that not only best explains said evidence, but also fits with other accepted explanations, offers the most explanatory value in general, and, often times, is the simplest.

This last criterion is a version of what is known as "Occam's Razor" which states roughly "other things being equal, the simplest explanation is usually preferable." It might not seem that Shawn uses this criterion, for example, when he claims a dinosaur was the cause of death of a John Doe who washed up on the shore ("Sixty-Five Million Years Off"), but given the available evidence, sometimes a seemingly crazy-sounding hypothesis, like a mummy got up and walked out of a museum ("Shawn [and Gus] of the Dead") is the best and simplest explanation.

So we know that Shawn is pretty good at IBE, but how can IBE be used to determine the best hypothesis for explaining Shawn's amazing crime-solving ability? In the very first episode, Shawn tells Gus that the only way the police will find out that he isn't psychic is if he (Shawn) tells them, which he certainly doesn't intend to do. (Although he almost tells Juliet he isn't really a psychic in "Shawn 2.0" from Season Five, when he's trying to impress her with his honesty. Fortunately for Shawn, Declan Rand beats him to the punch and tells Juliet that he [Declan] is a fake first, so Shawn doesn't actually confess.) But what *should* Shawn's friends and colleagues believe regarding his psychic ability? We can employ IBE to question what the people who know or work with Shawn should believe.

Should they believe he's psychic if they follow this technique? What evidence do they use to draw their own conclusions about Shawn's psychic ability? Using IBE, we can evaluate two competing hypotheses for Shawn's amazing crime-solving abilities:

1. He's psychic,

and

2. He's using abilities that are "natural" rather than "supernatural" (like HSP and IBE, for example).

What Lassiter and Juliet *Should* Believe

IBE tells us we should believe what we have the best evidence to believe. Given this, what should Lassiter and Juliet believe about Shawn's crime-solving abilities? Should they believe that he is psychic or should they pursue an alternate hypothesis? And should they have the same beliefs?

It certainly seems that Lassiter doesn't believe Shawn is psychic whereas Juliet does believe he's psychic. Based upon the evidence they have, they seem to have drawn conflicting conclusions. Does this mean one of them has reasoned poorly? Perhaps they don't have the same evidence. Or perhaps their conflicting beliefs have more to do with their background beliefs about the supernatural in general.

Lassiter's belief system appears to exclude any supernatural claims whereas Juliet seems to believe in the existence of supernatural entities. It's clearly "easier" for someone who believes in supernatural entities or powers to believe in one more. But is it the *best explanation* for a general believer in the supernatural to believe Shawn is psychic as opposed to believing Shawn's talents can be explained by science? Again, Lassiter certainly doesn't believe Shawn has psychic abilities, although his skepticism originally leads him to think that Shawn is somehow involved in all of the crimes he purports to have solved ("Pilot"), whereas later on he seems to accept that Shawn has impressive reasoning abilities, but he just can't figure out from where he gets the evidence ("From the Earth to the Starbucks").

What about Juliet? Why does she believe Shawn has psychic powers rather than the seemingly more plausible claim that his abilities can be explained by science? Perhaps part of Shawn's charm and attractiveness to Juliet is his purported psychic ability. Or perhaps she really wants to believe that he isn't lying. Also, given that it's not unheard of for police departments in California to hire psychics, belief in psychic abilities might be a "cultural" belief of sorts for some police in the state. It's strange, however, that Juliet, who is often at crime scenes with Shawn and Gus, doesn't notice him looking at real-world clues before he has a psychic episode. Nor does she seem to notice that Gus sometimes feeds Shawn his psychic clues, like the combination of a lock ("65 Million Years Off") or the direction in which a smelly shark can be found ("The Head, the Tail, the Whole Damn Episode"). The most likely explanation for Juliet's mistaken belief in Shawn's psychic ability is probably a combination of not wanting to believe he's lying, a set of background beliefs in the supernatural, working within a cultural climate in which people believe in psychic phenomena, and just plain old-fashioned ignoring of the evidence in front of her. She shouldn't believe he is psychic.

What Henry, Vick, and Gus *Should* Believe

Henry Spencer obviously knows Shawn isn't psychic and he isn't particularly crazy about the ruse, even though he's secretly proud of his son. Henry raised Shawn to be super-observant, assuming that Shawn would be a police detective when he grew up. It would be strange indeed for Henry to believe that Shawn is psychic, although he vouches for Shawn's psychic abilities after he is confronted by Chief Vick to verify Shawn's "powers" in the pilot episode. But Henry Spencer has considerably more information on Shawn's abilities, or lack thereof, than most other people. Given the evidence he has, it would be strange indeed for him to believe Shawn has supernatural abilities.

Chief Vick seems to believe that Shawn can give her detectives "psychic leads" or insights into investigations. If she doubts that Shawn's abilities are supernatural, she doesn't appear to let on, although she only hires Psych's services when her detectives are stuck or overwhelmed (as opposed to when Lassiter is on a crime-solving streak, as in "65 Million Years Off"), which fortunately for Shawn and Gus, happens quite often. It's surprising that a seasoned police officer and experienced crime-solver would believe in supernatural phenomena like ESP. It does seem plausible, however, that Chief Vick doesn't care how Shawn manages to solve so many crimes. If he claims he's psychic and his crime solving makes her department look good, then she just might not care whether he really is psychic. But she shouldn't believe in a supernatural explanation for his abilities any more than Juliet should.

Now Gus obviously knows that Shawn isn't psychic, but yet Gus believes in ghosts ("Who Ya Gonna Call?"), werewolves ("Let's Get Hairy"), UFO abductions ("Not Even Close . . . Encounters"), demonic possessions ("The Devil's in the Details, and in the Upstairs Bedroom"), and probably many other supernatural phenomena. However, he knows Shawn better than anyone so he obviously knows Shawn isn't psychic. Even though he believes in lots of other supernatural phenomena, he doesn't have any good evidence to believe in a supernatural explanation for Shawn's talents and indeed is one of the two people (the other being Henry Spencer) who are in on Shawn's psychic ruse. In Gus's case, having the set of supernatural background beliefs could not reasonably outweigh his other evidence for believing Shawn's abilities can be naturally explained.

Why Are People So F-ing Stupid?

There are some people Shawn and Gus encounter who are obviously unconvinced of Shawn's psychic ability. While Shawn and Gus lecture on "psychics" at a high school for the gifted ("If You're So Smart, then Why Are You Dead?"), a student boldly suggests that Shawn's psychic tricks can be explained by "hyperobservance." Shawn uses his HSP, along with IBE, to infer that the young man has bad dandruff *and* that he doesn't want his classmates to know about it (hence, the white sweatshirt he always wears over his burgundy school uniform) to effectively end the conversation quickly.

During the same lecture, the thirty-year-old-pretending-to-be-a-teenager killer suggests a psychic test for Shawn: writing the answer to a complicated chemistry question on the board so the psychic detective can psychically deduce the question. Shawn responds with the all-time classic response of all those who claim to have supernatural abilities: *negativity interferes with the psychic process*. So clearly some people don't believe Shawn's abilities are supernatural, although Shawn and Gus's clients on this case are two other teenage geniuses from the gifted school, which shows that some really smart people believe the psychic ruse as well.

The easiest answer for explaining the amazing number of people in the US who believe in ESP and psychics (and they're not all in California!) is that most people misunderstand the scope as well as the limits of science and the scientific method. Many people think that science is just another belief system, like a religion or like belief in the paranormal or supernatural, and also think that there are just as many good reasons to believe in the paranormal as there are to believe in scientific explanations. They underestimate what science can explain while overestimating the strength of scientific "proof." This leads many people to think that since what we take to be "laws" or "truths" of science have changed, sometimes drastically, over the centuries, proof in science is no more sturdy than proof from intuition or belief in the supernatural. And—let's face it— it's also considerably more fun to believe in psychic abilities than to either look for a scientific answer or to believe that boring old science can supply a better answer. *Mythbusters* aside, scientists are typically really bad at making science as interesting and fun as fortune-telling or paranormal claims.

And we've already seen that a set of firmly-held beliefs in other supernatural phenomena makes it easier to assimilate one more belief in supernatural phenomena, especially if the believer cannot imagine a natural explanation for Shawn's amazing talents.

So the moral of the story is: you too probably have some HSP abilities, you can definitely learn to use IBE more effectively, and the supernatural and paranormal are more fun than science. (But not more fun than autopsies for Woody.)

II

Quite the Talent You Have There

4

Thin-Slicing through All the Baloney

Daniel Yim

The virtues of *Psych* are endless. It features clever writing and numerous allusions to the plot lines of famous movies. It has arguably the most epic riff ever on the cult classic *Twin Peaks* in the Season Five episode "Dual Spires." There are engaging, wisecracking characters who do co-ordinated happy dances when they solve mysteries. In their daily lives, fans find themselves using *Psych* mantras such as "What? You know that's right!" as life imitates art. Even the coolness of the hackneyed fist bump is somehow still preserved by the *Psych* universe. A totally and completely unsubstantiated rumor has it that President and First Lady Obama got their fist-bump from *Psych*.

Psych's theme of the private-detective-and-side-kick borrows from the classic Sherlock Holmes and Dr. Watson set-up. Shawn Spencer plays the Sherlock-esque role with seemingly supernatural powers of observation and deduction. The Dr. Watson role is played by Shawn's best friend Gus, a slightly unwilling partner who happens to be tangentially connected to the medical profession (in this case, pharmaceutical sales) and who often cracks cases with his uncanny sense of smell and encyclopedic knowledge of drug chemistry and human physiology. Shawn even has an infamous nemesis pair in Yin and Yang, *Psych*'s counterparts to the Moriarty character in the Holmes series. This familiar set up is immediately recognizable as the classic "whodunit?" trope.

But it's the deeper subject matter of the show that is universally interesting.

Everyone Lies

The *Psych* theme song is about lying. Human beings lie all the time. We lie about really important things like our moral virtue. We say, "I would *never* treat someone that way," even though we do on a regular basis. For example, I know this guy who once gave a family visiting downtown the wrong directions when they asked him how to get to Westminster Presbyterian Church, a historic city landmark. He gave them directions to Sex World, the largest adult superstore in the Midwest. Later that day, when one of our friends joked about pranking tourists during the summer, he emphatically denied that he's that kind of person.

We lie about trivial things, such as what we did or didn't do this past weekend. The lies we tell can be explicit, such as when we simply contradict what we know to be the facts. The lies we tell can be really subtle, such as when we blur a detail or slightly bend a narrative to lead our listener in a direction that she otherwise would not go. A lot of times we're not even fully aware of the way we lie even while in the middle of lying, which often results in us believing our own lies!

Not all lies are with words. In season one episode "Cloudy . . . with a Chance of Murder," Shawn and Gus are watching the news when Shawn says that he just can't watch Channel 8 anymore. He complains that the newscaster wears a toupée, making every newscast start with a lie. This might seem like a stretch for Shawn to apply the word "lie." A toupée seems more like marketing and advertising a product—in this case, a television persona. If this counts as lying, then attempts at deception are on a continuum with make-up on one end, cosmetic surgeries probably somewhere in the middle, and outright disguises on the other end. Perhaps lies should be treated like a color: many shades but no clear *singular* cut off point between, for example, red and pink. If we treat it that way, then we might agree with Shawn that some form of lying is involved in wearing a toupée.

The name of the game is image-management in a world of limited resources, whether they involve careers, material goods, or meaningful relationships. The systems in place that reward or punish us all depend on whether we send the right signals. The stakes are high, and in desperate times (such as in covering up a crime), the resource is plain old survival. In this game, lying is the primary skill that we practice from our earliest memories.

We never have to teach children to lie. Their "make believe" play counts as dress rehearsals en route to becoming mature actors for the many different stages on which life requires their performance.

(Supernatural?) Powers of Observation

Psych is all about a very specific arena of this competitive performance involving liars and lie detectors. Much of crime is a form of lying and staging. Lies are perpetrated during crimes and afterwards, as criminals lie to cover their tracks and mislead the investigators. The cops are doing their best to sniff out the lies. What about Shawn? He's both a liar and lie detector, making him a unique protagonist.

In the pilot episode of *Psych*, Shawn is portrayed as an expert lie detector. The scene opens with Shawn in his apartment with his television broadcasting a news interview of the manager of a store that has been plagued by a string of unsolved burglaries. Shawn can tell, just from glancing at the television interview, that the manager being interviewed is guilty of the crime. He does this with the most causal of attention. In fact, he's in the middle of an amorous encounter (with another person) when he just happens to glance at the television.

This kind of instantaneous insight seems like a fictional device that cannot exist outside of the fantasy world of *Psych*, but there's a real world example. Dr. John Gottman is a retired professor of psychology, and he heads the non-profit Relationship Research Institute. People are drawn to Dr. Gottman's research because of his uncanny ability to make predictions about the long-term success or failure of marriages. After only about fifteen minutes of observing a couple having a normal conversation, Gottman can predict with ninety-percent accuracy whether the couple will still be together fifteen years down the road. He notices details that jump out to him—tiny coded signals that most people don't or can't perceive.

When Shawn shows up at the police station after he phones in the tip that cracks the case, he finds that the police think he's the crook in the series of store burglaries! Their theory is that he committed the crime and then "solved" it to grab some headlines. What else explains the consistently good leads that Shawn has been leaving at the tip-line for so many other crimes? Like the real life observational powers of Dr. Gottman, Shawn's powers appear magical to those without his gifts. In an act of desperation, Shawn claims that he possesses super-natural psychical abilities. The truth—namely, that he is an amateur detective with uncanny abilities at snap judgment— is unacceptable, because it *sounds* too unbelievable. Never mind that it's true. And we all know what happens next. He is enlisted into the service of the police to use his psychic abilities to help solve additional cases.

Thin-Slicing a Crime Scene

Malcolm Gladwell popularized awareness of an innate human power called "thin-slicing" in his 2005 best-seller *Blink: The Power of Thinking Without Thinking*. Thin-slicing is an uncanny ability to find patterns and connections in events and circumstances based on short glimpses, brief experiences, or, well, thin slices, of these events or circumstances. Think Sherlock Homes. Gladwell explains the various ways that thin-slicing appears in our daily lives. A very specific kind of thin-slicing is deception-detection, and this power is what Shawn has in spades. Shawn is an expert lie detector at crime scenes *because* he is an expert thin-slicer.

In "9 Lives," Shawn walks into the scenes of alleged sui-cides. The police have already been at these scenes for hours and presumably the area has been investigated. At the first scene, Lassiter asserts, "It was a suicide. There is no crime." But Shawn, with only a few glances at the scene, notices that something is not right. Objects in the crime scene just pop out of the background into his vision.

When he does this, it's not quite right to say that he's *thinking* in the way that we might interpret the term. When I *think* about something—say, about whether or not I should buy that new car—I imagine myself sitting somewhere quietly mulling over the decision, weighing all the pros and cons, calculating budgets and deliberating. That's not what Shawn does when he *first* glances at the scene of the alleged suicide. He engages in a different type of cognition that primarily involves things that we sometimes call "gut-instinct," "snap judgment," or "intuition." Obviously these things can go wrong, but we all have stories we can tell about how something like a special intuition that saved us from a major mistake. We can't really explain rationally why we felt suspicious about that situation right at the moment when we experienced the insight, even if we are convinced that we were correct.

We made a judgment with very little information, but somehow we made the right call. Shawn exhibits this power to a shocking degree, so much so that people are willing to believe that he's a psychic. This ability that people mistake for psychic powers in Shawn is "thin-slicing." Let's go back to the alleged suicide scene. Imagine that you're one of the police officers investigating the scene. You arrive, you scope out the scene, and begin taking notes to give to Lassiter. As you study the scene, you're aware of the passage of time, the notes you are writing into your pad, the other officers talking to you, and the morbid jokes that cops make about the dead. You experience all of these individual elements *all at once* as a single, continuous 3D streaming media file. Later, you might be able to split it up in your memory into different pieces, but at the scene you don't experience it as discrete, separated moments. Your brain instead gives you the entire experience as a continuous motion picture.

Shawn shows up to the scene. How does Shawn experience the scene? On one level, he experiences it just exactly as you do. His awareness is located in time just as yours is, but he has another special power that is more developed than yours. He thin-slices. He surveys the scene and, for lack of a better phrase, opens himself up to unforced information, analogous to a spiritual medium channeling ghosts, except that he's channeling tiny, overlooked details.

That little jingle and chime that anticipate these scenes have conditioned fans to immediately concentrate really hard on the scene, almost as if they're participating with Shawn in the act of observation. During these thin-slicing scenes, objects and details are highlighted to visually lift them into the foreground. Every episode has these magical moments, whether it involves Shawn perceiving some residue from the bottom of a shoe or some nervous tic in a witness that suggests she's not telling the whole truth. He allows these tiny details to jump out from the larger moving context without those details being *polluted* by the larger context.

What do I mean by *polluted*?

Can't You See the Trees for the Forest?

For most of us, the moving context determines what we see. Our brains are wired to see the forest more than the trees, and in fact once our brains decide that it's a forest, even our interpretation of the details are biased in line with the meaning of a forest. We begin to see what our brains tell us is supposed to be there. For example, imagine you are in a forest. In the distance you see a large black animal moving under the trees. If you're already thinking "black bear," then the concept of *forest* has already influenced your judgment.

That's how important a larger context can be, and this is where it connects back to lying, deception, and staging. The criminals in *Psych* are trying to fool the police. The way they do this is by staging the larger context of meaning in a crime scene to force an interpretation-bias in the minds of the investigators. They're trying to get the police to see the scene as a suicide. Once that initial judgment is formed, it can begin to bias the interpretation of the smaller details of the scene, just as a judgment that something is a forest influences how someone interprets the smaller perceptual details she sees inside the forest. Black bears are *supposed to be in forests*, so moving black smudges in the horizon become black bears in our perceptual interpretation. Suicides are *supposed to have guns near the person's hand*, so what could be a murder weapon becomes a natural piece of the scenery. Never mind that the refrigerator contains a recently marinated steak and other signs that the suicide victim was making plans for a future.

Shawn is going to notice small details like this because he is a freakishly skilled thin-slicer. These smaller details jump out to him in ways that simply do not for those of us who are overwhelmed by the larger staging. The premise of the show is that most of us are easily deceived, that we would miss such important details.

Granted, most of us also have flashes of some thin-slicing skills. I mentioned the familiar yet inexplicable sense of unease that we sometimes feel around a person or situation, even though we just met the person and know very little about him or her. That gut-instinct is our *unconscious* brain reacting to a thin-slice. We're picking up on something that feels a bit "off," but we are not able to become consciously aware of exactly what it is. It doesn't jump out to us with a chime and jingle and hence doesn't register in our rational awareness.

Shawn's thin-slicing skills are special in that his slice comes in *two* stages. First, his gut-instinct is activated because he's perpetually open up to unforced information. But he also enjoys a second stage that is very rare. He almost immediately can *consciously* interpret the strangeness of a crime scene. He knows why he feels that something is wrong because he *subsequently* perceives it in a rational way. As the elder Spencer routinely tells Shawn, "Sometimes, Shawn, the answer is right in front of your eyes. You just need to *choose* to see it." He sees how the thin-slice fails to fit with the larger staging. In that way, he isolates a narrow band of information sliced out of the larger context, and in doing so he prevents that narrow band of information from being biased by the larger moving context. That's how he beats the deceiver's intentions so quickly on the basis of very small perceptual slices of a crime scene.

Shawn also has the added bonus of a freakish brain. Not only is he a rare two-stage thin-slicer, but he also has an eidetic memory, also known as a "photographic" memory. With a little concentration, Shawn can remember everything he has seen in excruciating detail. This enables him to take the details of his thin-slicing episodes and compare them to the event narratives in search of inconsistencies.

Thin-Slice Boot Camp

Shawn is not simply gifted with this power. While it's true that he has more of this innate power in his mind than anyone else on the show, a good deal of his natural ability has been enhanced by training.

As a fan, the most enjoyable scenes for me are the flashbacks to Shawn's childhood when his dad is running Shawn through the paces of mental training. His dad knows that Shawn has a gifted memory, but what's he trying to do is further develop Shawn's thin-slicing powers to combine with his gifted memory. In "Shawn Versus the Red Phantom," young

Shawn is giddy with excitement over the special toy prize awaiting him at the bottom of the cereal box. He is crushed when the packaging turns out to be defective; it has no ring. Shawn's drill instructor decides to use the moment to drill the young boy. He gives Shawn an unopened box of cereal with a ring at the bottom. He challenges Shawn to get the ring.

Shawn is stumped. He wonders whether his dad is asking him to eat all the cereal. The elder Spencer suggests that he turn the box upside down to open it from the "wrong end." The point is that there really isn't a "right" or "wrong" end for opening cereal boxes. There's no cereal box police that enforces proper etiquette. You might think that the little cardboard closing fold on the top end preserves the freshness of the cereal, and that's why it's the "right end." Do you really believe that little cardboard flap will keep out the atmosphere?

The larger context of conventional expectation often dictates what we're willing or able to consider possible. The conventional rule is that cereal boxes are opened at the "top." In fact, just imagine you have in your cupboard a brand new box of cereal. Now picture your spouse or friend opening that brand new box of *your* cereal *from the bottom*. If you're feeling yourself getting a bit annoyed *just by the thought of it*, then you're experiencing the power of conventional thinking. It creates an artificial frame of possibility and even desire. But cereal boxes *can* be opened at the bottom. The elder Spencer is training Shawn to think outside the (cereal) box. He is training Shawn to block out conventional contexts from limiting Shawn's vision of the possible. The elder Spencer is freeing the younger Spencer's gut-instincts so that he can thin-slice more effectively and hence beat the deceivers who stage crime scenes to throw off the police.

I told you about the real-world research of Dr. Gottman. He has discovered that the natural ability to thin-slice other people can be trained in a clinical context. Dr. Gottman now runs a clinic that trains professional psychological counselors to become better at thin-slicing couples who seek relationship counseling. This makes for better relationship counselors because they're better at using their gut-instinct to help interpret the patients while thinking outside of the box. This is necessary because patients often do not know what they believe and they often subtly (or not so subtly) misrepresent themselves by saying what they think they should say to fit with conventional expectations. A good thin-slicing counselor can read the complex cues of human behavior and put them into a more accurate framework that makes sense of the couples' real troubles. This is not that far off from what Shawn can do with the kinds of people he encounters in the show, whether they are criminals, witnesses, or cops. One way to interpret the flashback scenes of young Shawn is to see them as a clinic for thin-slicing.

Tinted Windows to the Soul

This training turns out to be especially important because it takes a great deal of skill to thin-slice a person reliably and consistently. Consider highly skilled poker players. Among other things, they are studious bluff-detectors as well as skilled bluffers themselves. They are looking for "tells," the idiosyncratic behavioral ticks or signs that someone makes when projecting a misleading image.

In the flashback scene in "Poker? I Barely Know Her," the young Shawn is playing a game of poker with some police officers in the police locker room. He thin-slices his opponents, reading their "tells," that range from nervously chewing a toothpick, rubbing an earlobe, and brushing the corner of a card with a thumb. His opponents have no chance, because they are not monitoring their own behavior to suppress their own tells.

They've not mastered the "poker face" that in reality requires more than just controlling your face. A poker face is a whole body-monitoring enterprise, and even the smallest movements can give you away to a skilled thin-slicer, but most of the action is in the face. Dr. Paul Ekman is a psychologist who studies facial expressions. Different emotions and thoughts elicit specific and tiny muscle movements in the face. These movements cannot be consciously controlled or limited. For example, if a person's smiling but not sincerely happy, then not all the smiling muscles will be activated in the smile—hence, our phrase "fake smile." The tiny visual differences between a fake smile and a real smile may be as brief as one-twenty-fifth of a second. Our unconscious mind thin-slices facial expressions, registering a snapshot of that momentary facial expression, and sometimes that's enough to tell our gut-instinct whether or not someone is really smiling. Dr. Ekman has cataloged an impressive list of human thoughts and emotions that register in predictable and involuntary micro-expressions on the human face: contempt, guilt, pride, disgust, relief, excitement, happiness, fear, and shame—just to name a few.

Psych illustrates this real-life research in "Lights, Camera, . . . Homicidio," when a Mexican telenovela actor is accused of murder. He claims that he's being framed by someone who switched a real knife for the fake prop. He has been caught on tape plunging the knife into the victim's chest. Shawn thin-slices the innocence of the actor on the strength of the video evidence—namely, the micro-expressions of genuine surprise of the alleged murderer. Shawn claims, "That is not the face of a premeditated killer."

In April 2010, Dr. Ekman was a guest on *Philosophy Talk*, a call-in radio talk show, to discuss how thin-slicing facial expressions is a natural skill that can be improved with training. While we might be natural-born liars, we're also engineered by evolution as lie detectors. Some of us are better at it than others, and Shawn is portrayed as a master of these micro-expression "tells," partly because of his childhood of training by the elder Spencer.

Psych again references this type of thin-slicing in "Cloudy . . . with a Chance of Murder," when Shawn and Gus are discussing why he is so confident that a person accused of murder is innocent, despite some pretty damning material evidence.

> SHAWN: She looked at me right in the eyes. Now there are a lot of "tells" that people have when they are trying to appear not-guilty: the way that they sit, crossing their legs, uncrossing them, crossing them back, eye-lines to inanimate objects, twitching, itching, rubbing—all of these affectations, I'm an expert on all of them! But there is one thing that you cannot change no matter how hard you try. And that is the "tint on the windows to the soul."

Cheesy but Effective

In his typical cheesy way, Shawn's saying that, "he just knows." He has thin-sliced the defendant's micro-expressions. Even Shawn can't always explain why his gut-instinct can be trusted. Fundamentally it comes down to that mystical mix between his thin-slicing gut and a childhood spent informally under the elder Spencer's benevolently draconian tutelage. Those flashback scenes reinforce our appreciation of Shawn as both boy and man—he is a manboy. He refuses to grow up, yet he somehow bumbles into success. Shawn is the unifying fantasy for both Gen X-ers and Millennials: the perfect blend of juvenile irresponsibility and prodigious talent. You know that's right.

5
Cocky Confidence Versus Careful Conviction

GRAHAM D. SENOR AND THOMAS D. SENOR

An ideal detective finds the crook with efficiency and diligence. So what makes us trust Shawn Spencer's instincts more than Detective Lassiter's careful conclusions? It could be the difference in confidence levels.

Shawn's claims, though sometimes far-out, are said with assertiveness, strength, and most importantly conviction—a belief in himself that he is right. And while the actual words that come from Shawn's mouth sometimes make no sense, they are easy to believe because Shawn has self-confidence—a characteristic Lassie lacks.

Detective Lassiter's claims, rare as they are, are often not conveyed with confidence. Why? Because Lassie doesn't have (or maybe just doesn't trust) gut instinct. Even when he has a hunch that foul play is at work, he will hold back simply because he doesn't yet have good evidence.

Shawn Spencer has kiddie-pool deep knowledge of the world. And that may be giving him too much credit. We laugh hard at *Psych* partly because of its sharp-witted writing and carton comedy, but also because of Shawn's laughable, though confident, ignorance. He is all the more comical because the one area he does know something about (bad 1970s and 1980s TV shows and movies) comes back to bite him by providing opportunities for confusion. For example, when Clive Prescott replies to Shawn's challenge to define "relationship" with a word-for-word dictionary definition that he then attributes to Webster, Shawn gets confused and wonders why Emmanuel Lewis should be taken to be an expert on relationships ("Chivalry Isn't Dead but Someone Is").

Detective Lassiter isn't the quickest car in the race but he's got a lot on Shawn. Lassie is a careful, methodical thinker who believes in following up on leads and keeping hunches in their place. Better still is Detective O'Hara. Jules is bright and thorough; she comes to conclusions only after getting serious evidence. If you were the victim of a crime, and you had your choice of Shawn, Lassie, or Jules, who would you want to be responsible for finding the perp? Jules. You'd want Jules. Or at least we would.

But she isn't always right. Sometimes Lassie is. And, of course, often it's none other than the bumbling, idiotic (though funny as hell) Shawn who pieces together the evidence and solves the crime. How does that happen? How is it that careful Lassie and smart Jules get out-detectived by the likes of Spencer? His confidence might explain why we are likely to believe him, but it doesn't explain his success.

Good Detectives Are Rational

Good detectives aren't just smart alecks who try to solve crimes. They solve them. And while they may get the occasional lucky break, if they rely solely on luck, they won't be good detectives because they won't be successful very often. To be an effective detective requires critical thinking; and critical thinking leads to rational beliefs. And rational beliefs are likely to be true—that's why we care about rationality.

We want to accomplish our goals but we aren't likely to do that if we begin with false beliefs. Whether it's solving a crime, getting a good job, or finding a good taco truck in a new city, we are much more likely to get what we want if we have true beliefs; and our best way to get true beliefs is to have rational beliefs.

While philosophers disagree about what is sufficient for knowing, just about everybody thinks that belief and truth are necessary. In other words, if you don't *believe* that Little Rock is the capital of Arkansas or it just isn't *true* that Little Rock is the capital, then you can't *know* that Little Rock is the capital. You can't know what you don't believe and you can't know what's false. And while there's agreement that belief and truth are needed for knowledge, pretty much no one thinks they are enough. As philosophers say, belief and truth are necessary but not sufficient for knowledge. I might believe that Little Rock is the capital of Arkansas, and that belief might be true, but I won't know it if my belief is based on nothing but a lucky guess.

Unfortunately for Shawn, many of his true beliefs fail to be knowledge because of this. As Gus says when Shawn is about to make an outrageous allegation: "Let me guess: You've got a loosely formed idea that shouldn't work on paper but ultimately proves to be reasonably successful" ("He Dead"). Alas, true belief without justification is, well, just true belief.

For instance, in "Shabby the Sea Lion," when a funeral is held for a sea lion named "Shabby" (or "Shabby Thesealion" as Shawn tells Detective Lassiter before he realizes that the suspicious death he is being asked to investigate is that of a marine animal) that was reportedly killed by a natural predator, Shawn notices what looks like a stab wound in the underbelly of the creature and believes that Shabby was murdered. In the end, Shawn turns out to be right. But his true belief in the human cause of Shabby's demise certainly didn't count as knowledge. You can't come to know something on such (pardon the pun) shabby evidence.

Believing the Truth Isn't Enough

So something else is needed for genuine knowledge. Intuitively, there should be something that hooks together the belief and the truth. For instance, when I see the bright yellow of the black-eyed Susan flowers on the Fayetteville town square, I naturally come to know that there are yellow flowers on the square. In part, that's because I have a true belief that there are yellow flowers there, but that's not the whole story. My true belief is knowledge because it is based on what I saw, on my visual experience of the flower. This connects the belief with the truth. I believe as I do because I had the visual experience; and I have the visual experience because there really are yellow flowers where I'm looking.

It is tempting to think that justified true belief is all you need for knowledge. Isn't being justified in my true belief that there are yellow flowers on the square enough? No, it's not—

and you don't need a psychic episode but only a scene in *Psych* to see it. In "He Dead," Shawn and Gus are invited to dinner at the mansion owned by a recent widow, Mrs. Clayton. Mr. Clayton was recently killed when a plane that he owned and piloted crashed in the mountains.

Because of his remarkable powers of observation, Shawn has good reason to think that the plane was sabotaged. Furthermore, he has good reason to think that the Mrs. Clayton had both the motive and opportunity to kill her husband. Furthermore, the Claytons' son Garvin was hostile toward his father and stood to gain by his death. This leads Shawn to believe that Mr. Clayton was killed by a member of his family. We learn at the end of the episode that while a family member did murder Mr. Clayton, it was not his philandering wife. Instead, it was the son-in-law who was married to a daughter that Shawn reasonably believed to be dead.

Not only did Shawn have no reason to suspect the son-in-law, he had no reason to think the guy existed! So clearly, when he justifiably believed that a family member murdered Mr. Clayton, Shawn didn't know this even though the belief was true. Knowledge is more than justified true belief. What more is needed remains an unsolved mystery in epistemology.

A Psychic's Justification

Were Shawn what he claims to be—a genuine psychic—we would have an explanation for how he comes to know important clues for solving crimes. And that explanation would be surprisingly like what's going on when we see flowers on the square.

A genuine psychic is someone who has a sixth sense. And like our other five senses, his psychic sense comes with a distinctive kind of experience and is generally reliable. Now we have serious doubts about whether anyone really is a genuine psychic; more likely the folks who claim to be able to see into the future and talk to the dead are either deluded or con artists. But that's neither here nor there. The point is that if there were such a sixth sense, it would produce knowledge just like its five cousins do. But alas, even if there are psychics, Shawn isn't one of them. If his hunches are justified, it must be because of something else.

What Is Justification?

So a good detective is a rational detective and a rational detective will have beliefs that are ideally knowledge. But when those beliefs fail that high standard, they should at least be justified beliefs. In the flower case, my justification was my experience of seeing the flower. But what is it about that experience that makes it good reason for me to have the belief? That is, why does that experience justify?

Philosophers are divided about what's required for justification. While there are many different theories, there are, at bottom, two ways of approaching the issue.

Evidentialism

An evidentialist thinks that what matters is the evidence you have. Think back to the flower example. The evidentialist will say that what justifies me in believing that there are yellow flowers on the town square is my visual experience of the flowers. To put the matter slightly differently, when I looked at the flowers, what I experienced—you might think of my experience here as a mental snapshot—had a certain content and as long as the belief I base on the experience has that content too, then I'll be justified. So since the content of my mental snapshot when I looked at the flower was "yellow flower on the town square" and that is what I came to believe, my belief is justified. But if on the basis of that experience I were to believe instead that "there is a daisy on the town square" when I don't know how to distinguish daisies from black-eyed Susans, then my belief won't be justified.

The evidentialist thinks that all that matters for justification is good evidence. As Chief Vic tells Shawn when he asks her to trust him: "Trust requires evidence, Mr. Spencer" ("He Dead"). As long as your belief is grounded on sufficient evidence, then your belief is justified. The thought is that most of the time, beliefs that are based on good evidence will be true.

Even good evidence can be misleading, so there can be justified false beliefs. In "True Grits," from Season Six, a man named Thane is wrongly jailed for two years and eight months on a bum murder rap. He is released when the eyewitness testimony falls through. The evidence against him was overwhelming. There was motive, apparently reliable witnesses to the crime, and physical evidence against him was found at his house. Yet he is later exonerated and the real killer found. Jules had been the lead detective in the original case and while she reasonably regrets that a terrible mistake was made, she isn't guilty of bad investigative work—her belief that she had the right man was justified although false.

Reliabilism

The second primary theory of justification is called "reliabilism." According to the reliabilist, what matters for justification isn't the evidence you have but whether or not your belief is likely to be true. As we've seen, the evidentialist thinks that having good evidence will generally produce true belief; but what matters for justification is the evidence and not the likelihood of truth (if you were in the Matrix and didn't know it, you'd have lots of good evidence and justification even though your beliefs about your surroundings are all false). The reliabilist thinks that what matters is general success at getting at the truth. Being justified in your belief means you've been reasonably successful; your belief is at least probably true. So if you were in the Matrix, the reliabilist will think you don't have justification since your beliefs will be almost entirely false.

Suppose that Shawn were to suddenly acquire genuine psychic powers. His hunches are somehow connected to the world in a way that reliably (though not necessarily infallibly) produces only beliefs that are true. The evidentialist will think that until Shawn learns that he now has this power and has evidence of its reliability, the beliefs it produces aren't justified. Merely having a weird psychic experience isn't enough even if such "readings" usually lead to true belief. On the other hand, the reliabilist will think that as long as this brand-new power is reliable—that is, can be counted on to generally get things right—then the beliefs are justified.

So Who Is Justified on Evidentialist Justification?

Good detective work involves the proper gathering of evidence and understanding its implications. Comparing the investigative methods of Shawn against those of detectives Lassiter and

O'Hara, there is no doubt that the evidentialist will be much more impressed with the latter than the former. One reason for this is that Lassie and Jules are guided not only by the evidence they uncover about a particular crime but they are also sensitive to what are called "base rates" and "prior probabilities."

Here's an example: the caps of the baseball teams of the University of Arkansas and the University of Alabama are very similar. When seen from even a slight distance, it can be very hard to tell them apart. Let's assume that there are roughly as many Arkansas hats as there are Alabama hats in the United States. Assume also that there are many, many more Arkansas hats than Alabama hats in Fayetteville and many, many more Alabama hats than Arkansas hats in Tuscaloosa. Now if you see a red and white hat in Tuscaloosa, you'll reasonably believe it is an Alabama hat; if you see one in Fayetteville, you'll reasonably believe it is an Arkansas hat. And if you see one in Portland, you'll be reasonable only if you withhold belief.

What makes the difference in what you can reasonably believe in these cases are the prior probabilities of what you're seeing in the different towns. In Tuscaloosa, it's vastly more likely that the hat is an Alabama hat; in Fayetteville, it's vastly more likely that it is an Arkansas hat. And in Portland, neither is more likely than the other.

The reason that detectives Lassiter and O'Hara find it hard to take seriously that Shabby was murdered is because the prior probability that any given dead sea lion that washes up on the beach has been murdered by a human is much, much lower than is the probability that it died naturally or was killed by a predator. Or take the death of Mr. Clayton. Shawn initially believes that it is murder on the basis of very scant evidence. When he tells Lassie what he thinks, Lassie replies by citing the NTSB preliminary report indicating that the crash was an unfortunate accident due to pilot error, and that the black box shows he descended too rapidly on his approach to Santa Barbara. A plane crash is rarely a murder—particularly when the NTSB reports that it was an accident.

To regularly fail to take into consideration base rates and prior probabilities is to adopt a policy that runs counter to what evidentialism says is necessary for justification. So poor Shawn doesn't look so good given this theory of justification.

Who is Justified on Reliabilist Justification?

You might think that Shawn would fare better on the reliabilist understanding of justification. After all, at the end of most episodes it's Shawn who solves the crime. Even if he doesn't do such a great job handling evidence, in the end he gets it right. And that is what reliabilism emphasizes. You are justified in your belief if you've come to the belief via a reliable method.

Unfortunately for Shawn, there's a problem with this reasoning. Yes, what matters is getting at the truth, but it isn't just *ending up* with true belief that matters. If you form ten different beliefs about who the guilty party is and always end up with the right answer after nine mistakes, you aren't reliable. Shawn's trigger-happy approach to coming to conclusions means that he is regularly wrong in his beliefs about whodunnit. The reliabilist will note this and say that if being rational is necessary for being a good detective, then Shawn isn't a good detective!

Perhaps surprisingly, detectives Lassiter and O'Hara come out well on the reliabilist theory of justification too. While their methods are in keeping with evidentialism, the fact is that their careful, systematic approach to police work means that they are relatively likely to only form beliefs when they have very good evidence. They don't put much stock in hunches.

Lassie's relative lack of self-confidence noted at the beginning of this chapter is actually a virtue: he doesn't believe confidently until the evidence justifies confident belief. And when you wait until all (or at least an awful lot) of the evidence is in and then you carefully weigh the evidence (and if you are reasonably intelligent), your beliefs will generally be true. So Lassie and Jules come out as winners on the reliabilist account. And Shawn? Well, not so much.

So How Does Shawn Have a Job?

At this point, you might be thinking that something has gone very wrong. We began by asking what it is that makes someone a good detective. We argued that being able to figure out who committed a crime was crucial. That led us to a think about knowledge and justification. The two main competing models of justification that epistemologists endlessly debate were explained, and it turns out that Lassie and Jules are judged successful by both models while Shawn strikes out twice.

How can this be? After all, it's Shawn (with some help from Gus) who puts the pieces together at the end of every episode— often against the resistance of the detectives. So if being a good detective requires being rational and being rational means having justified belief, and Shawn rarely has justified belief, why is he so successful? Why do Lassie and Jules need him?

When philosophers talk about justification, they're focusing on a certain, narrow assessment of belief. But there are positive qualities that, while not directly relevant to justification or knowledge, are nevertheless important and indirectly related. We'll finish our comparison of the detectives and Shawn by considering a couple of these virtues.

The only reason Shawn is able to make anyone believe he's a psychic is because of his photographic memory and, when he focuses, his perceptiveness. Shawn notices details that slip by Lassie and Jules. And given his ability to recall these details when they are relevant to the investigation, Shawn often winds up with evidence that no one else can get. And while he might be too quick to reach conclusions from the evidence he uncovers, that he gets and shares that evidence is extremely useful for the detectives. So they need him to generate clues that they themselves are unable to find (and of course this is why the psychic ruse works as much as it does).

The other virtue that Shawn has to offer is, ironically, dependent on his tendency to jump to conclusions. Because he becomes convinced so quickly and on so little evidence, he'll often look for clues in places that more rational detectives won't think of looking. Ironically, the fact that he ignores base rates and prior probabilities leads him to take seriously suspects whom Lassie and Jules ignore. And while factoring in prior probabilities is important when coming to belief, you also can't rule out altogether the improbable happening. While it makes sense for detectives to make certain assumptions based on what's likely, and to act accordingly, they need also to be open to possibilities that they are inclined initially to ignore. Shawn is helpful in large part because he follows leads that Lassie and Jules don't take seriously enough to pursue. He'll take sea lion murder as a serious possibility.

Good detectives are rational detectives. But not all rational detectives are successful detectives. To get the bad guy, you not only need to follow the evidence but also know how to look for it in unlikely place, spot evidence that's hard to see, and keep it all in your data base. When you add the skills and abilities of Lassie and Jules with those of Shawn, you get the complete package.

6

Should the Police Hire a Psychic Detective?

LAURA GUIDRY-GRIMES

When Interim Police Chief Karen Vick is confronted with Shawn Spencer, a self-proclaimed psychic who has an uncanny ability to discover overlooked pieces of evidence, she faces a quandary: Can she trust Shawn's claims that he can help bring about justice and make Santa Barbara safer? Even if she decides she can trust him, should she hire him?

These questions are partly ethical. In order to trust Shawn in this role, she must have reasonable evidence that he has psychic abilities along with the discipline and motivation necessary to work on cases for the department. Spending taxpayer dollars on a psychic detective has ramifications for the police department's public image, efficacy, and inner-workings. Hiring a psychic isn't like hiring a legal consult; psychics generally don't have reliable skills, and presumably taxpayers expect their money to be spent on more traditional investigational techniques.

As head of SBPD, Vick has numerous competing obligations. She's obligated to victims and victims' families to bring criminals to justice swiftly and with minimal collateral damage. For their sake, is she morally *obligated* to pursue unconventional options when standard methods are ineffective or inefficient? What if hiring a psychic gives victims false hope?

Vick also has obligations to the officers and detectives working for her. Her judgment calls can make the difference between a wild goose chase and a successful investigation, and, all the while, the police are putting their lives on the line. Lassiter frequently complains that hiring a psychic mocks detective work, and Vick has to worry about hurting morale. Further, Vick has to uphold the mission of the SBPD to the best of her ability.

The current real-world SBPD has the mission to "create a safe community where all people can live in peace without the fear of crime" and "ensure a professional quality of service and accountability to the citizens of the city." Vick needs to make decisions that promote the good of the community, making sure that she reduces criminal threats and does not recklessly waste resources. When she meets Shawn Spencer, Vick believes that he might just be a "miracle, or a facsimile of one" ("Pilot"). If Shawn can actually solve unsolvable cases, or if he can at least solve cases at a much more efficient rate, then Vick is stuck in an ethical dilemma of sorts. Especially with a desperate and high stakes case, can Vick really turn down Shawn's services?

Vick thus feels ethical pulls from three main directions—the victims, the department, and the community. Navigating ethical tensions is never easy, and we have to be careful how we judge Vick on this matter. After all, we know something she does not—Shawn is a fraud. Given what information she does have, hiring Shawn and Gus is ethically defensible, especially after they have established a remarkable success record.

Psychic Schmychic

It might seem that we can simplify this ethical messiness into one empirical question: Do paranormal abilities exist, or not? We might be inclined to think that hiring a purported psychic detective can only be justified if there is sufficient evidence to believe that psychic claims could be true.

If clairvoyance, fortune telling, telekinesis, telepathy, aura readings, psychometry, remote viewing, and all "powers" along these lines are a whole lot of hokum, then no police department should hire someone claiming to have these powers, right? The answer to this, hopefully we can all agree, is YES. These individuals would be perpetrating fraud, though some of them might be convinced that they actually do have powers. A police department should never knowingly hire a fraud who uses debunked methods.

Immediately after soliciting Shawn's help for the first time, Vick cautions him that she will prosecute if he is lying about his abilities. As much as it pains me to say it, Vick's warning is clearly appropriate.

Two views within parapsychology dominate: the *Psi hypothesis* and the *Null hypothesis*. According to the *Psi* hypothesis, psychic phenomena really do occur, and they aren't attributable to any known natural mechanism or operation. This view requires that we acknowledge new entities, properties, or processes in the universe to explain the phenomena. Proponents of the Null hypothesis assert the opposite—that all of these phenomena can be explained by reference to natural events. It's generally believed that *parsimony* (simplicity) is a virtue of any scientific theory. This is the point of Ockham's Razor: If one theory will force us to accept more stuff existing in the universe, but another theory can explain the same phenomenon without adding more stuff, then we should choose the simpler, minimal-stuff theory. For decades researchers have tried to determine whether psychic events are explainable in natural terms. It appears that they are.

No study with scientifically appropriate controls and methodologies has proven that so-called psychic abilities are, in fact, paranormal. Studies reveal a number of other explanations for these phenomena, such as sleight of hand, misperception, or manipulations of electricity or magnetism. However, absence of evidence does not mean evidence of absence. In other words, even though no study has proven *psi*, we cannot automatically conclude that *psi* does not exist.

We can't conclude too much from that line of reasoning; I could use a similar argument to insist that we have to be open to the possibilities of Gravity Elves and Mitochondrial Fairies. Still, scientists who believe in *psi* believe that they will be able to produce repeatable observations under controlled conditions of paranormal phenomena. The burden of proof certainly lies with them, given all the evidence in favor of the Null hypothesis.

Stupid Americans?

A 2005 Gallup poll found that 73 percent of Americans believe in the paranormal, and extrasensory perception was the most frequently cited belief (41 percent). The 59 percent who don't admit to believing in ESP are divided into those who are uncertain and those who flat out don't believe in it. The majority of

Americans (roughly 66 percent) either *believe in* or are *unsure* about the existence of psychic abilities; only a minority is completely unconvinced. Moreover, from 1990 to 2001, the percentage of Americans who believed in ESP increased. The percentage from 2001 to 2005 decreased, but this downward trend could be temporary. It seems that beliefs in the paranormal are either deeply recalcitrant or ill-informed. Scientific studies do not give us reasons to believe in these phenomena.

Now let's assume the role of a police chief: Should we turn to what scientific studies say on the matter, or should we consult the people? Another piece of evidence would help us out here: Has an alleged psychic ever provided conclusive leads on a criminal case? There are some conflicting reports in response to this question. In 1928, the purported clairvoyant Elisabeth Günther-Geffers was accused of fraud but acquitted following repeated demonstrations of her eerie ability to find bodies and track down thefts. Peter Hurkos, the "man with the radar brain," claims he solved numerous cases in the 1960s and 1970s, and one New Jersey police chief reports that Hurkos did provide leads and the complete name of a killer. However, Hurkos also falsely accused a man of being the Boston Strangler. Gerard Croiset might have helped Tokyo law enforcement locate a child's body, though Croiset was embarrassed in other attempts to help police around the world. In the 2002–2003 search for Elizabeth Smart, over a thousand psychics (some of them famous) called in with tips, and none of them led police to her.

Vick's Predicament

Let's return now to Vick's predicament. The studies discussed above should recommend against hiring a psychic detective. Even though the majority of Americans would apparently be at least open to psychic claims, it's simply too unlikely that anyone professing to have these powers actually does. Police departments have limited resources, so spending money on a psychic consultant will be an imprudent waste of time and money in almost all cases.

Vick initially requests Shawn's help because she's desperate to prevent the feds from taking over a kidnapping case. Vick is open to Shawn's claims of psychic ability because he has a record of calling in critical tips, and while at the department he accurately "senses" evidence in a man's boot. This demonstration is certainly impressive. He's in a completely different room than the boot guy, and his information is specific and immediately verifiable. When Vick brings Shawn onto the McCallum kidnapping case, she tells him that this is a test run, meaning she won't use taxpayer funds on his services. In the course of this case, Shawn gives precise information about the location of the kidnappers and details of an accidental murder. The police did not have other sources of evidence that would have uncovered all of these facts, so Shawn's help was crucial.

This striking display of abilities convinces Vick to hire Shawn as a psychic detective for future SBPD cases. Given how supremely unlikely it is that Shawn's tips were actually due to paranormal sensing, Vick should have vetted Shawn more thoroughly, and she shouldn't have let him and Gus run around on their own in the SBPD's name. Still, Shawn proves to be *extremely* useful, even if he occasionally mucks up a case here and there.

Shawn's usefulness, though, cannot settle the matter. His "powers" might not always help, and having a purported psychic on staff has ramifications for how the PD functions. The police chief still needs to consider her wider obligations to the victims and victims' families, police department, and community.

Victims and Their Loved Ones

Vick owes it to victims and their loved ones to locate and prosecute criminals in a professional and efficient manner. To uphold the public trust, to maintain professional integrity, and to prevent future crimes and recourses to vigilante justice, the police department's responsibility in this regard is significant. Furthermore, the police should carry out their investigation in a respectful manner—particularly when the case is a sensitive one concerning heinous crimes or life-and-death matters.

Even when the victim is no longer alive, we disrespect the dead if we do not properly appreciate loss of life. In a criminal case, one way we can show our appreciation of this loss is by bringing the perpetrators swiftly to justice. Hiring a psychic could aid or thwart this effort, depending on how accurate and efficient the psychic is. The police chief should also consider

whether bringing a psychic onto a case could offend the victim
and the victim's family.

As we know already, psychics generally don't have the
greatest track record. We shouldn't expect them to provide
accurate or helpful guidance on cases, and trusting them too
readily can end up wasting time and money on a wild goose
chase. Shawn, however, proves his abilities repeatedly. He and
Gus have solved over fifty "unsolvable" cases, and even though
they often provide false leads, they almost always direct police
down the right path. They find previously overlooked evidence,
and they frequently solve the case faster than the detectives.

Shawn and Lassiter even have competitions to see who can
crack the case first, and Shawn's repeatedly besting him is one
of the main reasons why he and Lassiter have such a strained
relationship. Hiring Shawn might actually save the department time and money in many instances, since he prevents
cases from going cold, and his tips can bypass the immediate
need for sting operations, lab results, and the like.

Every Tool in the Arsenal

It might be ethically permissible to hire Shawn and Gus, but is
it morally required in desperate cases? At the Twenty-First
Century Law Enforcement Seminar, Lassiter actually defends
Vick's choice in having Shawn as a consultant by saying: "We
at the Santa Barbara Police Department believe in using every
tool in our arsenal to combat crime" ("Zero to Murder in 60
Seconds").

If traditional methods have failed, and time is ticking on a
high-stakes case, it seems that it would be irresponsible not to
even consider other techniques. Imagine a similar situation in
a medical setting. Suppose a patient has a terminal illness, and
no standard therapy has made a positive difference. There is
mixed opinion on the efficacy of alternative medicine, and
many traditionally trained Western doctors scoff at unconventional treatments. Even if we understand their skepticism, we
might think that doctors are doing a disservice to their
patients if they do not even mention the possibility of other
options. We should be even more inclined to criticize a closed-
minded doctor if there are practitioners of alternative medicine
nearby who have exceptional success rates. Likewise, if a police

chief knows a psychic with an outstanding success record, we might worry if she never mentions this option to victims or victims' families—especially in desperate, high stakes cases.

In "Meat Is Murder, but Murder Is Also Murder," Vick decides to follow Shawn's hunch because the department has "gotten information in stranger ways before. Never hurts to check it out." But does it never hurt to follow a psychic's lead? I have provided reasons for thinking that a psychic could easily end up wasting a department's resources. There are other considerations too. A victim and the victims' loved ones could actually be harmed by having a psychic called. For one, hiring a psychic could result in false hope. False hope can be cruel, especially when life and death are at issue. Given that most people are open to the existence of psychics, hiring one could give most people the impression that the odds have turned. Since this is generally not true, people who are vulnerable and distraught are being led into having inappropriate expectations—even though this is surely not the police chief's intentions.

Marc Klaas, father of Polly Klaas and President of the Klaaskids Foundation for Children, resented calls from psychics who gave his family false hope when his daughter was abducted. He said in an interview that alleged psychics "know that people are grasping at straws, and they put a hand out and offer the straw." Out of respect for the distress involved in these sorts of crimes, the police should obviously take care to prevent unnecessary heartache. Additionally, some people might think that hiring a psychic could actually "jinx" the case. They might worry that the cosmic forces (or something like that) would be disrupted by hiring a psychic to interfere. A police chief should be sensitive to the personal preferences of the victim and the victims' family when the proposed technique is controversial.

Arguably, a police chief is ethically required to use every tool in their arsenal, including hiring a psychic when a. the psychic has a decent success record; b. the victim or victims' loved ones do not object; and c. the case is high stakes and in a desperate state. There will be other instances when hiring a psychic is ethically *permissible*, though not ethically required. Vick frequently hires Shawn on cases that are not really desperate (yet), though most of them are high-stakes. Particularly since Shawn and Gus can effectively and efficiently close a case, hiring them can be in the best interests of victims and their loved ones.

Police Department Protocol

In the Season Two episode "Black and Tan: A Crime of Fashion," Lassiter tells Shawn and Gus that he would rather "shower with a bear" than work with them on a case. Lassiter's hostility towards Shawn is partly due to Shawn's unprofessional and immature behavior, but he also expresses bitterness about hiring any psychic. For example, in "You Can't Handle This Episode," Lassiter orders Shawn to let him assess the situation before Shawn "turns it into a psychic crapfest." He seems to think that a psychic detective demeans the work that he has trained for, and Shawn regularly impedes his work and throws a case into upheaval. Instead of Shawn learning how to adapt his methods based on the protocol in the department, Lassiter and everyone else have to adapt to Shawn and Gus's disturbances.

A police chief needs to minimize interpersonal conflicts and distractions, since they can result in low morale and increased errors. Lassiter's disgust with Shawn is an almost immediate obsession, and Vick cannot have her head detective losing sight of what really matters—solving his cases and following protocol. But despite his reservations, Lassiter solicits Shawn's help when he is accused of murder ("Lassie Did a Bad, Bad Thing"). As much as Lassiter resents Shawn's intrusion into his cases, he cannot deny that Shawn could find the crucial bit of evidence needed to exonerate him. Lassiter's respect for Shawn, though, comes and goes. To preserve the integrity of the innerworkings of her department, she should hesitate (more than she does) before hiring Shawn and Gus.

Ain't Swimmin' in Dough

As much as we moan about paying taxes, we can make peace supporting certain services, such as a police force. But what about taxpayer dollars going into the pockets of a psychic detective? Since most Americans are open to the existence of psychics, perhaps paying one with our money will not be all that controversial. In Vick's Santa Barbara, people's willingness to believe in psychic powers might even be higher than the national average, considering the positive publicity that Shawn repeatedly receives. This willingness to believe him could translate into a willingness to pay for his services.

We have to wonder whether that money could be better spent on other goods for the community, but especially since Vick's city is apparently chockfull of murderers and thieves, hiring Shawn might just be the best use of these public funds. What obligations does a police department have in virtue of receiving funds through taxes?

If Shawn had horribly ineffective or inefficient sleuthing skills, then Vick would be misusing public funds on hiring him on so many cases. Police departments ain't swimmin' in dough, and resources could be better spent on equipment, staff, training, or other necessities. Moreover, if Vick could reasonably infer that the Santa Barbara community would not want their taxes used to pay for Shawn's services, then she should reconsider hiring him. She has a duty to maintain the public trust, and she must carry out investigations in a professional manner. Public perception seems to matter—at least a little—for what counts as professional conduct. If the community overwhelmingly viewed psychics as charlatans, then using their money to hire one could be counterproductive to serving the community. Vick runs the risk of befouling the PD's image, and public trust is too fragile to lose on a controversial consultant. Luckily, the media keeps tabs on Shawn's numerous successes, and he usually receives praise and support from the city. So at least at this point in Shawn's career with the SBPD, she is ethically justified in using taxpayer dollars to pay him . . . though she is walking a fine line.

So Hiring Shawn . . . A Good Decision?

Taking a walk in Vick's shoes isn't the easiest thing. We know something she doesn't: Shawn is a fraud. A lovable, lovable fraud. All Vick knows is that Shawn and Gus prove their usefulness time and time again. But she can't endorse just *any* strategy that has a high success rate. She has to be more discriminating than that. Her obligations to victims and their loved ones, the department, and the community all add additional layers of complexity to her quandary. If she dismisses

Shawn out of hand for being a charlatan, then she loses his valuable skills in solving cases quickly and effectively. Especially when traditional methods have failed on an important case, it seems irresponsible not to keep an open mind to unusual techniques. At the same time, hiring Shawn really grinds the gears of her head detective. Although Lassiter certainly needs to have a stick removed from a certain orifice, Vick all the same should be sensitive to the effects that hiring a psychic could have on her staff. Whether hiring Shawn is ethically permissible will also largely depend on what the taxpayers in the area think about it. It is their money, after all, and Vick needs to maintain their trust and uphold the professional image of the SBPD.

Vick demonstrates her conscientiousness on this issue by interrogating Henry about Shawn's purported abilities ("Pilot"), hiring Henry as a liaison to oversee external consultants ("Mr. Yin Presents . . ."), and insisting that Shawn and Gus enroll in police academy training to minimize their screwups ("We'd Like to Thank the Academy"). In order to ameliorate the ethical concerns, Vick should further investigate Shawn's abilities and continue to train Shawn and Gus. Every time they embarrass themselves, they also embarrass the department. Hopefully, if Vick does discover the truth about Shawn, she can then find a legitimate way to keep him on staff. He's too useful and too much fun to let go easily.

III

Thus Spoke
Shawn
Spencer

7

The Three Metamorphoses of Shawn

DANIEL P. MALLOY

Shawn Spencer has been called many things, most of them uncomplimentary. So it may seem a bit off to hold him up as the pinnacle of what human beings can be. And while we might envy Shawn's extraordinary abilities, they are not what make him exceptional. Shawn is a higher type, an *Overman*, because of his attitude toward life.

The Overman is Friedrich Nietzsche's (1844–1900) ideal of what human beings could become. Nietzsche sees the modern world threatened by complacency and mediocrity. To combat these threats, humanity needs a new goal. Enter the Overman— the goal of overcoming humanity.

So how do we become an Overman? According to Nietzsche, a spirit must pass through three stages—the three metamorphoses. The spirit must become a camel, a lion, and finally a child to become an Overman. Shawn has undergone these three metamorphoses and has become an Overman. The key to Nietzsche's three metamorphoses and to the three stages of Shawn's life is the question of values.

What Have I Told You a Thousand Times Before?

Nietzsche's first stage of development is the camel. Camels are known as beasts of burden, and that is exactly what the spirit is at this stage. The camel seeks loads to carry, the heavier the better. The reason for this is that the camel must test its strength. Fundamentally, being a camel teaches the spirit discipline.

What better way of describing Shawn's childhood with Henry? Henry's training may not have been pleasant for young Shawn, but it did instill discipline. Yes, adult Shawn seems undisciplined, but the fact is that he can seem that way precisely because he is so disciplined. Think about it: Shawn's abilities aren't magical or mysterious in any way. He's simply better—more disciplined—at observing and recalling details than those around him. Possibly he also has an edge in his reasoning abilities, but all of those exceptional qualities are the result of his upbringing with Henry.

Shawn carried two heavy burdens in his childhood. First, there were the lessons. Everyone learns lessons as a child—that's part of what defines childhood. But Shawn's lessons were a bit more rigorous than most of ours. The other burden, and perhaps the worse one, was that his lessons had a specific goal: Henry was training Shawn to be a cop, just like dad. Some people grow up with these sorts of expectations, but not all of us.

We can see these expectations throughout the series, but two flashbacks make it explicit. In "Shawn vs. The Red Phantom," Henry catches Shawn reading superhero comic books and admonishes him about the true heroism of police officers, effectively quashing every little boy's dream of wrapping a towel around his neck and flying. Then, in "Earth, Wind, and . . . Wait for It," young Shawn approaches Henry with the more realistic dream of becoming a firefighter, only to be told explicitly that he's being trained to be a cop.

Each of these burdens, like all the burdens the camel must carry, represents the values of someone else.

It is this burden that best exemplifies what's wrong with being a camel. The burdens that camels carry all belong to others. Shawn carried his father's expectations and demands all through his childhood. Although he struggled under them and strained to get out from under them, he could not throw them off. Camels cannot free themselves. That's why the spirit must become a lion.

I Didn't Realize Experience Was Necessary

Many spirits remain camels forever. Most of Shawn's friends and family are still camels. To become a lion requires strength and motivation. It's one thing to have the strength to carry a burden, to accept the values of others, but it's something else entirely to have the strength to throw off those burdens. In fact, throwing them off isn't the right imagery. The lion does not cast off the burdens of the camel—the lion destroys them.

Shawn always displayed some resistance to the values of others, but most of that can be explained as struggles he suffered under the weight of his burden. It's only once Shawn enters his teens, particularly once his parents' marriage gets into trouble, that Shawn gains the strength and motivation to become the lion.

As the lion, Shawn has to destroy the values he's been burdened with—Henry's values. Nietzsche describes this destruction as the battle between the lion and a dragon, the great dragon "Thou shalt." "Thou shalt" is covered in scales and each scale is inscribed with a different commandment, a different value imposed on the spirit. The only way for the spirit to be free is to slay "Thou shalt."

Henry is Shawn's own personal "Thou shalt." Obviously, Shawn hasn't killed him. But he has disappointed Henry time and again. The great battle, though, happened when Shawn was eighteen and stole a car. That put the nail in the coffin of Henry's dreams for Shawn—there was no way Shawn could become a police officer with a felony record. "Thou shalt" was done for.

Since most of Shawn's lion phase is only mentioned in passing, and rarely shown, it might help to look at a different character. In "Shawn and Gus in Drag (Racing)," we're introduced to Tommy Nix, the leader of a gang of street racers. At one point Tommy tells Shawn, "You tell me I can't do something, I'm going to show you that I can. Or I'm going to die trying." This is the essence of the lion: defiance, even to the point of death.

Tommy also epitomizes the lion's main problem. With "Thou shalt" gone, the spirit has a problem. The purpose of the lion is to destroy old values. With that done, the lion has no purpose. But a spirit needs values. Without any values, the spirit falls into nihilism—it is lost, wandering, without any goals. In other words, after the death of "Thou shalt," the spirit is like Shawn after high school, wandering aimlessly.

Defending his string of fifty-seven jobs, none of them held for more than six months and some of them worked for only a weekend, Shawn says that he took those jobs because "they were all fun" and he "wanted the experience." But then he "mastered it and moved on." ("Pilot") Shawn's jobs were fun, but nothing more. That's one of the reasons he's so excited about founding Psych—it's more than a job, it's a chance to use his unique skills for a purpose of his own. The purpose is similar to Henry's, but a great deal more fun. This also explains his attitude toward Tommy at the end of "Shawn and Gus in Drag (Racing)": Shawn turns very quickly from admiring Tommy's approach to life to pitying him. This is because Shawn has surpassed the lion—he has become the child.

I Think Children Are Sticky

Shawn's often been called a child, but rarely as a compliment. When people say that Shawn is childish or immature, they are talking about his seeming inability to bring the appropriate level of seriousness and decorum—or any level of seriousness and decorum—to any given situation. This is perhaps best on display in his first encounter with Mr. Yang ("An Evening with Mr. Yang"): facing down a serial killer who has kidnapped a woman, Shawn insists that Gus keep up their usual irreverent quipping. He can't work without it. A serious attitude actually hinders his process.

However, when I say that *Psych* represents Shawn's spiritual childhood I do not mean just that he's immature. For Nietzsche, the essence of the child is creativity. Where the camel accepts the values of others as its own and the lion destroys those same values, the child creates its own values. This is what creates the association between the child and the Overman.

Shawn's creation of his own values can be seen most easily in his tendency to focus on details of questionable relevance. For instance, in the Season One finale "Scary Sherry: Bianca's Toast," Shawn and Gus discover that a woman they thought they had seen commit suicide was in fact alive and well. Instead of being happy that Scary Sherry survived, they're excited that they started an urban legend. Or again in "Black and Tan: A Crime of Fashion," Shawn obsesses over the fact that no one believes he could be a model. Or in the Season Three episode "Any Given Friday Night at 10 pm, 9 pm Central," Shawn seems more interested in being a part of the

Los Angeles Thunderbirds organization than solving the murder of their kicker.

The only times Shawn seems to really focus are when his partner, the usually dependable Gus, jumps to an outlandish theory, believing the culprit to be a ghost ("Who Ya Gonna Call?"), the devil ("The Devil's in the Details . . . and the Upstairs Bedroom"), or aliens ("Not Even Close . . . Encounters").

If Shawn is indeed the child, then he is also the Overman. Following his tutelage under Henry and his time spent establishing his independence, Shawn has now moved beyond having values imposed on him and aimlessly destroying values. But he can't live without values. So he must create his own.

Some might say that the sort of values that Shawn embraces—fun, laughter, silliness—are not the ones Nietzsche envisioned for his Overman. One of the reasons the juxtaposition of *Psych* and Nietzsche seems a little off is because most people don't associate Nietzsche and fun. This is unfortunate, because while Nietzsche does espouse some values that don't appear in *Psych*—strength, nobility, courage—he also espouses some values that we can recognize in Shawn. In particular, Nietzsche warns us against what he calls the "spirit of gravity." The Overman must overcome heaviness and seriousness, and embrace lightness and laughter. And neither Nietzsche nor the Overman was above a little good-natured mockery.

Gus, Don't Be the Last Man

One thing you may have noticed about our discussion of Shawn's path so far is that it has been largely solitary. Aside from Henry in his role as "Thou shalt," none of the stages in Shawn's evolution has included anyone but Shawn. But Shawn's life is all about others. Shawn without Gus wouldn't be Shawn. So, we have to ask ourselves what role others play in Shawn's status as an Overman.

We can divide these others into two kinds: Shawn's friends and his rivals. We'll look at his friends first: Gus and Lassie (I know I'm stretching the definition of "friend" by including Lassie, but Gus and Lassie have enough in common that it makes sense).

None of Shawn's regular associates is a fellow Overman. None of them even come close. Some of them, in fact, are almost the antithesis of the Overman—the last man. Gus and Lassiter, in particular, are last men. The last man, as Nietzsche describes him, is the ultimate herd animal. He is mediocre, passive, and complacent. Plainly, this is not a perfect description of either Gus or Lassiter, but in their relations to Shawn, they are last men.

It may seem cruel to call Gus a last man. In some ways it is. But Gus does have one of the defining characteristics of a last man: he's fundamentally passive. "Doing cruel things to Gus" could be an alternate title for both the show and Shawn and Gus's business. Gus doesn't do things—things happen to him, usually because of Shawn. Occasionally, Gus protests this condition, but he never takes serious steps toward overcoming it. It is a running theme in *Psych* that even though Gus is the more responsible of the two, Shawn basically runs his life. As he tells Gus at one point, "You still owe me for your entire life" ("Shawn Has the Yips"). The examples are myriad of Shawn's influence on Gus. Shawn reserves the right to vet Gus's girlfriends ("Thrill Seekers and Hell-Raisers"), kidnap Gus ("Who Ya Gonna Call?"), sign a lease in Gus's name ("Pilot"), do Gus's job for him ("Pilot"), and manipulate Gus's bosses ("Ghosts"). Throughout all of this, Gus weakly protests, and then goes along.

We could ask two questions here: why doesn't Gus object? And why does Shawn bother? Gus doesn't object because it isn't in him—he's passive. As for Shawn, his relationship to Gus is essentially one of pity. He does what he does for Gus's own good. The one thing he rarely does is treat Gus as an equal. Because Shawn and Gus are not equals, Shawn actively shapes his own life and values and chooses his own path, where Gus simply allows himself to be guided and manipulated through life, and that makes them unequal.

Our other last man is head detective Carlton Lassiter. Lassie isn't as passive as Gus or as easily manipulated, but he too is a last man. Like Gus, Lassie is entirely defined by others—in his case, by police codes and procedures. He's even proud of that fact. He tells Shawn, "Seriously, I don't want to be you, not even for one minute. I don't want to throw out five crazy theories to get one right. I am a police detective." ("The Head, the Tail, the Whole Damn Episode")

Like Gus, Lassiter is never treated as an equal. Instead, he is treated alternately with contempt and pity, depending on the episode. Generally Lassie is treated with contempt—so much so that Shawn at one point decides he must be right because Lassie thinks he's wrong ("The Devil's in the Details . . . and the Upstairs Bedroom"). Shawn and Lassie are normally at odds, but they're not rivals. Rivalry implies equality, and the fact of the matter is that Shawn and Lassie are anything but equals. Shawn is plainly the superior of the two. That is why he inspires Lassie's *ressentiment*—a word Nietzsche used to mean something like resentment combined with a strong will to revenge. The fact that Lassie actually keeps a crap list ("Not Even Close . . . Encounters") shows how central resentment is to Lassiter's character. Lassie usually resents Shawn, and Shawn usually treats Lassie with contempt.

There are times, though, when Shawn and Lassiter set aside their differences and work together. What's important to note about these occasions is that Shawn helps Lassiter either because Lassiter swallows his pride and asks for the assist, or because Shawn decides to help without Lassiter asking. When Lassie's car is stolen ("Zero to Murder in 60 Seconds"), when he is accused of murder ("Lassie Did a Bad, Bad Thing") and when he suspects his apartment is haunted ("Heeeeere's Lassie!"), he turns to Shawn for help, implicitly acknowledging that Shawn can do things he can't. Shawn jumps at opportunities to show off. In other cases, particularly the Season One episode "From the Earth to Starbucks" and the Season Five episode "Dead Bear Walking," Shawn helps Lassie solve cases without Lassie knowing, purely out of pity. In either case, Shawn and Lassiter aren't friends. Lassie doesn't pay Psych—he barely even acknowledges the help most of the time.

Shawn and Lassiter's relationship is best displayed in "The Head, the Tail, the Whole Damn Episode." Lassiter begins the episode deciding that he is going to out-Shawn Shawn, announcing that a shark attack victim was in fact murdered. Shawn jumps on the bandwagon because he sees this as Lassiter's evolution—Lassie is trying to become the kind of detective that Shawn is. Throughout the episode, Shawn encourages Lassie to come up with crazy theories, follow slight threads, to be great. Shawn tries to make Lassie an Overman. Lassie, however, doesn't have it in him. By the end of the episode, he has reverted to Detective Dipstick.

In his dealings with both Gus and Lassiter, Shawn is moved by pity. Pity is the great danger of the Overman. Pity is a danger because it tempts the Overman to give up his advancement and overcoming and retreat to his life as a camel. This temptation lurks around every turn, for Shawn and other Overmen. Just think about how Shawn and Gus choose their cases. If you examine each episode, it becomes apparent that there are two predominant motives for accepting or rejecting a given case: pity or ambition. The cases Shawn takes out of ambition (admittedly a strange word to apply to Shawn) are those that allow him to show off. A prime example, and also one that allows him to show up Lassiter, is in the episode "65 Million Years Off," from Season Two, where Shawn, having been at the crime scene mere moments, announces (correctly, of course) that the victim was killed by a dinosaur.

I've Heard It Both Ways

When it comes to other people, the Overman doesn't need friends so much as rivals. Rivals are not enemies—they may even be friends. But what defines them from the perspective of the Overman is that they challenge him. Shawn occasionally shows flashes of this attitude, like when he praises Camden McCallum's plan to kidnap himself in the pilot episode. But Camden, and the rest of the McCallum clan, turn out to be not quite up to the task of challenging Shawn. For his real rivals, we have to look to later seasons.

We could divide Shawn's rivals into two categories: criminal and non-criminal. The non-criminal rivals, Lindsay Leikin from "Psy vs. Psy," Declan Rand from "Shawn 2.0," and "One, Maybe Two, Ways Out" tend to be disappointing, and don't seem to understand the rivalry at all, so we'll set them aside and focus on Shawn's criminal rivals: Pierre Despereaux and Mr. Yin.

Yin and Shawn don't consider each other rivals. Yin doesn't think Shawn is his equal, and therefore he cannot be a rival. He tells Shawn that he considered him good enough to be amusing, plus "You had a black sidekick, and that seemed fun." ("Mr. Yang 2 in 3d"). Yin considers Shawn an inferior, but good enough to be worth challenging.

Shawn, for his part, doesn't consider Yin to be a rival because of the nature of his actions. He has no question that Yin is his intellectual equal, perhaps even his better, but Yin crosses a line for Shawn. While Shawn has created his own value system, and he doesn't hold others up to it, murder is kind of a deal breaker.

This can be seen clearly in the second appearance of Shawn's other rival, Despereaux. In "Extradition II: The Actual Extradition Part," Shawn comes close to treating Despereaux as a friend, up to the point when he suspects that his rival may have murdered the crown prosecutor. Before that, Shawn is nothing but impressed by Despereaux—even when the art thief manipulates the Psych team into aiding his jailbreak.

Once Shawn is convinced that Despereaux is not the killer, their rivalry and mutual respect returns. Notice that being rivals doesn't preclude helping each other out—Shawn is instrumental in proving Pierre innocent, just as he was instrumental in capturing him in the first place.

But the key to any good rivalry is a challenge. Shawn presents that to Despereaux and vice versa. In "Extradition: British Columbia," Despereaux challenges Shawn to catch him, even writing down clues to his upcoming crimes. The fact that Despereaux still manages to pull off those same crimes, in spite of Shawn solving the clues, only inspires Shawn to be better. When Shawn does figure out Despereaux's scam, he's markedly disappointed in the art thief. This disappointment, in turn, inspires Despereaux to be a better thief—hence his brilliant heists in "Extradition II: The Actual Extradition Part" and "Indiana Shawn and the Temple of the Kinda Crappy, Rusty Old Dagger." As he says in "Extradition II," "Well, gentlemen, I need you to know that I am capable of all the things you thought I could do, and more, I'd like the opportunity to prove it to you."

Despereaux and Yin both, like Shawn, have strong claims to being Overmen. Both forge their own value systems, and view their actions in terms "beyond good and evil," as Nietzsche would put it. Yin sees his crimes as grand puzzles, where Despereaux views his as works of art. He doesn't kill, or tries not to, not because murder is wrong, but because it is messy and inelegant. This is fitting, since to rival an Overman, you must be his equal: another Overman.

You Know That's Right

Shawn is the Overman, but that fact is only tangentially related to his unique abilities. Had Henry put the same amount of time and effort into making Shawn a world-class juggler or mime, it would have had largely the same effect. The basic problem of *Psych* is that Shawn is an Overman, and no one else around him is. That single fact explains most of Shawn's relationships and most of his treatment of both his friends and enemies.

The trouble with being an Overman is that it is not a static state. Once Shawn became an Overman—once he had entered the stage of childhood—it became necessary to constantly choose to be the Overman. But being an Overman is lonely. So, Shawn finds himself confronted with three possibilities: remain a lonely Overman, backslide into the herd, or encourage others to be Overmen as well.

Shawn tries this final course of action through much of the show, particularly with Gus, but in recent seasons he's been backsliding.

8

The Overman Is Available for Hugs

ROBERTO RUIZ

Shawn seems to be a walking contradiction: he's perceptive yet absent-minded, irritating and lovable, deceitful and honest.

If we're charitable, though, perhaps instead of contradiction we'll find what philosophers call a dialectic—the coming together of conflicting sides to produce a synthesis greater than the sum of its parts—and we'll see that Shawn transcends the dualisms of ordinary morality to reach a greater nobility.

Friedrich Nietzsche (1844–1900) identified something he called Slave Morality. Detective Lassiter is a good example of someone in the grip of Slave Morality. According to Nietzsche, slave morality is the kind of attitudes and behavior we adopt when our self-image is threatened by greatness in others. Instead of looking within ourselves when we don't measure up to some ideal of excellence, we find it easier to point fingers at others or to pretend that our own failings are really virtues.

While noble morality develops from a triumphant affirmation of itself, slave morality rises when people fall prey to a feeling of masked enviousness. So the person governed by slave morality reacts to the superior people he is jealous of, and compensates himself with an imaginary revenge against them.

You Want Me to Come with You to Awkward Class?

Despite Lassiter's awkward personality, emotional problems, and social ineptitude, he's a great detective. The problem, according to Nietzsche's description of Slave Morality, is that

Lassiter has come to define himself in terms of an opposition to Shawn, and lives vicariously through him. Before they ever crossed paths, Lassiter used to feel powerful and respected. Through time and circumstance, however, and especially because he's constantly undermined by Shawn's buffoonery and spot-on "divinations," he has unwittingly become parasitic and now depends on Shawn for his continued sense of self-worth. His action is now pure reaction.

In "The Head, the Tail, the Whole Damn Episode," Lassiter is obsessed with beating Shawn to the punch, so when a body washes ashore full of deep and deadly shark bites—and a single apparent knife wound, Lassiter jumps at the chance to one-up Shawn, and admits to Jules: "It's now or never, O'Hara. Week after week, I sit idly by doing life-sucking, soul-eating detailed police work while he just bounces in and hops from one wild conclusion to the next, only to be right. This knife wound is good, and I'm going to jump on it before he does."

While he does turn out to be right about the murder, the instinct that drove him to take that leap in the first place was motivated by a need to stand out and define himself *in opposition to* Shawn. It's a manifestation of the slave instinct in him. Now, this instance of slave morality may seem trivial, and it kind of is, so you might be thinking 'Big deal, so what?' But Gus, don't be a myopic Chihuahua! Let's take a step back and look at the big picture, because it can get much, much worse . . . So now, a little history.

Gus, That Is So Two Thousand Five Hundred Years Ago

If you take a look at any civilization throughout history, you'll find a predictable pattern: the gods have an uncanny resemblance to the people who lived in those places. It's almost as if they were made up. . . . If you look at the ancient Greeks, for instance—especially before Socrates ruined everything by making everyone insecure about not being as smart as he was—you find a people so full of life energy and unfettered freedom that they could easily make Sodom and Gomorrah look like a bunch of uptight goody two-shoes: the Greeks engaged in orgiastic bacchanals full of dance, song, and frenzy. And what did their gods do? Well, go figure: they also got drunk, partied like it's 1999, and screwed any hole they could find—no matter the gender . . . or the species!

Kudos on the Child Rearing. Let Me Know How the Therapy Goes

When you look at the Judeo-Christian tradition, on the other hand, the story looks rather different. This is where Nietzsche finds the seed of the most abysmal and macabre expression of what he calls *the slave revolt in morality*—an inversion of values motivated by *ressentiment* in which strength is seen as evil and weakness as virtue. Why should that be the case? Because historically, they had very little to celebrate: whenever they crossed paths with other civilizations, they were almost invariably made the laughingstock and turned into slaves. To them, existence was a burden. These were a people who needed to get psychologically clever, and who were in need of some major self-defense mechanisms in order to survive the contemplation of their deplorable circumstances. Thus, as Nietzsche tells us, "when submission begins to appear to a people as the prime necessity and it becomes aware of the virtues of the subjugated as the conditions of self-preservation, then its god *has* to change, too."

It should come as no surprise, then, that these people imagined a god who praises the meek and downtrodden, and who views humanity as condemned and naturally flawed. Ever hear of concepts like original sin or the fallenness of man? Ever notice Lassiter's negative outlook? Just look at the kind of advice he gives Jules in "A Very Juliet Episode" and what it says about his default outlook:

> I want you to listen to me, O'Hara. And believe this, because I mean it from the bottom of my heart: all romance ends in despair . . . or death, but mostly despair, gut-wrenching despair. And it's just going to make you a better cop to realize that all people are essentially just out there to destroy any chance of happiness you will ever have.

This kind of slavish mentality also explains why most biblical commands are orders about what *not* to do: our natural inclinations cannot be trusted, and salvation can only come from without. And it follows from the same principle that the "appro-

priate" way of dealing with our wickedness isn't through reasoning or by invoking the better angels of our nature but by
coercion, through severe and vengeful punishment. Just think
about who first comes to mind whenever you hear things like
wrath, fire and brimstone, wailing, the gnashing of teeth, apocalyptic destruction, and eternal punishment. And let's not even
get started with the Lassiter examples here, but suffice it to
say that his best friend is his gun.

Gus, Don't Be a Rabid Porcupine!

Nietzsche claims that "the slave is suspicious of the virtues of
the powerful" and vilifies them, but then what's the slave standard of good? Traits born of weakness: pity, patience, humility,
justice, cunning, industriousness, obedience, and faith, "for here
these are the most useful qualities and virtually the only means
of enduring the burden of existence." The only major difference
between the traditional slaves of religious lore and Lassiter is
that Lassie is always packing an enormous amount of firepower
that allows him to boss others around and treat them conde-
scendingly. Without it, we have to wonder how he would behave.
Actually, when we see flashbacks of his early days as a rookie
officer, we find precisely that kind of insecurity.

The Chips Say You're a Cheater, Cheater, Pumpkin Eater!

Nietzsche has often been accused of anti-Semitism. That
charge is unfair and not something we have room to deal with
here, but whatever he may say about the Jews, he thinks the
greatest crime and inversion of values ever committed against
humanity is actually Christianity because "this Jesus of
Nazareth, the incarnate gospel of love, this 'Redeemer' who
brought blessedness and victory to the poor, the sick, and the
sinners—was he not this seduction in its more uncanny and
irresistible form?" And can *you* think of a more petrifying form
of reverse psychology and hypnosis to equal "the overwhelming
and undermining power of that symbol of the 'holy cross,' that
ghastly paradox of a 'God on the cross,' that mystery of an
unimaginable ultimate cruelty and self-crucifixion of God?" As
Shawn would say, "that is some dark juju-magumbo!"

Are You a Fan of Delicious Flavor?

Nietzsche thinks that unlike slave morality—which requires the presence of an "other" against whom to measure itself—master morality springs from self-affirmation. A master is confident, spontaneous, radiant. He is a self-propelled wheel that doesn't need to look to others for vindication or approval, and that's what we find in Shawn. Yes, he may be a bit of an attention whore sometimes, but he is his strange and irreverent self whether others approve or not, even if there's no one else present, like that time he baked a pineapple upside-down cake and it took him nineteen hours because he decided it would be fun to use an Easy Bake oven ("Psy vs. Psy").

Audience or not, Shawn is always himself. Yes, he often impresses everyone, but that's more a side-effect of his personality than the motivating force behind it. Ultimately, what he does care about is solving the crime, getting the right culprit and going out with Gus to get some Fries Quatro Quesos Dos Fritos.

The Good News? I'm Available for Hugs

While Shawn doesn't require approval, he's not blind or indifferent to the circumstances and needs of other people, and even though he doesn't make a big deal out of it, he tends to go out of his way to help others. What we have here is "the consciousness of a wealth which would like to give away and bestow." Shawn is an overflowing cup—he helps others not from pity but from "an urge begotten by superfluity of power."

Think of all the times Shawn has been kind and generous to others without any expectation of reciprocity—especially because he often helps others without their knowledge. At one point, he even gave the credit for solving a series of murders to a cat! ("9 Lives"). And think of all the people he has helped when no one else would: innocent people mistakenly accused of murder, people who claimed to have witnessed ghosts or alien abductions, or people who believed themselves to be werewolves or vampires.

Say what you will about Shawn, he's got a big heart, and he's generous to a fault because he believes in people, and he's willing to give them the benefit of the doubt for *their* sake, not his. He doesn't suffer from that slavish pre-emptive mistrust of humanity that afflicts Lassie.

Like My Dad Says, Real Men Take Bubble Baths

Nietzsche made a big deal about the dichotomy of passivity and physicality embodied in slave and master morality:

> . . . the knightly-aristocratic value judgments presuppose a powerful physicality, a flourishing, abundant, even overflowing health, together with that which serves to preserve it: war, adventure, hunting, dancing, war games, and in general all that involves vigorous, free joyful activity.

We don't have to dig deep to find a stark contrast between Lassiter and Shawn in this respect. Lassiter is stiff as hell: he's self-conscious about his movements and doesn't want to risk humiliation, like that time when he started taking tap-dancing lessons with Gus and didn't want anyone to find out ("Feet Don't Kill Me Now"). Shawn, on the other hand, can't *not* move! And it's not like he's an elegant and graceful panther. He's more like a drunken monkey on drugs. But he doesn't care; he expresses his individuality through movements that are entirely his own, and dances to the beat of his own drum.

While Lassiter is limited by his fear of what others might think of him, Shawn has no inhibition improvising and incorporating into his personality unconventional traits that may suit the occasion, like that time he told Gus to try Chief Vick's pregnancy chair: "we have got to get one for the office. My birthing canal has never felt so alive!" ("Woman Seeking Dead Husband, Smokers Okay, No Pets"). Lassiter would never be that comfortable in his own skin.

I Decided to Be and Therefore I Am. Socrates Said That. No, That Was Descartes

And while Shawn isn't exactly the epitome of classical Hellenistic physicality Nietzsche had in mind—and he does tend to scream like a little girl from time to time—he's also not afraid to throw caution to the wind in genuinely dangerous circumstances, like that time in Season Five's "Romeo and Juliet and Juliet," when he chased and fought a Chinese gang leader and martial arts expert, or that time in Season Three's "Gus

Walks into a Bar," when he went *into* a hostage situation to save Gus. One could argue that Shawn's bravery may be foolish, impractical and dangerous, all of which might be true, but that would be an objection made from the point of view of that knavish utility in which all that matters are the practical consequences of a heartless cost-benefit analysis.

For Nietzsche, safety and the will to survive are only a step to something greater: the will to power. This doesn't necessarily refer to power over *others* but to self-mastery: "the noble human being honors in himself . . . the man who has power over *himself*, who understands how to speak and how to keep silent." Okay, fine, maybe Shawn doesn't know how to say no to food, and he *definitely* doesn't know how to keep silent, but you get the point. "One must test oneself to see whether one is destined for independence and command," and the way to do this is, as Shawn proves repeatedly, by actively taking those risks, foolish though they may seem: the process is more important than the outcome.

The Devil's in the Details, and in the Upstairs Bedroom

Now, this drastic contrast between Shawn and Lassie, while generally true, is also a bit of an exaggeration made for illustrative purposes. There are many examples of Lassie behaving in noble ways, like that time in "From Earth to Starbucks" when, under the influence of some scotch, he confessed to Shawn:

> You astound me . . . it's beyond astounding. It is some of the most impressive reasoning I've ever seen. . . . I don't know how you do it. I mean, it's not psychic-ness. We both know *that's* a crock of crap, but you sir, are unstoppable.

Yes, he was wasted at the time, but doesn't that make it all the more impressive?

On the flip side, Shawn has his share of slavish moments too, like his obvious daddy issues, or like that time in "Shawn 2.0," when Declan—a good-looking, filthy rich philanthropist and successful fake criminal profiler—managed to consistently steal Shawn's thunder and woo Juliet. Shawn actually developed a minor obsession with him, and admitted to Gus: "Trust me on this, Declan is no ringer . . . and if making him look sucky somehow diminishes his appeal in Juliet's eyes, I'll take it." Boo! Moreover, during that same episode, Declan profiled Shawn:

> You're highly intelligent, but you're shameful of that fact, so you play it down with the use of inappropriate behavior, and you live in fear of showing weakness, so you hide behind a constant barrage of jokes and sarcasm.

Although begrudgingly, and only to Gus, Shawn ultimately had to agree that Declan was right.

Lieutenant? Actually, I've Been Promoted. It's CAPTAIN Crunch

While Shawn may have his moments of weakness, however, he's still a master: this isn't an either/or, all-or-nothing scenario. In fact, we *all* fall somewhere along a spectrum, embodying different proportions of master and slaves qualities. The extremes may be impossible idealizations, but we can use them as goal posts so we can do what Nietzsche thought was essential: "To 'give style' to one's character—a great and rare art! It is practiced by those who survey all the strengths and weaknesses of their nature and then fit them into an artistic plan."

This seems to be precisely what Shawn has done: he has moved *beyond* the dualistic false dilemma of good *and* evil, following *or* rebelling, and has simply given his own brand of flavor to his character—grapelicious, in case you're wondering.

Don't forget the cost, though. Being an individual may sound great, but the sacrifices that must be endured are momentous. One of these is a forlorn loneliness. That may sound strange given the fact that Shawn is a social butterfly, but since he creates his own values, he stands outside of conventional modes of intelligibility and can't really be understood. Even now that they are romantically involved, Shawn can't reveal the secret of his identity to Juliet, and must keep that distance between them. Despite being his BFF, even Gus can't really understand the *what-it's-likeness* of Shawn's freedom and individuality, even though Shawn continuously tries to unshackle him from the mental prison that prevents him from becoming his own person. You heard about Pluto? That's messed up, right?

I'm a Psychic. I Can't Lie

I'm trying to make the case that Shawn is the most authentic character in *Psych*, but doesn't the entire show revolve around his *lying* to everyone about being a psychic? Isn't he just a lying liar from Liarsburg, even if his pants aren't on fire?

This is the dialectic paradox I mentioned at the beginning: in the same breath, Shawn is and isn't lying to everyone. How can that be? Think of art: in lying to you about what it is, in its admission of representation, great art can bring out a reality hidden beneath the surface of appearances. Similarly, Shawn lies to everyone and pretends to be a psychic to bring out the truth behind crimes that, due to official protocol, the SBPD cannot always discover or prove on its own.

Now that you know a little bit about paradoxes, let me pose one to you. Obviously you don't want to be part of the herd, right? You probably want to stand out and be your own person, a real individual, so become one. Be a self-propelled wheel! Overflow with abundance! Spread your wings and soar! As Nietzsche himself would shout, "Live dangerously! Build your cities on the slopes of Vesuvius! Send your ships into unchartered seas! Live at war with your peers and with yourself! Be a robber and a conqueror as long as you cannot be a ruler and possessor!"

And above all, don't be a follower. Of course, if you do what I say and try to become such an individual, aren't you just following what some jerk you've never met says?

IV

Psych You Out in the End

9
Psychic or Psycho?

BENJAMIN MCCRAW

Shawn's weird. When he starts on one of his "psychic" experiences (maybe psychic "convulsions" or "spasms" is better), all sanity goes right out the window. He uses strange voices, strange words, and often totally inappropriate movements.

In any other situation, we'd think he was completely insane or having some kind of mental breakdown. His psychic psychosis makes for really funny television, but it doesn't really help most folks' evaluation of his mental status. We pity or institutionalize people who act like that. We would never consider *believing* folks that act the way Shawn does in his psychic fits.

But, is that true? Shawn may go off on wild goose chases and act like someone on a psychotic break, but about ten to fifteen minutes from the end of each episode he has one of those *aha!* moments. Because of those moments, Shawn becomes remarkably reliable as a crime-fighting super-sleuth. What do we make of a psychotic Sherlock like him?

Should We Trust What Shawn Says?

Should we trust Shawn? Should a person accept or believe what Shawn says when he finally comes out with whodunit? That question doesn't seem to have an easy answer. On the one hand, we have remarkably good reason to trust Shawn. Any fan of the show knows that Shawn is always (or nearly always) right about the criminal. We have really good evidence for trusting Shawn because he has a very successful track record of nabbing the bad guys (and gals) in the past. Shawn is a very effective detective and that gives us good reason to trust him when he tells us whodunit.

On the other hand we also have good reason *not* to trust him. Shawn chases down many bad leads before the final *aha!* moment, so if you trust him too soon then you'll end up following the same dead end. Unless you know that his current claim is his *last* claim, you'll probably end up being wrong. But how can you know that any given claim is the last one?

And, then there's the problem of the way he communicates his knowledge. He doesn't present evidence the way a typical person does or in a way that most reasonable folks accept. Shawn's communications are wildly entertaining but they don't inspire confidence that he's all there. He's not even making 'normal' psychic claims—Miss Cleo or Dionne Warwick style. No—he comes up with outrageously over-the-top ways to convey his psychic communications.

Season One has Shawn channeling a cat ("9 Lives"), writing on a glass door as he fakes being possessed by a woman ("Who Ya Gonna Call?"), and Season Two has Shawn clucking like a chicken to uncover the culprit ("65 Million Years Off"), just to give a few of the inventive ways Shawn has his psychic episodes. His communications often come by strange, clairvoyant spasms and those types of communications typically give us good reason to *dis*trust the person in question.

So, we have good evidence to trust Shawn and good evidence not to trust Shawn. In philosophical terms, we're considering Shawn's *testimony* and when it's *justified* (okay) to trust it. There's no clear or easy answer to the question of whether we treat Shawn as a genuine psychic (and someone to trust or believe), or as a psychotic loon (and someone to distrust).

Other regular *Psych* characters display different attitudes towards Shawn that can help us make sense of trusting him. Many of the main characters embody different approaches to how we can view Shawn's testimony and how we should think about trust.

Gus

Gus is clearly the first person to think about since he's the other main character in the show. But, he won't help us here because he's never in a position to trust Shawn about who did the dastardly deed. He's always in on the answer since he's the one who always helps Shawn figure out the criminal's identity in the first place. He has evidence for whodunit independently of Shawn's psychic (or psychotic) communication. Like Shawn, he *knows* the identity of the criminal and doesn't need to rely on Shawn's testimony for that fact.

But everyone else needs Shawn's testimony because they, unlike Gus, don't have that independent evidence. Since Gus doesn't need to trust Shawn, his attitude won't help us answer the question of trust in Shawn.

Lassiter

Anyone who watches *Psych* picks up on Lassie's attitude towards Shawn from the get-go. Lassie never believes what Shawn says until either he gets evidence independent of Shawn's testimony or the circumstances of the episode force him into action. Unlike Gus, though, Lassie is in a position to trust Shawn since he doesn't have independent evidence to know who's the bad guy. But, he never trusts Shawn unless he gets confirming evidence not based in Shawn's testimony.

Lassie takes on the *dis*trusting or skeptical view of Shawn. He may end up believing what Shawn says eventually, but he never actually trusts in Shawn. He stays constantly suspicious and doubtful of pretty much everything Shawn says until he can see things for himself.

Lassie provides us with an answer here: *dis*trust or suspicion or doubt is the default mode or attitude until you have independent evidence for what someone says. Trust is never justified, or acceptable, without confirming evidence. Lassie discounts the good reasons to trust Shawn and accepts the reasons to distrust him (probably due to the psychic basis of Shawn's testimony). But is his attitude of suspiciousness or his position of distrust a good answer to the problem of Shawn's testimony?

No. Lassie's answer is a bad one. He's forced to act on Shawn's testimony by Chief Vick or Juliet. Or he waits almost too long to act because he won't accept Shawn's words until he's got the evidence himself. If the investigation were left up to Lassie, most of the crimes would never be solved or they would be solved too late. Either the criminal could escape or a victim would die before Lassie's traditional evidence would come through. Lassie's approach won't get him what he wants—a quick, successful solution to the crime. His skepticism or suspiciousness prevents him from effective police work and it works against the very thing he wants most. So, his answer to the question of whether to trust in Shawn won't work.

McNab

McNab is a lovable character but plays only a back-up role. He has no real authority and ends up just tagging along on the investigation. But what he lacks in character development and plot significance, he makes up for in how he views Shawn.

McNab plays the role of the gullible or naïve believer. McNab always seems to believe in Shawn no matter how crazy Shawn may be acting or speaking. In the very first episode, McNab is the first to buy Shawn's claims as a psychic ("Pilot"). Whereas Lassie *never* trusts Shawn, McNab seems to *always* trust him. McNab never questions Shawn's claims or his psychic outbursts. Evidence for or against Shawn's claims never really comes up for McNab.

McNab is the opposite of Lassie—he trusts without thinking about evidence or reasons or anything like that. McNab has blind faith in Shawn. Where Lassie requires independent evidence to believe Shawn, McNab trusts him from the very beginning. McNab, from the first episode on, sees Shawn as reliable and trusts him from there on out without seeking evidence for Shawn's testimony. McNab's attitude towards Shawn involves trust in his testimony beyond any thought of evidence for or against what Shawn claims during his psychic testimony.

Like Lassie, McNab gives us a bad answer. If we imagine McNab leading a criminal investigation, then we won't get a successful conclusion either. Since McNab trusts Shawn indiscriminately, the police will end up spinning their wheels chasing down each of Shawn's early and false leads. If the cops chase down that many wild geese, then they will never get to the later and correct answer until it's too late. The criminal will escape or someone will die before the police can hit on the true culprit.

McNab will also end up trusting the wrong people. Shawn may have a reliable track record, but other self-proclaimed psychics will probably not have that kind of success. Since McNab trusts so easily and so uncritically, he will most likely end up trusting someone who often leads him astray. So, the police will also end up tracking down bad leads from unreliable psychics in addition to Shawn's early guesses.

McNab's answer won't work for the same reason that Lassie's fails—neither will actually allow the police to do their work successfully. Just as Lassie is wrong in *never* trusting, McNab is also wrong in *always* trusting. McNab's attitude of gullibility and credulity actually prevents effective police work. His naive and gullible acceptance of testimony gives the wrong answer to the question of trusting that testimony.

Juliet

Juliet walks a middle path between McNab and Lassie. Unlike Lassie, she actually does trust in Shawn eventually. She sees that Shawn's talents can be helpful in solving the crime, but she won't allow him to get away with too many of his unfounded psychic insights. In many episodes, she will listen to Shawn's claims but she will take up a "wait and see" approach until he can give her something besides his outlandish psychic testimony. Trust comes in the end but it is not placed in a naive way. Juliet's willing to trust under *some* circumstances but not *all* circumstances.

Her trust develops over the course of the investigation. She doesn't *begin* by trusting Shawn. Her Lassiter-like suspicion at the beginning of his investigation forces him to do more work to get some evidence or reasons for her to accept his testimony. But, she also has a McNab-like trust in Shawn at a certain point that spurs the capture of the criminal as Shawn becomes more believable. She won't go on wild goose chases, as would McNab, but her eventual trust in Shawn allows for the capture of the bad guy in ways that Lassiter's suspiciousness won't.

Juliet's trust also develops over time. Early in the show, Juliet's attitude towards Shawn looks more like Lassie's, although she never adopts Lassie's *extreme* skepticism. At that point, she seems to have a "What can it hurt to let him look into it?" approach and, when he makes his case, she believes him. But, as the show progresses through the various seasons (and as she grows closer to him), her trust grows from a more suspicious position to a more trusting one. She never hits the naive degree of McNab, but her attitude towards Shawn moves from a Lassie-like lean to a more trusting approach.

Between Lassie's suspiciousness and McNab's gullibility, Juliet's approach seems a much better answer. Her early suspicious attitude prevents the police from chasing Shawn's less-than-educated guesses. So her attitude avoids the problems with naive trust like McNab's. But she does come to trust Shawn later on, which spurs the police's actions to follow Shawn's testimony and capture the criminal. Her trust hits a Goldilocks zone between Lassie and McNab and it's in that zone that one can capture the bad guy successfully and efficiently.

Trust Me, I'm a Philosopher

So far, we've talked about different ways to think about trust in Shawn. Philosophers talk about this in terms of testimony. How do we best think about how we believe the words of others? Thinking about testimony in philosophy is thinking about how we accept information that others transmit to us. When do we trust the words of others? Talking about trust in Shawn finds its place in these general philosophical questions about trust and testimony.

Humean, All Too Humean

The (in)famous Scottish philosopher David Hume (1711–1776) thinks that you can accept someone's testimony or trust in that person only if you have good evidence for that person's reliability independent of their words. Hume's approach to testimony runs parallel to Lassie's approach to Shawn: you trust or believe someone only when you have positive, independent evidence for what that person's telling you. If you don't have that independent evidence, then your trust in that person is poorly placed and your belief in him or her is unjustified. For both Lassie and Hume, trust based on insufficient evidence is a recipe for having irrational, insane, or really *really* misguided beliefs.

But, as with Lassie's view, Hume's approach has problems. In particular, the main worry is that such a position on trust won't get us what we want. Inquiring minds want to know, and we need to rely on others to know a lot of the stuff that we want to know. I know that the Earth is round, but I have to take my teachers, parents, and astronauts at their word because I can't make it to outer space to check myself. We just don't have the time or the resources to find out everything first-hand and that makes trusting others crucial if we want to have knowledge. But, since Hume's view requires that we have positive evidence for the people we trust, we have to do too much work to back up our trust in others. Hume's view seems to imply that we can't know everyday things like 'The Earth is round'. And that approach takes what we want— knowledge—away from us.

Learning How to Reid

Thomas Reid (1710–1796), another Scottish philosopher, has a more relaxed approach to testimony and trust than Hume. According to him, humans have built-in tendencies to tell the truth and to take others at their word. We know that folks lie and that people can frequently make claims that are false. But Reid thinks that our *default* mode is to tell the truth, even if that default can be overridden to various degrees. We also have an innate tendency to believe others and accept their word—a sort of trust faculty. As part of our nature, we're just disposed to trust other people when they tell us things. If trust is part of our nature, we won't need independent evidence to belief people. We just do what we do naturally and we'll have all the knowledge from testimony that we want.

Like McNab, Reid's approach makes trust really easy for us and we don't need to have any evidence for the person in whom we trust. So long as we don't have overwhelming evidence *against* that person, trust is perfectly acceptable.

But, also like McNab, Reid's trust seems too easy and it can backfire on us. If we trust by nature, without *any* regard for having evidence for our beliefs, we can be easily deceived. McNab is lovable, sure, but he's also really gullible. And if you're too gullible, then you're too likely to fall for liars and deceivers. The gullible life isn't one that most of us prize, and Reid's approach to trust seems to make gullibility a virtue. So, he gives us a bad answer on testimony, too.

The Good, the Bad, and the Vague

What McNab and Lassie show us is that approaches to trust like those of Reid and Hume won't work. We must either be gullible or skeptical and neither of those options look very appealing. Instead, we need something like Juliet's approach. When put alongside McNab's and Lassie's attitudes, the main strength in her approach is its flexibility. McNab *always* trusts Shawn; even when that trust may lead him down the wrong path. Lassie *never* trusts Shawn; even when trust may lead him down the right path. Juliet trusts Shawn in *some* situations (unlike Lassie) but she doesn't trust him in *all* situations (unlike McNab).

Hume's view says that we should *always* have independent evidence for the people we trust. On the other hand, Reid says that we *never* need independent evidence for trust. But, looking at Lassie, McNab, and Juliet, we learn that we need a view that's more flexible than either of those provided by Hume and Reid. Some trust may require evidence to avoid being naïve or gullible but we can't require evidence for *all* trust or else we'll lose too much ordinary knowledge and become skeptics. McNab and Lassie give us case studies that help us understand how philosophers think of trust and, given what we see in them, help us determine that we need a view more flexible that the ones Hume and Reid give us—one modeled on Juliet's attitude towards Shawn.

But we're still left with a question: *When* and *how* should we trust? If it's not about having independent evidence (Lassie and Hume) or default trust (McNab and Reid), when is trust justified? There's no easy answer to that question, even if we think about Juliet's attitude towards Shawn. Each *Psych* case is different and, depending on what Shawn says, Juliet might trust him more or less. The same happens for testimony. Should you trust someone's testimony or should you remain skeptical? Like *Psych* cases, each situation is unique and differences in those situations mean that there is no cut-and-dried theory for trust for each and every situation.

To get the flexibility we want for trust and testimony, the good answer must be a vague one. When to trust and when not to trust must be nuanced to the circumstances in each individual case, in a similar way that Juliet trusts Shawn to a different degree depending on the details of the case. Hume and Reid give us answers that are definite, but ones that are bad. The answer we want may be vague but, with its flexibility, we can avoid becoming like either Lassie or McNab.

Is Shawn Psychic or Psychotic?

We began with the question of whether or not to trust Shawn. And if Juliet is the model here, then the answer is a yes and a no. Really, though, the answer is, "Well, it depends." The differences in particular cases make for differences in trusting Shawn, and Juliet's attitude towards him is flexible enough to take advantage of those differences. Sometimes you should trust Shawn and sometimes you should not.

McNab and Lassie embody hard and fast rules about trust: Lassie says never trust and McNab says always trust. But, the flexibility we want means we can't really have hard and fast rules here because we need some wiggle room to respond to different cases and situations in different ways. Nuanced, flexible trust is what we need even if we can't formulate handy-dandy or neat rules for it.

So, should we view Shawn's testimony as psychic or psychotic? Well, the answer is *both*. We should trust sometimes, and that requires us taking Shawn's testimony as genuine. That means seeing him as a reliable guide as he would be if he were the genuine ESP article. But we shouldn't trust him all the time, and that requires us taking his testimony as fallible and often misleading. In that case, we should see him as a bit crazy or at least misguided as we typically see the run-of-the-mill loony.

We should see Shawn as both psychic *and* psychotic, and trust in him should reflect both his (fake) psychic trustworthiness and psychotic blunders.

10
The Bigger the Lie, the More People Will Believe It

JAMES EDWIN MAHON and
CRISTINA CEBALLOS

In his autobiographical work, *Mein Kampf* (*My Struggle*, 1925–26), Adolf Hitler attacked what he thought were lies about why Germany lost World War I. He also talked about how people are more likely to believe a big lie than a small lie, since "they would not believe that others could have the impudence to distort the truth so infamously."

Josef Goebbels, Hitler's Minister for Propaganda, wrote in an article in 1941 entitled "Churchill's Lie Factory" that the "English follow the principle that when one lies, one should lie big, and stick to it. They keep up their lies, even at the risk of looking ridiculous." From this and other sources, Goebbels is commonly credited with the line: *The bigger the lie, the more people will believe it.*

To this line can be added another line: *Tell people the truth, and they won't believe it.* In Australia in 1980, Lindy and Michael Chamberlain told the police that their nine-week-old baby daughter, Azaria, had been taken from their tent by a dingo while they were on a camping trip at Ulruru (Ayer's Rock). They were telling the truth; however, many people did not believe that dingoes would be bold enough to do such a thing. A jury decided that the Chamberlains were lying about what had happened. Lindy went to jail for the murder of their daughter. She was only freed when a piece of Azaria's clothing was found in a dingo lair, and more reports surfaced of dingoes going after children.

If the Chamberlains had lied instead of telling the truth, they would have stood a better chance of not being accused of lying. And if they had told a big lie—say, a lie involving kid-nappers—they might have stood an even better chance of not being accused of lying.

Big Liar

Shawn Spencer is in a similar predicament in the pilot episode of *Psych*. While watching a story on the local Channel 8 news about recent thefts from a stereo store in downtown Santa Barbara featuring an interview with the store's manager, Shawn calls the police and tells them that the manager is responsible for the thefts. They arrest the manager, but they bring Shawn in for questioning. The manager needed an accomplice, and there is no way, they think, that Shawn could know about the manager's thefts without having been involved in the crime himself.

Shawn protests that he's innocent, but the police don't believe him. "So you're telling us that you can read guilt off of TV interviews?" scoffs Detective Carlton Lassiter. As Shawn is about to be booked and placed in a holding cell, Lassiter's part-ner, Detective Lucinda Barry, gives him one last chance: "Just give us a reason, Mr. Spencer, that's all we need. How did you get this information?"

The truth is that Shawn has heightened powers of observa-tion and a photographic memory, and that he's been trained to use these abilities since he was a child by his police officer father, Henry Spencer, in the hope that one day he too would become a police officer. Shawn knows that if he tells the detec-tives the truth about his special abilities, they will continue to think that he's a liar, because that explanation is too mundane to account for such a fantastic result.

Detective Barry says that what they want is a "plausible explanation" for his seemingly miraculous knowledge of the guilt of the store manager. Since the truth is completely implausible, Shawn knows that the only plausible explanation is a lie. Not wanting to tell the truth and be thought a liar (and go to jail), Shawn decides to tell a lie and be thought honest (and avoid jail).

But what lie to tell? This is the point at which Shawn reasons in the way referred to by Hitler and Goebbels. A small lie won't work. If he lies to them that he saw the store manager stealing things, or that he heard about the thefts from a friend, they won't believe him, or else they'll put him in the holding cell while they investigate his story, and eventually determine that he's lying. In order to get them to believe him, and to avoid being caught in his lie, Shawn must lie big—in fact, he must lie really big. Thinking on his feet, Shawn comes up with the biggest lie that could possibly be believed by the police: "I am a psychic."

Shawn then proceeds to tell each of the detectives and police officers facts about themselves that they had not disclosed to him—facts that were actually revealed by his keen observational and memory skills. He also tells them where they can find evidence that will incriminate a suspect for another crime. The police officers become convinced that Shawn's a psychic, and the detectives give him the benefit of the doubt. The police chief goes one step further, and hires him as a consultant to work on another case. Shawn, the *fake* psychic, becomes a *real* detective.

Note that big lies don't violate what Shawn's father calls *rule number one* about lying: "I've got a nickname at work. It's the Human Lie Detector. I spend my day analyzing lies and the people who tell them. Rule number one. Every lie is built on a kernel of truth" ("**Truer Lies**"). A big lie is built on a kernel of truth, just like a small lie. It's just that a big lie has an even smaller kernel of truth than a small lie. In Shawn's case, his lie that he has psychic powers has the small kernel of truth that he has truly exceptional powers of observation and a photographic memory.

Reverse Psychology

In the pilot episode, while talking to his best friend, Burton "Gus" Guster, Shawn explains the rationale behind his lie: "The best way to convince people you're *not* lying to them is to tell them you *are*." What Shawn's talking about is the reverse psychology of lying. People who aren't liars expect liars to stick as close as possible to the facts. They think that the less the liar deviates from the truth, the more plausible the lie will be, and hence, the greater the chance of success. They don't expect liars to tell lies that are implausible.

Liars, however, are well aware of how people expect liars to behave. They know that people expect liars to tell lies that are plausible. So, they know that the more the lie is unbelievable, the more the lie will be believed, because this isn't what people are expecting. The more implausible the lie seems, the more plausible it actually is. The reverse psychology of lying is that the more you seem to be lying, the more you must not be lying, since liars would never seem to be lying. The opening line in a scam is often "You're not going to believe this, but . . ."

In "9 Lives," Shawn and Gus gatecrash a crime scene that has a dead body. The police believe that it's a simple case of suicide, but Shawn believes that a murder has been committed. Not having enough evidence to support his suspicions, Shawn lies that he can communicate with the dead man's cat, which means that it is the "lead witness in a major murder investigation." Nobody challenges this outrageous lie, and he's able to proceed with investigating the case.

As he says to Gus afterwards about his meager evidence, "I didn't have anything substantial. A steak, the chain on the door, a stain on a carpet. . . . I wouldn't have believed me. We needed an in. Now we have one." The lie that the pet cat is communicating with him psychically about the murder is more believable than the circumstantial evidence of the murder in the victim's apartment.

Unfalsifiable Lies

Shawn's lies about having psychic powers aren't arbitrarily chosen. It's not enough for his purposes that a lie is big enough to be believed—the lie must also be of a certain kind. It must be the kind of lie that can't be proven to be false. As Shawn tells Gus in the pilot episode, "The only way they can absolutely prove that I am not a psychic, is if I tell them, and I can guarantee you that is the one thing I will never do." Shawn's big lies, then, can never be proven to be lies at all.

The Austrian philosopher Karl Popper distinguished between scientific and non-scientific theories on the basis of whether or not they could be proven to be false. If a theory is such that it can be proven to be false by some observation or experiment, then the theory is a scientific theory. To be scientific is to be refutable. If a theory is such that it can't be proven to be false by any possible observation or experiment, then the theory is a non-scientific theory (and if it claims to be scientific, it's a pseudo-scientific theory). Being scientific, therefore, is not about being true, but about being refutable. The name that Popper gives for refutability is *falsifiability*. The name for irrefutability is *unfalsifiability*. Scientific theories are falsifiable theories; unfalsifibale theories are non-scientific, or pseudo-scientific, theories.

The theory of evolution is a scientific theory, because there are observations that can prove it to be false. If hominid bones were found along with dinosaur bones in the same layer of rock, for example, then that would disprove evolution. As Charles Darwin stated in *The Origin of Species*, "If it could be demonstrated that any complex organ existed which could not possibly have been formed by numerous, successive, slight modifications, my theory would absolutely break down. But I can find out no such case."

On the other hand, the claims made in a horoscope, such as "This could be your lucky day," are not scientific, because there are no observations that can prove them to be false. A person might be hit by a car while crossing the street, and complain that her day wasn't lucky at all. A defender of the horoscope could tell her that this was indeed her lucky day, since she was lucky to still be alive. As Popper says: "It is a typical soothsayer's trick to predict things so vaguely that the predictions can hardly fail: that they become irrefutable." He argued that astrology, the Marxist theory of history, and the Freudian theory of psychoanalysis are irrefutable, and hence, are non-scientific theories.

Popper rejected confirmability as the mark of a scientific theory. No amount of observations that 'confirm' a theory make that theory a scientific one. As he says: "A Marxist could not open a newspaper without finding on every page confirming evidence for his interpretation of history; not only in the news, but also in its presentation—which revealed the class bias of the paper—and especially of course what the paper did *not* say."

How Many Fingers?

Shawn's lies about having psychic powers are unfalsifiable. It's not possible for any member of the police force, or indeed anyone else, to prove that he lacks psychic powers. In the episode "Woman Seeking Dead Husband: Smokers Okay, No Pets,"

Shawn and Gus get caught by a pair of ex-convicts they are trailing while they're peering through the window of the ex-convicts' motel room. Shawn lies that he's a window inspector and it's immediately disbelieved by the ex-cons. "Window inspector? In a motel?" Shawn's lie is both a small lie and one that is falsifiable. Shawn switches to a bigger lie, one that is unfalsifiable. "Okay, I lied. I did. The truth is I'm a psychic."

The ex-cons don't immediately disbelieve him. The big lie appears to be succeeding where the small lie has failed. One ex-con sends the other out to keep watch, and then turns to Shawn. "Can you prove you're a psychic?" This ex-con believes that it's possible for someone to be a psychic, but he's not convinced that Shawn is a psychic. "I'm talking about real proof! Like a test." Shawn's initial response is to refuse to agree to a test: "Here's the thing. It's not really a parlor trick." The ex-con is pointing a gun in his face, though, so Shawn agrees to a test. The ex-con puts his hand behind his back and asks Shawn to tell him how many fingers he is holding. Shawn sees the reflection of the ex-con's hand in the water pitcher, and tells him "four." The ex-con changes the number of fingers, and Shawn again tells him the correct answer: "three."

This keeps happening, until the ex-con shouts, "You can see my fingers, can't you?" At this point, Shawn tells him the truth, but as he does so he laughs, and throws up his hands, in a way that suggests that he's joking, and not telling the truth: "Yes, yes, yes, I can. It's the reflection of the TV bouncing off the mirror to the water pitcher here." The ex-con moves to another position, and says, "*Now*, how many fingers?" This time Gus can see the ex-con's hidden hand, and signals to Shawn that he is holding three fingers. Shawn tells the ex-con, "Dude, you need to stop picking three." At which point the ex-con finally believes that Shawn is a psychic. He smiles, and fist bumps Shawn, saying, "Respect."

In this scene Shawn's small lie isn't believed. Only his bigger, unfalsifiable lie about being a psychic is believed. The unfalsifiable lie is believed after it has been 'confirmed' by a test. But no amount of 'confirmations' of Shawn's supposed psychic powers can change the fact that Shawn's lie is actually a falsehood. Unlike a scientist, who hopes to be advancing a truth, Shawn wishes to advance a falsehood. Unlike a scientific theory, it is a virtue of Shawn's lie that it can't be proven to be false. It's better for his lie that it be an unfalsifiable claim, or a non-scientific claim.

Shawn doesn't believe that anyone has psychic powers. He's actually committed to a wholly naturalistic explanation for everything in the universe. He must believe this, otherwise he couldn't rely solely upon physical evidence to solve crimes, as he does. Consider the episode "Who Ya Gonna Call?" where Shawn and Gus take on a client who believes that a ghost is trying to kill him, and Shawn berates Gus for actually believing in ghosts. To justify his belief in ghosts, Gus proceeds to tell Shawn a story from his childhood where he was in his room one night and heard a girl's voice coming from the walls claiming to be a ghost. "When I asked her name," says Gus, "she said, 'My name is . . .'" At this point, Shawn interrupts saying, "My name is Wilting Flower. I died without knowing love. Will you be my friend?" Gus is perplexed. "How . . . how did you *know* that? I never told that to anyone before." Shawn replies, laughing: "*I* was Wilting Flower, Gus! I can't believe that you fell for that! I put an old walkie-talkie in the wall when your dad put in the new insulation. . . ." It's Shawn, rather than Gus, who is the resolute *dis*believer in all things psychic, committed to the explanation of everything in purely physical terms.

Blaming the Victims

Normally, when somebody is deceived by a lie, the liar is held wholly responsible for the deception, because when a liar tells a lie, the liar invites the victim to believe what the liar is saying on the basis of trust, and not evidence. Unlike cases of deception that don't involve lying, such as being fooled by a fake limp or a wig, the error involved in being taken in by a lie is the error of trusting someone, and not the error of failing to pay attention or failing to weigh evidence correctly. For this error of trusting a liar, victims typically aren't blamed.

However, there are certain lies where it seems possible to hold the victim responsible for believing the lie based on trust. Lies told in sales are a good example. In the case of a used-car salesman who lies to customers, philosopher Thomas Carson found that many Americans believe that "if the buyer is so stupid as to believe what he is told, then he deserves what happens to him." Most adults, and even some children, agree that we shouldn't believe everything we're told, and that we should take the words of a used-car salesperson, or any salesperson, with a grain of salt.

This is especially true in the case of Shawn's lies about having psychic powers. His lies are highly implausible, if not utterly absurd, on their face. People who are taken in by these lies are, at the very least, extremely gullible. They should know better than to believe that someone can have psychic powers. Those who are duped by Shawn's lies about his having such powers can be held responsible for their deception. Unlike the victims of other kinds of lies, those who are the victims of completely absurd lies may deserve blame for believing them. It's easy to imagine what Shawn would say if he ever revealed to his victims that he had been lying to them all along about his having psychic powers. He would tell them that *they* were to blame for believing such lies.

I Know You Know that I'm Not Telling the Truth

The theme song to *Psych* contains the line "I know you know that I'm not telling the truth." Assuming that this line refers to the show's premise, it's not clear who the "you" is who knows the truth. It could be Gus. But it could also be all of those people who believe Shawn's lies about his having psychic powers. If it's those people, then the people who believe Shawn's lies also know that Shawn is lying. And yet this seems to be impossible. Surely, if you know that someone is lying to you, you don't believe that person, right?

Yet when we examine the findings of social scientists, we find that many victims of deception claim that they participated in the deception. American sociologist Brooke Harrington surveyed investors who lost half or more of their savings as a result of financial deception by large companies, such as Enron. She was surprised to find that many investors saw themselves as participants in the deception, even though they were in no way involved with the companies' fraudulent schemes. One participant, Cate, said, "We sort of knew the books were cooked; I kind of saw it coming," and another, Greg, said, "I knew it was a sham back then. I was just riding it as long as I could." Perhaps the most revealing admission of all was that of a participant called Karen: "That's just human nature—why look a gift horse in the mouth?"

The same refusal to look a gift horse in the mouth was evident in those who invested their money in Bernard L. Madoff Investment Securities, despite the fact that, as Bernie Madoff finally admitted to his sons, "It's all just one big lie." According to journalist Andrew Kirtzman, whenever people asked Madoff's clients, who had invested millions of dollars with Madoff, how Madoff was able to deliver such high returns in good or bad markets, they admitted that they didn't know how he did it. The conclusion that Kirtzman reaches is that Madoff's victims were self-deceived.

Shawn is also a gift horse for the Santa Barbara Police Department. He solves cases for them that they could never solve by themselves. Sometimes, indeed, he solves cases for them that they don't even know are cases. By believing his lies about his psychic powers, they get to profit from his work for them. So they believe his lies. It's not merely that they are to blame for believing such lies, because these lies are incredible. They are also complicit in Shawn's deception. They know that nobody really has psychic powers. They know that he's not telling the truth. But they ignore this knowledge, and believe his lies anyway. After all, it seems to work. It is indeed a case of self-deception.

A Good Pineapple?

In this chapter we've compared Shawn Spencer to Adolf Hitler, pseudo-scientists, used-car salespersons, and Bernie Madoff. But there's an important difference between Shawn and all of these malefactors. Shawn only tells lies in order to help others—to catch guilty people, and to keep innocent people out of jail.

He's a *good* liar. That is to say, he's a good egg. Or perhaps we should say, he's a good pineapple?

11
Do You Remember that You Don't Remember?

SKYLER KING

To every person, "life" consists of recalling many memories and making new ones. This act of "making new memories" seems to stand as the primary, underlying impetus to every human action. But what if a new "memory," when challenged, comes across as erroneous or irreconcilably false? What if that new memory isn't really a memory at all, but an event conjured from imagination? How can a *real* memory be distinguished from a *false* memory? If *any* aspect of memory can fail or be proven false, can we trust it? Memory represents the fundamental building block of life: by it we *learn* to do different activities and what we do and don't like; by it we *judge* the potential outcome of a given decision or scenario; most importantly, by it we *live*. Yet how can we depend upon an innate mechanism so heavily, even though it often fails us?

These are all important questions to consider before boasting about the reliability of our memory. Memory *can* be used as an evidential tool, but, unfortunately, isn't as reliable as we think. Photographic memories, in the true sense, are actually rare and often not as reliable as Shawn's. Memory, much like our brains, is very impressionable; but, as with every other skill, it can be trained and honed for greater precision.

Flashbacks and Flashbulbs

There are two basic types of memory, short-term and long-term. But *Psych* typically demonstrates long-term memory. Before delving into the "reality and reliability of memory," as demonstrated by many of the characters in *Psych*, we need to understand the three types of long-term memory: procedural, episodic, and semantic.

Procedural memory is the type of memory that "never goes away," unless you experience severe psychological or mental trauma. This type of memory relates to tasks, activities, and skills, such as riding a bike or knowing how to properly type on a keyboard—or how to properly punctuate sentences and speak your native language.

Episodic memory is probably the type of long-term memory that most of us typically employ. It deals with *personal* memories, events, or sometimes "flashback" moments of life (hence the name "episodic"). Most of the time, episodic memory is a *visual recollection*—an important point to keep in mind. Also, episodic memory is not to be confused with *flashbulb memories*. Flashbulb memories are similar to episodic memories except that they are *vivid recalls* of one instant or event, usually either extremely bad or extremely good, that occurred in your life. Most people today probably have flashbulb memories of where they were and what they were doing on 9/11.

Finally, semantic memory is the category of memory that we usually take for granted: general knowledge, facts, names, and concepts. So, perhaps when you say the guy down the street lacks "common sense" you're actually saying that he is "semantic memory impaired"? Basically, semantic memory is the "boring" stuff—your name, your birthday, your cell phone number, your social security number, and the name of the first president of the United States.

Super Sleuth, Super Memory

So, what is the *true* "reality and reliability" of memory? Even though memory has been shown to be quite faulty, most people swear by their memory and the accounts of their memory—unless they suffer from smoking copious quantities of heroin and shooting up too much crack, or snorting too many cigarettes, or maybe Alzheimer's (but that's a special case because sometimes that person doesn't even remember that they're forgetting something or incapable of remembering).

The average person's memory isn't nearly as reliable as they think. For example, if I asked you to recite the third sentence of this chapter without looking back, you probably couldn't do that. Or, if I asked you to say what the eighteenth word of this chapter is without looking and counting, you probably couldn't do that either.

In *Psych* the super-sleuth character Shawn Spencer has memory lapses all the time. He forgets he has a dinner appointment with his dad ("Scary Sherry: Bianca's Toast"), and, in the *same* episode, he forgets that his best friend, Gus, is stuck inside the creepy Wispy Sunny Pines Mental Institute! In a later episode, Shawn forgets that he told Gus to take a vacation day so they could go to Scare Fest—and, I don't know about you, but to me, planning a trip to an amusement park seems like a *big* thing to forget ("In Plain Fright")! Yet Shawn's supposed to be "the master of memory, observation, and deductive reasoning."

Memory is *generally* reliable—meaning, basic day-to-day routines, *semantic memory*, and sometimes *episodic memory* are easily remembered and usually accurate. But what about the memories I have of my graduation or my wedding day, you ask? *Those* memories are usually incredibly accurate, mainly because they are either episodic memories or flashbulb memories. Unless you're a completely oblivious dunce who didn't pay attention to anything about your wedding, if the police were to come and interrogate you about the *exact* chain of events on your wedding day, you could most likely tell them everything right down to the smallest detail—just like Shawn does. So, in terms of specific *personal* events (especially the ones you deem highly important), memory can be very reliable and very useful as an evidential tool.

Memories Are Made of This

What makes memory unreliable, though? Okay, so we forget a few things here and there, but why should we change our view about the "precision and reliability" of our memory? Because memory is imperfect. For example, when Shawn tries to remember the plot of a Hitchcock movie to stop a serial killer, he agrees with Gus's conclusion and tells the Santa Barbara Police Department that the killer is going by the script of *Frenzy*, but the killer is actually going by *Psycho*. Shawn doesn't realize this mistake until he sees Mary murdered by Yin ("Mr. Yin Presents . . .").

This kind of recall confusion is what psychologists call *source confusion*. Source confusion refers to the accurate recall of information or a memory, but that information or memory is attributed to the wrong source; for example, you remember that Peter Parker decides to give up being Spider-Man for a while, but you think it occurred in *Spider-Man 3* rather than *Spider-Man 2*.

Source confusion actually happens quite frequently. We often attribute quotations to the wrong author or accidentally combine plots from movies, especially if it's a movie series or movies by the same director and in the same genre. Any time you have a "déjà vu" moment, you're actually experiencing source confusion at its finest. Usually, this occurs when you might visit a new place and suddenly think, "Hey, this building looks really familiar." You typically think perhaps you've driven by or visited it before, but you *probably* just saw it on a movie or TV show sometime and can't remember. So, basically, source confusion is forgetting *where* a memory or certain piece of information originated.

Actually, the phrase, "I forgot" bears no literal meaning. Your brain literally remembers *everything* that happens throughout your life, but your ability to *recall* and *retrieve* those memories is the mechanism that fails. Shawn demonstrates this "remembrance of everything" principle in nearly every episode, but particularly when he remembers his dad's training for escaping from the trunk of a car or how to lose an assailant ("Shawn Takes a Shot in the Dark"). The truth of "forgetting" is not that the memory doesn't exist in your brain; it's just that *you* can't physically order it "on-demand" with your mental satellite company. So, why can't we remember *everything*? Oftentimes, we remember what we *want* to remember. As a kid, did your mom or dad every say to you, "Why is it you can remember everything about everything else, but not when I ask you to turn on the dryer or to mail something or [insert whatever your parents told you to do here]"?

Ah Yes, I Remember It Well

We all have "selective attention" and that selectivity also impacts *memory*. Thus, sometimes we can't remember things because we weren't *consciously* paying attention to it. Also, many memories have *triggers*—or specific smells, sights, or sounds that prompt recall (and these recalls are most usually things that you might not have thought about in *years*).

In *Psych*, Shawn demonstrates this "triggered recall" incessantly. In Season Six after Henry and Lassie round up whom they think the prime suspect of the case is, Shawn flashes back to his first encounter with Thea which demonstrates she is color blind—a crucial element to solving the case ("Santabarbaratown"). Such a detail seemed trivial during the first interview, but, upon reading Ellis's case file (the paramour of Veronica Towne, a girl murdered twenty years earlier), the detail becomes vital. So, even small, seemingly inconsequential details can be triggered.

For most people, these "triggered memories" aren't as pristine as Shawn's. Shawn has an astounding eidetic memory, but most of us don't possess a memory half as powerful as his—even those of us who claim to have photographic or eidetic memories. Eidetic memory is actually a rare feature for adults to possess, especially concerning minute details. Generally, psychologists say that this "photographic memory" is more common in children. Sure, you remember the color of your graduation robe or the color of your first dog or whatever, but do you remember what you wore at 2:32 pm three weeks ago? Do you remember what your boss wore three weeks ago on Thursday? Probably not. Unless both you and your boss are incredibly boring people who wear the same outfit or same type of outfit for weeks at a time, you probably won't remember that.

If you looked at a map of a Civil War re-enactment for two minutes, could you create an *exact* duplicate of the map ten minutes later ("Weekend Warriors")? I know I couldn't. Yet Shawn is able to do all of that. Am I saying that Shawn's abilities are impossible? No, but for the average, untrained, and undisciplined (and, by undisciplined, I mean "not trained to recall precise details on demand") individual, such tasks *are* probably impossible.

One-Time Deal

Shawn's eidetic memory is *so* powerful that he can recall almost anything after looking at it just once. Shawn glances down at the serial number on a dollar bill suspected of being a counterfeit and recites it (probably the next day) to Chief Vick and the rest of the group sitting in the conference room (Psy vs. Psy"); Shawn mentally fast forwards through a movie in his head to see how many f-bombs are dropped and his guess is only *one* short of the actual amount ("Shawn 2.0"). The first example is impressive enough, but the second example shows how superior and well trained his memorization skills are.

If I asked you to go to a mall, look at the first person you see for ten seconds, and then describe to me *every* detail of their physical appearance five minutes later, you probably couldn't even tell me if the first person you saw was a man or a woman. Yet Shawn can walk into a bar or restaurant and randomly describe every hat in the building as well as the appearance of the owner of each hat. Does he stare at people as he walks by like some pedophilic creeper? No, he casually looks around like any normal person would—but he *remembers*. I don't think any of us can boast of possessing *this* powerful of an eidetic memory. Sure, we have the occasional flashbulb memories and several episodic memories, but those aren't *every day occurrences*. Our memories are like a snapshot or brief window to the past frozen in crystal. And, of the things we do *consciously* and *actively* remember, very few are as pristine and accurate as the "visions" Shawn has several times throughout every episode.

Memory, like anything else, is an *influenced* device. Every memory we have, obviously, is recalled from a first-person point of view, which also means that our *perspectives* or *beliefs* subtly affect memory. This is another reason why memory is typically only *generally* reliable: information we already have or to which we are exposed *ex post facto* (Latin, "after the fact") can literally *change* a given memory.

This happens when Abigail and Shawn meet at their high school reunion. Shawn tries to woo Abigail and Abigail says, "Do you not remember what happened between us thirteen years ago?" *She* remembers standing alone on a pier on what would've been her first date with Shawn and from that she draws the conclusion that Shawn stood her up and didn't *actually* like her. Her memory is correct—to a point.

What she didn't know was the Shawn was standing nearby watching her, afraid of approaching her because he "choked"— he couldn't speak around her. Shawn tells her that he was there that night, but she doesn't believe him—until he describes *everything* she wore, right down to the name brand of her heels ("Murder? . . . Anyone? . . . Anyone? . . . Anyone? Bueller?"). So, her *memory* was correct (Shawn didn't approach her that night), but her conclusion was incorrect (Shawn wasn't there or didn't care about her).

Stunningly enough, such confusions happen frequently with memory. Oftentimes, our *schemas* (or predispositions concerning "societal norms"—such as "boys play with action figures, not girls!") lead us to form memories with fallacious conclusions. These memories, though inherently true, often elicit false responses—and, from that, many problems or potentially *false* memories arise.

False Memory?

Information that you receive *after* an event can also influence memory. This is why suggestive questioning is deleterious to memory recalls. To illustrate, in Season One, Lassie hits a dead end on an investigation and encounters Shawn at a bar. Lassie tells Shawn his predicament and then Shawn decides to help Lassie solve the case of the astronomer's mysterious death; however, in order to help Lassie, Shawn teams up with Jules and they feed Lassie vital clues under the guise of, "Hey, Lassiter, what were you saying about clue x?" Lassie, being exhausted and ready for a big break in a previously cold case, at first says he doesn't remember saying *any* of the stuff he allegedly said, but then says, "I've said so many things the past few days, that must've slipped my mind" ("From the Earth to the Starbucks"). Here, the information Lassie received from Shawn and Jules caused him to develop a *false* memory.

Similar things happen in real life. Psychologists have done memory-based tests to assess this "lack of reliability" of memory. One such test is to show a group of people a car crash and then ask each person to take a multiple choice "test" over the video. For the sake of simplicity, let's just say that Car A was going seventy-five miles per hour when it crashed into the back of Car B, which traveled at fifty miles per hour. Car A crashed into the guard rail and nothing else happened, but Car B flipped over and burst into flames—and that's *all* the video showed. Surprisingly, many people put down that both cars flipped or exploded or that an ambulance came by to help or that one driver flew out of the front windshield—yet the video only showed one car flipping and *no one* flying out of the car! How can this be explained? Simple: information received *ex post facto* altered the memory and *imagination* blended a fake version of the events with the *actual* version of events—yet the two became inseparable in the minds of the people taking the test. Unfortunately, memory is very impressionable.

This "impressionability" of memory is another factor that should give us pause when assessing the accuracy of our memories. Typically, what psychologists consider "false memories" or likely to be false memories are recovered memories—meaning, memories that "resurfaced during a therapeutic session" or an interrogation. Psychologists are so skeptical of these "memories" because the person remembering the memory is basically being *told* what to remember ("Were you abused?" "What? I don't think so." "You show signs of abuse. Try to remember the first time you suffered from abuse." "Oh, wait, *now* I remember"). Memory, much like our belief structure, is often influenced by authority figures we regard highly or various family members or colleagues throughout our lives that influence us. Thus, they can *help* us "remember" something that never happened.

Two such questionable instances occurred in *Psych*: when Lindsey, a "psychic" working with the FBI, questions the Home Depot cashier and when Shawn questions a pet store cashier. In the episode where Lindsey questions the Home Depot cashier, the cashier says that he doesn't remember anything about the guy that paid in counterfeit dollars—then he says he doesn't remember if the guy was *actually* a guy! Right as the SBPD is about to give up, Lindsey says, "He had a scar three inches above the jaw and a diamond stud in his left ear" to which the cashier emphatically agrees and suddenly "remembers" exactly what the guy looks like ("Psy vs. Psy"). Later in the same season, Shawn is trying to solve the "babysitting burglaries" when he finds a lead that breaks the case. Unfortunately, the only person who can verify the lead is the cashier at a pet store and—you guessed it!—the cashier doesn't remember anything. So, to "spur" the cashier into remembering, Shawn uses a bunch of reptilian similes to describe the culprit and the cashier *suddenly* remembers *everything* about the customer ("Rob-a-Bye Baby").

Granted, in *Psych* these recovered "memories" always turn out to be true, but in real life such spontaneous *vivid* recalls are highly questionable. Thus, as I mentioned earlier, suggestive questioning is quite detrimental to the accuracy of memory—because our memory is easily tricked!

Google It, Beatch!

So, does this rather alarming unreliability of memory make it unfit for use as an evidential tool? I don't think so. But we should keep in mind that memory is only *generally* reliable and any time you try to press for very precise details—such as making someone spontaneously remember the exact model and inscription of a key a suspect was holding four days ago, which leads you to successfully apprehending the criminal ("Viagra Falls")—the memory-given account will likely break down and prove unreliable. In fact, the only *real* way to validate a given memory is to find physical corroboration—otherwise, *you* might remember the counterfeiter having a hotel key and Shawn will have to tell you that the criminal actually had a Nissan key in the Home Depot surveillance footage ("Psy vs. Psy").

Thankfully, memory, like any muscle group or skill, can be trained and honed over time with constant practice, thereby reducing its natural tendency to err. You can Google "memory training games" or some variant of that and you will find several useful sites that, if you train daily, *truly* help improve your encoding of memory and memory recall. You won't transform from a McNab to a Shawn in a week or two, but maybe your memory can become more reliable and loosely more eidetic, thus eliminating the easy impressionability of any old or new memory you make. After all, life isn't what happens *before* your eyes, but what happens *behind* them—so why not make your memory as good as possible?

V

Embrace the Deception

12
Lying for Justice

JAMES ROCHA

Just make sure you act in awe of me when they come to say I was completely right. Oh, and maybe a little afraid like my powers could possibly be used for evil.

—SHAWN SPENCER

Spoiler Alert. Shawn Spencer isn't psychic. Okay, that's it. That's the spoiler. I apologize for spoiling it for anyone who thought *Psych* was the greatest paranormal show since *Scooby Doo* . . . Actually, while we're at it, I should also let you know: those ghosts on *Scooby Doo*? Well, really, they are . . .

No, I'm just going to expose one supposedly paranormal show at a time. *Psych* actually has no paranormal activity at all. At least *Scooby Doo* had a couple of talking dogs. But *Psych* has nothing metaphysically bizarre about it. What about Shawn Spencer's uncanny ability to always figure out who the killer is, you ask? Well, I'm afraid to let you down, but that's all based on his rational inductive skills, including a keen eye for discovering and analyzing the relevant details of the circumstances around him. Shawn Spencer is no psychic; he's an acute observer of evidence with a rationally brilliant mind.

But, wait: if everything I'm saying is true, then I appear to be accusing Shawn of being a liar! *J'accuse* Shawn Spencer! You, sir, are a liar! You claim to be a psychic, but you are not. That is a bald-faced lie!

We all know that Shawn's a liar, but none of us holds it against him. Is something wrong with us? I mean, lying is immoral, and Shawn lies every week and once a year around Christmas. That's a lot of lies! Maybe we shouldn't be so forgiving.

On the other hand, Shawn is one of the biggest reasons murders get solved in Santa Barbara on a regular basis; Carlton Lassiter's not going to solve murder mysteries on his own, that's for sure. Murderers are kept off the streets of Santa Barbara, all because of Shawn Spencer. Maybe, given all the good he does, we can excuse Shawn all his lies.

This makes me wonder: when is it okay to lie? Some people think there are many cases where it's morally acceptable to lie: surprise birthday parties, when your wife asks you how she looks in her new outfit, or when you tell someone your partner's name is, "Benedict Arnold Jackson." Others believe that lying is never permissible: if you ever have to do it, then you have to admit that you've done something wrong by lying. Myself? I've heard it both ways.

One philosopher in particular, Immanuel Kant, seems to believe that lies are always immoral, regardless of the results the lies might produce. Some people seem to believe that Kant has an absolutist ethical theory, *especially* when it comes to lying. According to these theorists, Kant thought that you could never lie in any circumstances for any reason, *no matter what*. In the most famous example of this view, a French politician, Benjamin Constant, claimed that if a murderer showed up at your door and wanted to know where your friend was, then Kant would say it would be wrong to lie to the murderer. And, in his infamous paper, "On a Supposed Right to Lie from Philanthropy," Kant seemed to agree that this was his view. Maybe Kant wouldn't think that Shawn's success of catching murderers means that he is justified in lying. He apparently didn't think that you could justify a lie when it was told to prevent the murder of your friend!

At the same time, I would like to think that Kant would be able to enjoy a good episode of *Psych*. Kant's not the fuddy duddy that everyone believes he is, and in spite of harsh claims to the contrary, Kant's not an absolutist about morality at all. I actually think that Kant may have been able to see that Shawn Spencer's lies are justified. Not because the lies give good results, but because the lies are necessary to ensure justice is done in a world where bureaucracy and the supernatural are treasured above rationality and justice. When the core values of our society are upside-down, we may have to shake things up to get them turned right-side up. When it comes to shaking things up, no one is better than Shawn Spencer.

Not Inclined to Resign to Maturity

When Burton "Gus" Guster II first learns that their fake psychic detective agency is called, "Psych," he says to Shawn that they should have called it, "Hey We're Fooling You and the Police Department, Hope We Don't Make a Mistake and Someone Dies because of It." But Shawn explains that that name would be too long to fit on the window. More importantly, "The best way to convince people you are not lying to them is to tell them that you are" (Season One, "Pilot"). A career built on lies auspiciously begins with a giant lie right on the office window.

Shawn has to lie to solve murders because they wouldn't let him do so any other way. From an early age, Henry Spencer trained his son to be an expert detective who could spot clues and deduce the guilt of culprits based on those clues. When we first meet Shawn, it's in a diner where Henry is testing the observational abilities of Shawn as a young child. After Shawn has expertly described the three hats (and one beanie) of everyone in the diner, the waitress says, "I guess I know what you're going to be when you grow up," to which Shawn responds, "Oh, I'm never gonna grow up, Ma'am" ("Pilot").

Shawn never does grow up, and we all know he could never be a cop given all the formality and bureaucracy that becoming a cop involves. Shawn acknowledges he could never be a cop when he says, "If I was a cop, I'd be a bad cop. That much I know. Not because I'm tough or unscrupulous. Because of lateness. Just general tardiness" ("Six Feet Under the Sea").

It's true that Shawn scored a perfect score on the detective's exam at fifteen years old ("There's Something about Mira"), but Shawn showed he didn't belong in the police academy when he shot two cutouts of innocent women during the exam (in Shawn's defense, they were clearly suspicious: one woman had groceries in a library that didn't allow snacks and the second woman was a replica of the first woman darkened in to look like a minority, which is, "both offensive and suspicious"). The police academy teacher, Nick Conforth—played by Ralph

Macchio—questions how, given their inability to do well on the police exam, Shawn and Gus could have experienced so much success:

> NICK: How can you two be responsible for solving all these cases? I can't believe you get out of bed in the morning without hurting yourselves.
>
> SHAWN: Oh, but we do, and injury free since June of last year when Gus broke his finger flipping the injury-free countdown calendar. Wait, that's irony, right?
>
> GUS: Irony is you asking me what 'irony' means every time you say it.
>
> NICK: Alright. Maybe you'll do better in the field. ("We'd Like to Thank the Academy," Season Five)

But this attempt to make Shawn and Gus follow rules and accept the dictates of the bureaucracy fails. As the chief says, "Enrolling you guys in the academy was a good idea gone horribly, horribly awry. At least when you screwed up as detectives, you somehow end up catching the bad guys...[then, to Lassiter] I'd prefer they screw up while not wearing our uniforms" ("We'd Like to Thank the Academy").

That's the thing: Shawn and Gus succeed *because* they don't follow the rules. We all know that Shawn cannot be a rule follower who did what he was told even when he thought it wasn't the most rational way to catch the bad guy. Shawn can't be Lassie – a nickname Shawn gives to Carlton Lassiter in a way that suggests that Lassiter is a dog who does as he is told (though there is of course admiration in the name since we often want dogs who do what they are told to chase criminals). Shawn acts outside the rules, which are mere approximations of the most rational ways to behave. With his rationally trained mind, Shawn knows when he should be the exception to the rules, and he's usually right.

Even though Shawn could never be a cop, our society holds psychics in deep esteem. People put all kinds of trust into psychics while asking them to talk to the dead, break curses, read minds, speak to animals, predict the future, or view distant items that cannot be perceived by the five senses. Shawn has all of these abilities. Wait, no, he has none of them, but he can fake them all. For example, he fakes that he can talk to the dead in "Woman Seeking Dead Husband: Smokers Okay, No Pets," breaks a curse in "Bollywood Homicide," and talks to a cat in "9 Lives."

We take Shawn's skills of observation and critical thinking, combine them with a lack of maturity and an inability to follow orders without question, and put that person in a society that requires deference to bureaucracy in law officers, but that also esteems psychics. What do you get? You get a situation where the best way to help the police solve murders is to pretend you are a psychic. Shawn's in an odd situation where it seems like he has to lie to help catch murderers.

Does that make Shawn's lies justified? Well, he's doing it to solve murders. That means he's preventing future murders. His lies show no respect for honesty, but they show even greater respect for the sanctity of human life at the same time. Shawn's lies don't really harm anyone. Well, they harm the killers obviously—and they may drive Lassiter insane, of course. But, no *innocent* people are harmed. Many people, such as Officer Buzz McNab and Officer Allen (from the Pilot), believe in Shawn and seem to benefit from his psychic readings. Most of the others, such as Juliet and Chief Vick, seem less sure about Shawn's abilities, but they don't seem to be harmed by the deception. Shawn's lies don't hurt any innocent people, they help him capture killers and prevent future murders, and he's pretty much forced into the lies. Shawn's lies appear to be justified. So, why worry? We're all fans of delicious flavor, so let's just move on and enjoy some pineapple pizza.

There's a Lot of Obscurity

Wait just a second there. Before we move on to our pizza, we should pause and wonder whether a case could be made against Shawn's lies. Immanuel Kant would certainly be skeptical. When people first read Kant, they get the impression he's an absolutist about ethics, and that with lying in particular, he would not allow any exceptions. The common view is that Kant thinks that lying is absolutely wrong, all the time, no exceptions. His view isn't really that clear-cut, but Kant certainly does abhor lies. Let's try to get into his views a bit to see what Kant would think about Shawn.

Kant has some quite harsh words about lying, which could reasonably lead a person to think he has an absolutist position that lying is always wrong without exception. For example, in *The Metaphysics of Morals*, Kant says that lying is the "greatest violation of a human being's duty to himself," that "no intentional untruth . . . can refuse this harsh name," and that a liar, "throws away and, as it were, annihilates his dignity as a human being."

Then there's Kant's infamous example in "On a Supposed Right to Lie from Philanthropy." The case at hand is a little like this: we are to imagine that a murderer is pursuing Shawn. Shawn hides in Gus's home. The murderer knocks on the door, Gus answers, and the murderer asks, "Is Shawn there?" The question is whether Gus has a right to lie to the murderer. Kant, shockingly, says there is no right to lie even in this case. This seems like the best possible case of an exception to the never-ever-lie rule. No one's pants should be set aflame just because he lies to protect a friend from a killer in hot pursuit! If Kant doesn't believe you have a right to lie here, then when could you?

Philosophy requires careful reading: what is Kant really saying here? Kant is saying that Gus doesn't have a *right to lie* in this case (he mentions that he's talking about "a Supposed Right to Lie" right in the title). He isn't saying that the lie would be immoral or that it couldn't be justified. In this paper, Kant is not primarily interested in the ethical status of lies. He mentions that the ethical status of this lie is more difficult than it seems because a lie always harms someone. Even if we discount the harm to the murderer, it harms the liar. That's a bizarre thing to say, and we should look into it briefly, but remember that it isn't Kant's main point, which we will come back to.

Why does Kant think that every lie harms the liar? When Shawn says he's training for the Santa Barbara 1K (which admittedly doesn't require a lot of training), it certainly doesn't seem to *harm Shawn* ("Tuesday the 17th"). Kant believes that the liar shows (sometimes to others, but always to himself) a lack of respect for truthfulness in communication. We have to respect truthfulness in communication because we humans are social creatures who learn to be more rational by communicating with each other. We're not just born with fully developed rational capabilities. We are, of course, inherently rational, but we improve our rational skills through interactions with other rational beings. For those interactions to be fruitful, we must speak to each other honestly and openly.

Even when you lie to someone who doesn't deserve the truth, you still know, yourself, that what you have done is wrong because you have disrespected the need to always engage in honest communication. If you fail to respect honest communication with others, you aren't respecting your own rationality since that honest communication helps you improve your rational abilities. But your rationality is the most important thing about you: it is how you get yourself to act, how you motivate yourself to be moral, and the source of your value as a being that has dignity and who is worth more than any other thing of value. That's why Kant thinks that whenever you lie, you violate your highest duty to yourself by throwing away your dignity.

Wow, lying is really bad. I certainly wouldn't want to throw away my dignity for almost anything. But I'm not sure this argument means there couldn't be exceptions. Couldn't there be something important enough to risk an offense to your dignity for? What about Gus lying to save Shawn's life? Let's return to that case.

Remember, this ethical evaluation of lying is not Kant's primary interest in this essay. His primary interest in "On a Supposed Right to Lie" is how honesty and lying should fit into a legal system. Kant believes that a legal system has to reward truthfulness: if you tell the truth, you should not be held legally responsible for whatever results. This way, everyone has a path to avoid lawsuits and criminal prosecution: always be honest. For example, in the United States, you cannot be guilty of libel or slander if you're telling the truth.

If you lie and things turn out badly, then you should be held legally responsible. Kant explains this point by examining what could happen if Gus lies and says Shawn is not home. Suppose the murderer then leaves but finds Shawn escaping out of a window. If that happened, Shawn could sue Gus based on the fact that a lie led to a horrible result. Of course, Shawn would never sue the Chocolate Columbo, but the legal point remains: you have no *right to lie*. If you lie, you can be held legally responsible.

Well, it makes sense that you wouldn't have an unassailable right to lie. Maybe Kant's position on lying, while still harsh, isn't as absolutist as people think. As a matter of fact, Kant actually asks several questions about the morality of lying— questions that he doesn't think he can give answers to. This doesn't mean Kant thought some other philosopher could answer these questions. They are questions that he cannot answer because they are paradoxical enough that only a person who was facing them in concrete circumstances could untangle their solutions.

Kant was actually far from an absolutist about morality: there are no simple and absolute rules that always hold. Instead moral dictates depend on the agent's circumstances. Kant was an objectivist about morality because he felt that any person in the exact same circumstances would have the exact same moral duties. Your personal status (whether you are a royal, a noble, or the one percent) along with your emotions, desires, and reluctance to carry out the duty are all irrelevant to the fact that it's your duty. Lassiter may hate Shawn, but every week (and once around Christmas), he has a duty to help Shawn regardless of what he feels about Shawn. Circumstances are certainly relevant since lying for personal gain is clearly different than lying to save lives.

So, what questions does Kant ask about lying that he can't answer? In particular, in the *Metaphysics of Morals*, Kant asks whether untruths told out of politeness count as lies. It's not clear whether it's a lie for you to say, "Yours," at the end of an email where you have no intention to hand yourself over to the person receiving the email. Similarly, if someone asks you to comment on his work, would it be a lie to add an overall nice comment to soften the blow of the critical ones?

Kant leaves such questions open, not providing the answers himself. We know from what he says elsewhere that Kant believes it's not the philosopher's job to fill in all the details, but only to analyze what makes an action moral or immoral. A lie is immoral because it attacks the respect we ought to have for the value of social communication, which is key to helping each other be more rational. It's up to everyone else to figure out when a lie could be justified in his or her circumstances.

One thing's for sure: a lie could not be justified if it's made out of a bad intention. A lie done to take advantage of someone, to make a personal gain, or to feel good about yourself will always be wrong because these intentions show no respect for rationality or human life. Shawn's Uncle Jack (as played by Steven Weber) lies to obtain gold in Season Three's "The Greatest Adventure in the History of Basic Cable." No lie is ever justified if your goal is to get gold. That's pretty much a perfect example of an intention that will not in any way excuse or justify a lie.

Perhaps a lie could be justified if it showed respect for rationality and human life. Let's return to Shawn's compulsive lying to see if it qualifies.

Embrace the Deception

Shawn does lie in a way that respects both rationality and the value of human life. Shawn lies because he lives in a world where he could not solve murders, given who he is, unless he pretended to be a psychic. He only tells people that he's a psychic because he lives in a society where people have more esteem for psychic abilities than for keen observational and analytical skills. His respect for rationality lies in the fact that he only lies about his psychic abilities because his social world irrationally esteems those skills above logic and rationality.

This doesn't mean that all of Shawn's lies are justified. When Shawn tells people he meets that Gus's name is, any one of, "Lavender Gooms," "Paddy Simcox," "Art Vandelay," "Donut Holschtein," or "Jonathon Jacob Jingley-Smith," he's probably lying for the personal gain of lol's. When Shawn lies to involve Gus in a case, he probably could be honest instead of lying. He probably didn't have to tell Gus, in "Bollywood Homicide," that someone dropped off a bunch of bunnies on the doorstep, which meant Gus had to rush to the office since Shawn didn't know how to feed them—he perhaps could have just said they had a case. He also didn't have to tell Gus's wireless provider that Gus was a fugitive from justice so that they'd let him track the GPS on Gus's phone ("Meat Is Murder, but Murder Is Also Murder"). He probably could have found Gus some other way.

No, most of Shawn's lies are certainly immoral. All except the big one. The one lie to rule them all: Shawn's claim to be psychic. That lie at least would give Kant pause. Shawn has to tell that lie to solve murders. Solving murders shows respect for human life. And he only has to lie because he lives in a world that doesn't respect rationality. In that one case—Shawn's biggest lie—we perhaps should allow Shawn to bend the truth so that society's worst inhibitions don't psych us out in the end.

13
Shawn's Hocus Pocus Hokum

Jeffrey E. Stephenson

There's much to like about Shawn Spencer. He has a quick and clever wit, his one-liners are targeted, and his humorous persuasiveness in getting his way with his best friend is delightful. His refusal to take life too seriously, especially in light of his father's constant and tedious recriminations regarding the same, makes Shawn all the more interesting as a sort of rebellious Peter Pan figure. His is a sympathetic, brilliant, idiot-savant-like Casanova persona.

Yet for all of his goofiness and charm, for all of the delight we experience in watching his interactions with his childhood friend turned partner, Gus, during their crime fighting shenanigans, plenty can be said against Shawn. There's something that leaves us feeling somewhat uneasy about how Shawn is engaged in the world. This unease is in part rooted in how he uses his significant powers of observation and memory to manipulate others. For instance, he uses his powers of observation to deduce information about women so as to not just subtly impress but to sometimes outright trick them into dating him.

More egregiously, however, Shawn uses his gifts to get paid large sums of money to solve crimes by relying on the gullibility of those around him. Like a snake oil salesman, Shawn makes his way by telling people what they want to hear, by feeding into the deep psychological space humans fill with beliefs about all sorts of occult powers and objects: telekinesis, ESP, visiting spirits.

However, Shawn isn't merely a consultant. The premise of the show, of course, is that he explicitly portrays himself as a psychic consultant; he's paid by the Santa Barbara Police Department to deploy his psychic abilities for the purpose of solving complicated crimes. As such, then, he relies on deceit and lies in every episode of the series. Granted, some arguments can be mustered to account for the situation in which he unwittingly finds himself. For instance, one could argue that he was coerced, under threat of incarceration, into claiming his eidetic powers were actually psychic powers. In the Pilot episode he's accused of being an accomplice in an appliance theft, and he quickly conjures an explanation of his psychic abilities as a way of having led law enforcement to the proper perpetrator of the crime. But even this explanation does not reflect Shawn in an entirely favorable light, because he has come to the police department to collect a commendation for solving the crime. This selfish, self-aggrandizing motivation gives us a more complete, if less favorable, understanding of Shawn Spencer.

Shawn isn't about doing the right thing; Shawn is often interested in, well, Shawn, or about getting on in the world in obstinate opposition to his father's remonstrations to "grow up" and be responsible.

Now that I think of it, I like these features of his personality too.

Setting the Stage

As a well-compensated psychic consultant to the SBPD, Shawn is engaged in a fairly sophisticated and long-term deceit. And deceit is usually morally problematic. We are all familiar with white lies, those innocuous deceits that serve the important function of gluing our social networks together and maintaining our intimate relationships. When asked whether a pair of slacks looks flattering, the husband nods with happy approval even if he isn't sure about his fashion acumen. Or consider deceit in behavioral research, where revealing the actual aim of a study would influence the outcomes of what is being studied. Social and behavioral scientists frequently deceive or even lie to research participants for purposes of conducting unbiased research, and we generally accept these deceits as necessary for the progress of science.

These examples show us that not all deceit is morally problematic, and in some instances deceit is clearly justifiable. Yet other instances of deception strike us as clearly unjustifiable. Violating spoken, explicit commitments of exclusive intimacy with one's life partner, especially in the age of AIDS, is unjustifiable. And in general we recognize that truthfulness and honesty are necessary features for building trust in relationships, be it in the public or the private spheres. But these observations bring to the fore the following questions: How should we think about Shawn's deceitfulness? To whose judgment should we defer on this topic?

The Philosophers

Philosophers are a serious lot. Moribund, even. Concerned as they reputedly are with getting beyond appearances to truth and reality, one would imagine philosophers would take a fairly dim view of deceit and lying. And to be sure, many philosophers do. However, philosophers have held a wide variety of views on lying and deceit.

Probably the most famous defense and even justification of overt deceitfulness is given voice by Socrates in Plato's *Republic*. Socrates defends the idea of perpetuating what has come to be known as the Myth of the Metals, in which the citizens of the two lower castes constituting society—artisans, laborers, and soldiers—are told that people are made with one of three types of metals, and the metal of which citizens are largely composed dictates what function each will have in society.

Plato thought citizens of this society would be happier if they were not constantly struggling to become something they could not become. He also thought society would function more smoothly, with far less conflict and greater harmony, if all citizens believed the same myth about status and position in the social hierarchy. For political and social purposes, then, Plato embraced the idea not only of lying but of lying to subordinates paternalistically for purposes of controlling the populace. Of course, when we consider what Shawn is doing and what motivates him, we are hard pressed to conclude that he does so out of any sort of noble intention. Any attempt to justify Shawn's deceit along similar lines seems a stretch at best.

A similar position though—focusing on the outcomes of lying, minus the political paternalism—can be found in utilitarian lines of thought. Utilitarians hold that actions are right or good insofar as they contribute to the greater good of the greater number of people; wrong or bad actions are those that reduce the good for a greater number of people. Utilitarians can justify lying and deceit if the lies or deceits are contributory to the greater good. We can easily inagine a scenario that might meet general approval along this line of thinking. If a police officer knowingly lies about the guilt of a thief in order to stop a murderous riot from unfolding, the utilitarian holds this as justified.

But there's trouble lurking here, because there isn't a clear way to calculate long term consequences. There's clearly an argument against most instances of lying based on the same type of utilitarian thinking. If citizens eventually discover that the police officer has been deceitful, citizens will be less trusting of law enforcement officials and other representatives of local executive power, and an erosion of trust is precisely the kind of corruption against which we would want to secure ourselves in coming to a conclusion regarding justified lying. So maybe the utilitarian calculus isn't quite as helpful as we would wish.

Shawn's deceits and lies don't appear to be terribly harmful, and in some ways they bring about good, such as each time he catches a criminal. But the long-term consequences of his deceits are not quite as clearly beneficial. In circumstances in which lying is involved, taking the long view requires us to consider what happens if the lie is discovered. If Shawn is found out, there are a number of culpable people who are going to be socially and legally condemned with him, including his best friend, his girlfriend, his mother, his father, and many members of the police department solely by association. Clients will feel betrayed. There might be a loss of confidence in law enforcement officials, who, it seems, can't even catch a fraudulent criminal right under their noses. So utilitarian thinking doesn't quite provide the moral relief we would want.

Popper and Kant

In contrast to these positions defending or justifying the use of lies and deceit, Sir Karl Popper argued that deceits and lies—especially in the political sphere a la Plato—are opposed to what he called an "open society." Popper was giving voice to a position that was implicit in John Locke's argument against monarchies (which was a direct influence on the American Founding Fathers, including the author of the Declaration of Independence, Thomas Jefferson) and was given greater attention in the twentieth century with the advent of totalitarian rule.

Popper's position echoes that of an earleir philosopher, Immanuel Kant. For Kant, deceitfulness was deeply immoral. According to Kant no human can live in a society in which deceit and lying are advanced as principles for behavior and action, because no such society could continue to exist, or even get off the ground. It would be an untenable society, or perhaps it would even be a self-contradiction to propose that this would be a society at all.

Kant implicitly recognized that deceit and lying are actions premised on specific motives, and motives are difficult to assess, since they are invisible components of a person's internal states instead of observable aspects of his behavior. For Kant, the morally praiseworthy person is the one who wants to do only what could be a maxim for the actions of everyone.

To insert Shawn's actions into this Kantian analysis, we might imagine a maxim being formulated as follows: It is permissible to lie whenever a career opportunity is at stake. Or perhaps: It is permissible to lie whenever we might otherwise go to jail. We can readily see that neither maxim is viable.

For both Popper and Kant, Shawn's deceit would not be defensible. We can't universalize Shawn's efforts into a livable maxim; open and free societies depend on truthfulness. Then again, for Kant there would be no condition under which lying is justifiable, which strikes most reasonable persons as a kind of fanatical commitment to truth, come what may. This isn't to say that Kant's line of thinking is wrong, but only that it has problems. We've seen there are some lies and some deceits that are acceptable or even justifiable. The question is where Shawn fits in the philosophical landscape.

One Last Try

So, how should we characterize Shawn's deceit? Let's consider some further features of the situation Shawn has created. Isn't it true that the moral problem of Shawn's deceit is further compounded by the fact that he makes his father and best friend, and later his girlfriend, complicit in his lies? It seems that Shawn is digging himself deeper and deeper into a moral hole from which it may be impossible for any reasonable person to get him out.

However, there may be a way of looking at Shawn's deceit that will give us room to judge him less harshly. Recall that we have already acknowledged some few examples of lies that we can accept. Maybe Shawn's lies are acceptable based upon the idea that they are instances of mutual deceit.

Mutual deceit is a situation in which the parties involved have agreed to the deceit in question. Poker provides a perfect example of mutually acceptable deceit. Poker players understand that deceit is part of the game, and the rules of the game and the appropriate strategy even depend to some extent on deceit and bluffing. They are, in effect, onto each other from the start.

Likewise, those in power at the SBPD are skeptical of Shawn's powers. They are onto him. Detective Lassiter clearly is, and so is Police Chief Karen Vick. To some degree, Shawn's aware that they're onto him. It's a mutual game of tolerating the deceit that all know is happening, for the sake of playing the crime fighting game, so to speak.

Unfortunately, Shawn's interactions aren't limited to people in the police force who are onto him. Indeed, Shawn has expanded the breadth of his deceit by starting his own psychic investigative business and duping private clients into paying him for his psychic services. Shawn's deceit, then, not only fails to meet the standards for mutually agreed upon deceit, but as I've already mentioned he is evidently guilty of a kind of fraud usually perpetrated by charlatan palm readers. His may be a more sophisticated fraud, but it is fraud nonetheless.

I've appealed above to a "reasonable person" standard. That's usually interpreted as a philosopher's way of excluding the opinions of people he doesn't share. But the reasonable person standard is a very useful conceptual tool when assessing instances of deceit, tied as it is to the notion of public accessibility. One of the most recent contributions to the philosophical literature on deceit is *Lying* by Sissela Bok. Bok argues that one of the clearest ways of determining whether a lie is morally permissible is to judge the lie in light of a reasonable person standard. If a public test of the example can be met, then the moral culpability of the lie is removed or at least acceptably minimized.

This is why white lies, for instance, are acceptable to us. In a public forum, we can offer up most white lies and reasonable persons will acquiesce to the acceptability of the practice. Likewise, other types of deceit, such as failing to inform research subjects that they may receive a placebo instead of an investigational treatment drug, are not something that can be justified in a public forum constituted by reasonable persons.

Unfortunately, again, Shawn can't meet the standard of public acceptability. If in a public forum Shawn were to explain to a group of his peers what he was doing, there seems very little likelihood of reasonable persons concluding that it was morally permissible for him to continue to deceive his clients as he does. Shawn is, in fact, a liar whose lies can't really be justified according to the tenets of most traditional or contemporary moral philosophy.

Hocus Pocus Hokum

Shawn is engaged in deceit and long-term patterns of lying. He is constantly, if hilariously, being "struck" by visions and impressions that lead him to the solutions of crimes. Additionally, as we've observed, he orchestrates much of what he does for selfish gain. And he's also implicitly engaged in what might be considered something more sinister. After all, he is perpetuating false beliefs about extrasensory phenomena and communications from the spirit world. There doesn't seem to be much we can do for Shawn at this point, at least not philosophically speaking.

But this then brings me back to where I started this essay. I really like Shawn's character. Yet now we see that moral philosophers don't, indeed can't, view Shawn or his actions in the same way. Moral philosophers will likely condemn Shawn. Which gets us to the question: Why should we care what moral philosophers think?

Liking Shawn might be just fine, despite the fact that he deals in deceit. Even if you don't want to give Shawn a pass, say, because he actually does catch criminals and unmask charlatans with his ironclad deductive abilities and habituated powers of observation rivaling those of Sherlock Holmes, it's difficult to condemn Shawn outright because at some level we all recognize Shawn represents a kind of life force that societies need. Condemn him all you like morally, Shawn is an integral part of any healthy society. People like Shawn are not only entertaining. They push against the boundaries of belief systems. And society, as Nietzsche famously observed, needs individuals who push boundaries in order to thrive, in order to change.

I think the reason we like Shawn is the same reason we like the show in general, and that is that Shawn and the show represent an instance of mischief making to which we are all privy. Shawn's hocus pocus, his seemingly magical crime-solving abilities, are only an illusion; we know the truth behind this illusion. But Shawn's hokum is the truly interesting and praiseworthy aspect of what Shawn is doing, the real value of Shawn's character and the show *Psych*. What Shawn's doing, and what we as the viewers can see, is that people naively believe in fairly silly things like extrasensory perceptions and communicating with ghosts.

It's the *mischievousness*, the subversiveness of the show and the character, which makes us lean toward giving Shawn a pass. Just like nineteenth-century performers who with their "hokum" mocked the propriety of "acceptable" society and mores, and who drew in audiences by reveling in low comedy and embracing farce all with an eye toward capturing the audience's attention, Shawn's character draws us in with his wit and comedic idiocy while opening our eyes not only to the absurdity of people believing he has extraordinary, occult powers, but to more reasonable explanations for such phenomena than lazy intellects are willing to muster.

Against his stated desire, Shawn has been maturing as the show has progressed. His petulant relationship with his father is more nuanced in later episodes, just as his understanding of the relationship between his parents has deepened. A fitting end to the series would be to have Shawn reveal that he has realized, as some aspect of his own deep psychological motivation, that in part what he has been doing all along is giving an extended lesson against unreflective beliefs in occult nonsense. Most mature people of sufficient intelligence recognize that beliefs in extrasensory perceptions and witches and ghosts and ghouls are not only unwarranted but fairly idiotic. *Psych* is an extended trope dealing with just such a lesson delivered in a rather subtly humorous manner. And sometimes the best lessons, the ones we remember most readily, are lessons accompanied by a joke, a jest, laughter.

Uncomfortably Comfortable

Psyche is just a television show about fictional characters in unlikely situations. But like all works of fiction, the story in its details gives us pause to reflect and consider varied aspects of the human condition. In this instance, Shawn's situation, entertaining as it is, should probably leave us feeling slightly uncomfortable in praising Shawn. However, we find ourselves wanting to praise Shawn, to like him. Shawn's situation should also bring us to understand the importance of real individuals like Shawn who work "outside the box" to offer us a window into the human condition and oddities of beliefs.

People like Shawn are deceivers. So what? People like Shawn, and the television show *Psych* itself, force us to take a closer look at what we think is real and true. Mischief makers in general do this for society; through implicit and subtle communicative acts they force audiences to reconsider some belief or set of beliefs previously naively or even blindly accepted. No society is healthy, and no society can flourish, without such individuals.

14

I Know You Know that I'm Not Telling the Truth

GREGORY L. BOCK AND JEFFREY L. BOCK

Shawn Spencer is the lead psychic for the Santa Barbara Police Department, but he doesn't have psychic powers and his psychic detective agency is a sham. He's a crime-solving machine, however, which he proves over and over again in the cases he works for the SBPD.

Why doesn't he just become a cop if he's so smart? Well, even though he made a perfect score on the police detective exam—something even Lassiter and Juliet couldn't do—he's not cop material. Perhaps this is because of his troubled relationship with his ex-detective father, or perhaps it has to do with his criminal record (busted for car theft when he was eighteen).

Anyway, the only way Shawn can help the Department bust criminals now is to lie about the nature of his skills; hence, the name of his private detective agency, Psych. For this scam to work, Shawn has to pretend that he has supernatural gifts. His childhood friend, Gus, is reluctant to go along with the ruse, but Shawn ultimately convinces him in the pilot episode, saying, "Gus, let's be clear on one thing: the only way they can absolutely prove that I am not a psychic is if I tell them. And I can guarantee you that is the one thing I will never do."

In her noteworthy book, *Lying: Moral Choice in Public and Private Life*, Sissela Bok (no relation to us, and spelling not as cool) defines *lying* as any intentionally deceptive stated message. Defined this way, Shawn is clearly a liar, for he deceives others and does so intentionally. He lies to the SBPD, his father, and his close friends. He even lies to his girlfriend; for example, consider when Shawn asks Juliet's father for permission to

145

marry her in the Season Six episode "Heeeeere's Lassie." Her dad replies: "I don't know. You're sharp, but I've always dreamed that my daughter would marry someone unlike me, someone honest. Now look me in the eye and tell me you've never lied to my daughter. Huh? Yeah, birds of a feather."

Are Shawn's lies morally permissible? Might lying even be necessary in some cases? Is deception an essential part of police work?

You Should Never Lie

Two philosophers are famous for their absolute prohibition of lying: Augustine and Kant. Augustine argues that all intentional duplicity is evil. In *The Enchiridion*, Augustine says that every lie is a sin, even ones that might help other people. He argues that if we allow some lies to help others, then we could allow stealing for the same reason, adultery, and so on. Kant's prohibition against lying is even stronger: when a person lies, she violates her own human dignity. In "On a Supposed Right to Lie," Kant calls truth-telling a formal, *exceptionless* duty. To him it doesn't matter if lying harms someone or not; lying is a "wrong done to mankind generally."

Most philosophers have rejected Kant's view because it seems too easy to think of situations in which lying would be not only permissible, but even necessary. Consider the following standard example: you live in Nazi Germany and are hiding Jews in your attic. One day, two Nazi officers knock on your door and ask whether you are hiding Jews upstairs. Kant would insist that you tell the truth; it's not your responsibility what murderers do. But most of us think this is a bit extreme. There's at least one other duty that outweighs the duty to tell the truth: the duty to protect innocent life.

Lie Like a Rug!

Two philosophers are known for their views on the other extreme: Nietzsche and Machiavelli. Nietzsche thinks that everyone lies because truth telling is impossible. In other words, all language is metaphorical. The problem, according to Nietzsche, is that the scientist and philosopher don't realize this fact and so lie unintentionally (which, considering Bok's definition, would not be a lie). The artist, on the other hand, understands the metaphorical nature of language and "lies" intentionally, creating her own reality. Young Shawn comes to realize this in the Season Two episode "Lights, Camera . . . Homicidio":

> SHAWN: So, acting's really just a lie?
>
> HENRY: Of course, Shawn! What, you think those goofballs on CHiPs are really cops?!
>
> SHAWN: Wow! Anything else you want to ruin for me?

Nietzsche would probably commend Shawn for artistically creating his own psychic reality, but Shawn doesn't live out a Nietzschean philosophy consistently (neither does Nietzsche) because he believes in both lies and truth. For example, Shawn says, "Every good liar's lies are rooted in a kernel of truth" ("Truer Lies").

Machiavelli thinks the end justifies the means to that end, and the end he has in mind is winning and maintaining political power. For him, dishonesty is one of the means available to the one seeking power. In the following passage from Machiavelli's *The Prince*, you can almost hear Shawn speaking:

> Men are so simple and so ready to obey present necessities that one who deceives will always find those who allow themselves to be deceived.

However, Machiavelli and Nietzsche fail to adequately consider the harms and injustices that might result from lying. Shawn learns this from his dad in "Christmas Joy" after Shawn has a falling out with Gus. Henry says, "Of course Gus is going to overreact. He's more than just your friend; he's your partner. There's a special kind of trust there. When you find out you've been lied to by your partner, you get angry."

Bok's position on lying is somewhere in the middle of these extremes and is more reasonable. She says that there's a presumption against lying: lying in general isn't morally permissible, but there are exceptions. She gives three questions we should ask in deciding whether a lie is morally permissible:

1. whether there is an option that doesn't involve a lie,

2. whether a moral reason can be given as an excuse, and

3. whether the reasonable public would condone it.

These conditions will help us decide whether Shawn's lies are good lies.

The Amazing Psych Man

Shawn has something in common with superheroes: superheroes lie. Superman needs his Clark Kent, Batman needs his Bruce Wayne, and Spider-Man needs Peter Parker. While not of the superhero caliber of Batman and Robin, Shawn and Gus need alternate personalities too. If the police were to figure out that Psych was a scam, the gig would be up. In "Truer Lies" from Season Three, Gus pleads with Shawn: "If your psychic powers disappear, Vick won't need to hire us anymore. There's no way we can subsist on the private jobs we get."

When the guys are away from the cops, they're just two ordinary guys who struggle to make ends meet. Whenever they're with the cops, the psychic cape and colorful verbal tights go on.

Shawn and Gus's run-in with the Mantis in the Season Six episode "The Amazing Psych Man & Tap-Man, Issue #2" brings out the comic book shenanigans of our heroes, and Shawn feels a bit insecure in being bested by a superhero:

JULIET: You have to admit [the Mantis] has done a better job than we have in slowing down the Caminos, and he's just one guy.

SHAWN: I'm just one guy. I've solved more crimes than I can count, because I've solved a lot of crimes, not just because I can't count very high.

JULIET: Yes, but you have a supernatural psychic gift. The Mantis is solving crimes using his natural instincts and sharply honed abilities.

GUS: She's right, Shawn. I mean, if you were a regular guy solving these crimes—that would really be impressive. But everyone knows that you're a psychic. I mean, it's really an unfair advantage.

SHAWN: [*laughs*] I guess you're right, Gus . . .

GUS: Why are you bothered by this guy?

SHAWN: Because there's already a badass crime fighter in a cool outfit running around this town, and his name is ME!

While they're more like fans of superheroes than superheroes themselves, a closer examination of traditional superheroes might help us decide the question of lying.

For example, take off Superman's tights and cape, add thick-rimmed glasses, and sweep the bangs up and over to the side, and Clark Kent is born. This disguise is a bit weak, but it seems sufficient to fool the good citizens of Metropolis. This disguise is necessary to ensure that Superman can live a normal life outside of the daily stresses of fighting the evil that threatens all who live under his protection. Bruce Wayne lives his lie as Batman. In reality, he is an extravagantly wealthy trust-fund playboy who has taken on the cowl of the Batman to save Gotham from the hardened criminal set. His lie is that he's a fearsome bat, prowling the Gotham streets striking fear in the hearts of those who would live a life of criminality. He takes his wealth and creates the illusion of superpower.

In Season Three's "Truer Lies," Shawn appeals to Batman's actions when trying to convince Lyin' Ryan to stop lying and trust him:

SHAWN: Stop it! This is real! Your life is in danger! Okay? Even Batman takes off the cape and the cowl when he is in the Bat Cave with Alfred. So, just pretend that I'm Alfred and you be Ryan . . . Wayne.

What this shows is that Shawn (and Batman, too) knows when lying is inappropriate and that Shawn uses superheroes for his moral compass.

In contrast to lying superheroes, take a look at a super villain. The Joker, for instance, is evil incarnate, a being whose primary goal in life is to cause chaos. He delights in mayhem and violence, and to him, the joy of living is murder and violence. But he doesn't live a lie. He's out in the open, telling the truth wherever he goes. He is unapologetically evil. In seeking to be true to himself, not once does he try to hide behind a false persona. No one doubts his evil nature, and he delights in spitting in the face of those who would attempt to counter his chaotic image. What does this say about his foe, Batman, who must lie and cover his tracks to protect his true nature? Is he also a villain? Of course not, but what this demonstrates is that dishonesty is not as pernicious as actions that harm others.

Lying for a Good Reason

One of the main reasons superheroes lie is the ever-present need to protect their loved ones. If it were common knowledge that Superman was Clark Kent, then Lois, Jimmy, and the rest of Clark's human friends and family would be at considerable risk. Peter Parker lost his Uncle Ben early on in his superhero career, but his Aunt May and love interest Mary Jane would certainly benefit from his not revealing the truth, the lie that he's not Spider-Man.

This said, how does Shawn and Gus's lie affect their loved ones? Shawn's dad, Henry, is an ex-cop, who is in no need of protection, but it's possible that Shawn's lies (if uncovered) could ruin Henry's reputation at the SBPD. Henry shared his feelings about the sham early on, in the pilot episode:

SHAWN: Dad!

HENRY: So, are you going to continue with this little charade?

SHAWN: Well, it sort of gives me carte blanche, you know? I mean, I can work cases for the department, I can do private jobs. In fact, I've already got another case.

HENRY: Be aware. This is the last time I cover for you, pal. I'm not okay with this, Shawn, any of it.

Although Henry struggles with the deception, he's probably willing to go along with it because his son is finally doing detective work, which is what Henry has always hoped for. In fact, he shouldn't be surprised by the charade because he's the one who taught Shawn how to lie in the first place. In the following scene from Shawn's younger years in season three's "Six Feet Under the Sea," he catches Shawn scheming to break into a dolphin enclosure at the aquarium:

HENRY: If you're going to take time to create a deception, do it better.

SHAWN: Wait, Dad, I'm confused. Do you want me to lie to you?

HENRY: No, I want you to make it more of a challenge for me to catch you . . . because I always will.

Like a superhero, Shawn's work does put his loved ones at considerable risk. Consider that in Season Four, "Mr. Yin Presents . . .," both of Shawn's love interests, Abigail and Juliet, were kidnapped by the evil Mr. Yin, and Shawn was forced to choose only one of them to save. Also, his mom was kidnapped in "An Evening with Mr. Yang" in Season Three. However, unlike a superhero, his lying doesn't serve to protect his loved ones, it only serves to protect Shawn himself, in order to keep up the facade. Lying for oneself (egoism) isn't as defensible as lying for others (altruism), and only altruism would satisfy Bok's second condition. In short, Shawn's deception seems neither justifiable nor heroic.

Lying for Some Greater Good

One vital aspect of police work requires that detectives go undercover to gain the trust of their suspects. This usually requires taking up a lie to gain the trust of those who are being targeted by the sting. Although this method has proven to be an effective tool in the fight against crime, it involves some questionable tactics that allow officers to deceive their targets. Are the police then guilty of some great moral sin? Should law enforcement personnel avoid getting their hands dirty, ethically speaking?

In "Scary Sherry: Bianca's Toast," Juliet infiltrates a sorority house to determine who was involved in the death of a coed:

JULIET: It's crazy. I have spent the entire morning planning a mixer. And yesterday, I went and I had a Himalayan Mani-Pedi. Yeah, at first it was to get the other girls to talk, but then I realized that my cuticles have been completely taken for granted.

SHAWN: Jules, you realize that we're the only ones that can see . . . or hear you.

Yes, Juliet definitely gets too far into her deception, but the fact remains that she has to lie to the sisters of the society to guarantee success. Their trust is gained, and she's taken in as a fellow Beta Kappa Thetan.

In "Talk Derby to Me," Juliet infiltrates a roller derby team to track down a team of thieves. Somehow, the even-keeled Juliet manages to fool the current members of the derby team with tough talk and posturing. She's accepted and manages to help Shawn crack the case. This deception is just par for the course in undercover work.

CHIEF: Did you break somebody's nose?

JULIET: Yes, I did, thank you. Oh, but it was a clean hit. It was actually more of a dislocation. You know, it just popped right back in. Yeah, she curled into my wingspan, so I was totally justified. We're friends now. She has a cat.

Shawn and Gus do undercover work too. Their consistent *modus operandi* is pretense and deceit. In addition to psychic ability, they've gone so far as to pretend to be supermodels, bounty hunters, and firemen, not to mention the numerous witty jobs Shawn comes up with to explain himself to people he's just met: "Psychic and treasurer of the American Wicker counsel. I'm up for re-election; I'm running on a Rattan platform" ("Talk Derby to Me").

Lying for undercover work seems justifiable under Bok's conditions, at least on a case-by-case basis. The first condition is satisfied since there may be few effective alternatives to good undercover work. If there are better options, like eavesdropping technology, these would be preferable since they involve less risk to the detectives involved. Second, undercover work can prevent great public harm by preventing future crimes. The moral reason here is "the greater good."

As the moral philosophy of utilitarianism states, we should do things that maximize happiness and minimize suffering. If deceiving a few criminal suspects results in a safer and happier society, then we should. This is connected to satisfying the third condition, that the general public accepts this kind of police work since it results in a lower crime rate; however, as the reaction to the recent Patriot Act shows, the public wants limits. We aren't comfortable with a police force that has unchecked power and uses deceptive tactics like the Soviet-era secret police.

So, if it's morally permissible for the police to lie for the public good, should they expect Shawn to tell the truth when it's clear he's helping solve crimes too? As the chief warns Shawn in Season One's "Psych," "If this psychic thing is a scam, we will prosecute. You know hindering a police investigation is a criminal offence?"

This apparent double standard raises questions. But while the target of Shawn's deception includes criminal suspects, it also includes the police. The public grants the police limited powers to deceive some of the population for the purpose of keeping us safe, but lying to the police is another story. While there might be cases when it's okay to lie to the police (consider the Nazi example above), a ruse like Shawn's doesn't satisfy Bok's conditions, especially the first and second.

First, there are other (non-lying) options: join the Department the normal way or start a private detective agency that isn't based on a lie. Second, while Shawn could cite the greater good as a reason, this isn't really why he does what he does. As Shawn's dad tells him, "You work hard to have fun, to show off. Look, I'm not an idiot!" ("Truer Lies") Shawn lies for his own self interest, and this isn't a good reason.

I Know You Know

Some could challenge our assessment that Shawn's lies aren't justifiable by arguing that Shawn doesn't really intend to deceive the SBPD at all. As he says to Juliet in "The Amazing Psych Man & Tap-Man, Issue #2," "I know you know I'm not telling the truth." In other words, he means he's been telling bald-faced lies, or undisguised lies.

Recently, philosophers have become interested in this type of lying because it doesn't fit the standard definition—that a lie is an intentionally deceptive statement. Bald-faced lying isn't deceptive, nor does it seem as reprehensible as a lie that is. Bald-faced liars know their listeners don't believe them. That's not the point. They're dishonest for some other reason. In Roy Sorensen's very readable article, "Bald-faced Lies! Lying Without the Intent to Deceive," Sorensen describes members of Saddam Hussein's regime who were telling bald-faced lies leading up to and during the 2003 war. While speaking to members of the press, regime officials would deny the patently obvious such as the high Iraqi casualties. They did so because in the culture of the regime, loyal members were expected to never say anything negative about it, but the liars never expected their listeners to actually believe them. Tom Carson, in "The Definition of Lying," tells of an example of a student who is caught cheating. Even though the student is caught red-handed, the student denies it because he knows that he will only be punished if he confesses.

There's evidence that Shawn is a bald-faced liar. For one, his psychic episodes are ridiculous. If his goal is to deceive, he would tone down the antics a bit, especially in front of Chief Vick. However, he saves some of his most absurd shows for her. For example, in "Truer Lies," from Season Three she says, "I am not having a conversation with your pinky!" As Sorensen remarks, "One of the marks of a bald-faced lie is that the speaker allows (and sometimes even welcomes) the increase of absurdity."

We could argue that nobody really believes Shawn. Lassiter's disbelief is obvious. He says in "You Can't Handle This Episode," "You know, Spencer, why don't you zip it and let me assess what's going on here before you turn it into a psychic crap fest!" Nobody in the department ever truly defends his psychic powers. There's no denying he's a crime solving genius, but when given the opportunity to defend the supernatural nature of the gift, no one takes a stand. Juliet and McNab have the opportunity to defend Shawn when Mrs. Clayton asks whether Shawn is "for real" in "He Dead." Instead of validating Shawn's psychic gift, they cite the results he produces, which are obvious to everyone. They defend Shawn's abilities as a crime solver, but not his psychic powers. So, maybe the Department is just playing along, something they're willing to do because they know they need his natural crime solving skills.

Bald-Faced Liar!

On the other hand, there's good evidence that many of Shawn's lies are, in fact, meant to deceive. If he were a bald-faced liar, the truth would come out more often to people closest to him, but he doesn't come clean with Juliet until her suspicions force him to. The fact that Juliet and others have their doubts about his psychic powers only means that they're skeptical, not that they recognize Shawn's dishonesty. Also, in spite of evidence to the contrary, Chief Vick believes in him. In "Rob-A-Bye Baby" from Season Two, Chief Vick privately hires Shawn and Gus to find her a nanny. She says, "I want to hire you both to psychically read the best candidate." She has everything she needs to do a proper background check, so she wouldn't need Shawn unless she, in fact, is deceived.

So, Shawn is telling real lies, and his lies would probably fail Bok's conditions: there are better, more honest options available, his reasons are morally deficient, and the reasonable public would not allow it if they knew. But are we being too hard on him? Remember that he has solved numerous cases and kept the public safe, a feat that the SBPD may not have been able to accomplish without him. Should we overlook his lies for the greater good?

VI

I Know You Know

15
Duped into the Truth

RONDA BOWEN

One of the more humorous aspects of *Psych* is when Shawn has to dupe the Santa Barbara Police Department (SBPD) into believing he's psychic rather than observing details with acute skill. The problem with Shawn's strategy, even though he delivers the truth, is that he's lying in the *delivery* of the truth. Shawn isn't psychic; his father trained him to observe every aspect of a scene. If the SBPD have the right suspect, but their justification for this knowledge is based upon a lie, can we then say that the SBPD *know* that the suspect is guilty?

Figuring out what constitutes knowledge is not a new question for philosophy. In ancient times, the Greek philosopher Plato (429–347 B.C.E.) wrote a dialogue, *Theaetetus*, and in it three guys named Socrates, Theodorus, and Theaetetus discuss the nature of knowledge. They agree that perception alone can't be knowledge, as perception can be mistaken. Imagine for a moment you are looking at a glass of water. When you place a stick in the glass, the stick appears to bend. Because perception can trick us in this manner, it can't count as a form of knowledge.

Next, the question of a true belief comes into question, for we wouldn't say that a false belief can constitute knowledge. This is because we could learn a new piece of information that would make the false belief obsolete. For example, imagine you believed that the present king of France was bald. However, you then learned there is no present king of France. You would be able to replace the first statement "The present king of France is bald" with a replacement statement "There is no present king of France."

However, just as Shawn wouldn't get away with simply telling the SBPD who committed the crime, we can't get away with calling true beliefs *knowledge*. We must also have an account *justifying* the truth of the belief. In the series premier, Shawn is on the verge of arrest due to his statement that he knows who the guilty party is. Shawn calls in tips to the SBPD in order to help solve crimes. These tips he provides are based upon observations he makes while watching the evening news. The problem is that the SBPD detectives don't have the keen sense of observation Shawn has. Shawn must provide the SBPD with an account of how he arrived at his conclusions. When the SBPD believe that Shawn's account must stem from being an accomplice to these crimes, he then uses his observational talents to convince them that he is psychic. The justifications Shawn has used in order to arrive at his conclusion are different from the justifications the police have in arriving at their conclusions based upon Shawn's reporting.

Smith, Jones, and Shawn Spencer

In 1963 Edmund Gettier called into question the usual theory held by philosophers—that knowledge consists of 'justified true beliefs'. Gettier pointed out that there can be beliefs that are justified, and true, but not knowledge.

In the example from *Psych*, when Shawn and the SBPD have different justifications, it seems odd to say that the police are justified in their belief in the way that Shawn is justified in his belief. Gettier points out that there need to be good reasons for believing a particular statement is true for it to count as knowledge. He provides his audience with two examples.

In the first example, two men, Smith and Jones are up for a job promotion. Smith believes that Jones will get the job, and he believes that Jones has ten coins in his pocket. Because these two sentences involve the same person, Jones, these beliefs also lead to the belief that the man with ten coins in his pocket will get the job. Unbeknownst to Smith, he has ten coins in his own pocket too. When Smith gets the job, it seems fair to state that his belief that the man with ten coins in his pocket will get the job was correct. However, it seems strange to call this belief *knowledge* since Smith believed the person being referred to was Jones. So it seems that Smith's belief was false.

Likewise, when the police believe that the psychic will tell them who committed the crime, they have a false belief, even if the information provided by Shawn is true. For example, in the Season One episode "Spellingg Bee" Shawn believes that Miklous is responsible for the death of the former champion, Elvin Cavanaugh, as well as the collapse of one of the participants in the spelling bee. He bases this belief upon an observation involving analysis of Chinese food, determining that Cavanaugh was going to spill the beans about Miklous and Jiri cheating, and determining that the cheating was occurring by an electrically rigged asthma inhaler. When the police arrive on the scene, Shawn acts out his psychic belief and points to the inhaler held by Jiri. The police then formulate their conclusion that Miklous must be guilty based upon Shawn's demonstration of the proof.

Add Brown to the Mix

In the second example Gettier uses, Smith believes that Jones owns a Ford and he has good reasons for believing this. So, Smith goes ahead and constructs three statements after selecting three random places where his good friend Brown may be located. With any statement that is true, by adding the proposition "or" and a second statement, the new statement is also true. For example: "All unmarried men are bachelors" is true. "Martians exist" is not true. But "Either all unmarried men are bachelors or Martians exist" *is* true. By using the same logic in the previous example, Smith forms the following statements:

A: Either Jones owns a Ford, or Brown is in Boston.

B: Either Jones owns a Ford, or Brown is in Barcelona.

C: Either Jones owns a Ford, or Brown is in Brest-Litovsk.

Just as in the first example, it turns out that Smith is correct by accident. It turns out that Jones doesn't own a Ford, instead the Ford Jones has given Smith a ride in was a rental. Brown is in Barcelona. Now, this would seem like a lucky guess, and once again, we would be hard-pressed to call this odd stroke of truth-generating luck *knowledge*.

By the same token, such either-or statements come into play within *Psych*. Either Shawn has some secret talent for determining guilt, or he is on the inside. Well, Shawn does have a secret talent: a highly defined talent of observation for determining guilt in crimes. But it isn't the talent the SBPD believes it to be, namely, psychic ability.

So then there exists a problem. The problem is that while Shawn may know who committed the crime, it seems difficult to state that the SBPD know who committed the crime because as it stands, there is a problem with the sufficient conditions for knowledge. Someone can be justified in believing something that is false or someone can have a lucky belief. Because it seems difficult in many episodes of *Psych* to state that the SBPD have knowledge about the guilty party, it also seems as though the arrests they make are unjustified (after all, it would be difficult to say in court, "The psychic led us to the guilty party"). Therefore, conditions for justification must exist.

The Lottery Paradox

"I know that I won't win the lottery this year" is a problem statement for the justification of knowledge. Lottery paradoxes involve statistically improbable events. For example, it's statistically improbable that Shawn is psychic. Then again, it's statistically improbable that Shawn can note all the details he does, even with his father's training drills. When he recalls the number and types of hats in the restaurant for his father, we are all amazed that he has the attention to detail to do this (Season One, "Pilot").

It's this improbability principle "I know that people don't notice details to that extreme extent" that gets Shawn into trouble. It's actually *more believable* for most of the police officers for Shawn to be psychic. Detective Lassiter is skeptical. He looks at Shawn and thinks, "I know that he's not psychic." How, then, can he justify the arrests that take place as a result of Shawn's investigations?

In his 2004 book, *Knowledge and Lotteries*, John Hawthorne described such "lottery propositions," or propositions where the statement seems likely to be true, but we wouldn't necessarily claim that we have knowledge of it. For example, even though the statement "Shawn isn't a psychic" seems to be likely, it's difficult to say with certainty that we know that "Shawn is not a psychic." Contrast this with the statement "All men who have never been married are bachelors." In this second statement, it seems clear that the statement is true and it seems clear that we can rightly make the statement, "I know that all never-married men are bachelors."

It is on this uncertainty that the SBPD allows Shawn to continue to assist with crime investigation as a "psychic." They allow for the possibility that the statement "Shawn isn't a psychic" may be false. When Shawn can convince the police that he received the information relating to the crimes he's tipped off on through psychic activity, they have no way to prove that this claim is false ("Pilot"). Chief Vick buys into this idea so strongly that she assigns him his first case.

What lottery propositions do in justification is add in a sense of probability. While the probability of the statement "Shawn isn't a psychic" is very high, Shawn produces information that makes it appear as though he *is* psychic. This is called a *counter-example*, and it serves as a defeater (a statement that overrides the seemingly true lottery proposition). In the statement "I won't win the lottery," the defeater would be a counter-example where I do win the lottery. Perhaps I watch one person after another lose, and my doubt grows stronger, so that I perceive the possibility of winning the lottery as a very small one. Even so, it is difficult to completely give up and say, "I know that I won't win the lottery." That is because there's a chance, albeit a small one, that the statement "I won't win the lottery" is false.

When Shawn continues to solve crimes, and it seems as though he's doing so using psychic abilities, it produces a defeater to the statement "Shawn isn't a psychic." While Shawn, his sidekick Gus, Henry, and the audience all know that Shawn isn't a psychic, the police don't. This produces an interesting irony for the viewer—at once, the statement "Shawn isn't a psychic" is true, yet the police have good reasons to believe the statement is false. Even so, it appears that this defeater isn't enough to give the officers sufficient reasons to arrest the guilty party.

Your Testimony, Please

When it comes to justifying what you know, there are two camps. The *internalists* believe that reasons for believing something to be true come from inside; that is, through thinking through any particular subject, we can determine whether we are justified in our beliefs. The *externalists*, on the other hand, believe that there need to be factors outside of an individual that contribute to whether or not a belief can be justified.

For the externalist, justification comes from many sources, one of which is testimony. In the real world, court cases hinge upon whether an individual's testimony is true or false. This is so in *Psych*. The police officers feel justified in arresting suspects that Shawn points out because they believe that "Shawn tells the truth." However, Shawn is lying to the officers. He is claiming to be psychic when he isn't. This calls into question whether his testimony is reliable. For instance, we might call into question a teacher who believes in creationism but teaches evolution. We might ask whether her testimony is, in fact, reliable. After all, while she may be speaking about scientific theories in an accurate manner, she may believe they are utterly false. We might wonder whether her testimony is then clouded by this belief, regardless of whether the students take her testimony to be justified true beliefs.

By this same token, the reliability of Shawn is called into question. He is, after all, purporting to be an individual who makes our radars go off. "I am psychic," he says. By all accounts, it's highly unlikely that this is the case, while at the same time we don't want to say "I know that he's not psychic." The idea behind testimony is that ideally, if an individual knows something and tells another person, then the hearer ought to also know that statement to be true. With testimony, there are several things to consider, which Detective Lassiter calls into question. The first important facet of credible testimony is the consideration of the testifier's honesty. Detective Lassiter does not believe that Shawn is being sincere. The second facet of credible testimony is whether or not the individual is a competent testifier. This is not questioned by Detective Lassiter, but not for the reasons we would suspect.

In the teacher example, we might say that she isn't a competent testifier. Because she has beliefs differing from those, which she teaches, she might be considered incompetent. However, one might make the argument that even though she does not herself believe the theories she shares with the class, she has attained enough education to qualify her as competent in this regard. At this point, her sincerity might be called into question. The audience, Gus, and Henry know that Shawn is competent, because we know about his gifted skill as an observer. However, we call into question his sincerity and honesty.

Detective Lassiter calls Shawn's sincerity into question and does not trust Shawn. He does, however, believe that Shawn does have the experience to testify—but this is because he believes Shawn to be in cahoots with the guilty parties. It would appear, then, that even though we might see Shawn do the work in order to come to the conclusions he comes to— Shawn isn't a reliable testifier, in that he is not being sincere. This is the case both in the eyes of the audience and in the eyes of those close to him, Gus and Henry. We need more thorough justification before the police can justify their belief that the suspects Shawn catches are indeed criminals.

In the End, It's What's Inside that Counts

The police cannot rely upon the testimony alone they are provided with. Instead, they have to have further reasons to believe that Shawn tells the truth when he points to the criminals. In "Spellingg Bee," Shawn does his psychic dance and points to possibly poisoned Chinese food as the cause of death as opposed to what police have called a heart attack. Chief Vick tells Shawn, "We need more than a hunch." Shawn then has to do more work in order to help the police see that it wasn't a heart attack, but a murder that took place.

Shawn winds up deducing that the inhalers used by two of the children participating in the spelling bee were identical, but one of the children, Jiri, doesn't have a prescription on record for an inhaler. When the child with the prescription collapsed, even after using the inhaler, the inhaler disappeared, and according to one witness, "it did not feel like a normal inhaler." At the end of the episode, Shawn spots Miklous sending signals to Jiri through the inhaler, and at this point, he calls the police. When he acts out his psychic dance, pointing to the inhaler Jiri is using, he hopes that the police will come to their own conclusion that Miklous is the guilty party. In other words, Shawn's testimony isn't enough. He must create a situation where the responding officers can deduce the guilty party on their own.

While much of the evidence presented in the case is external to the individuals involved, the rationality and reasoning leading to the conclusion happens internally, and it is the product of correct logical thinking. Internalism is often criticized as being circular, meaning that the conclusion of the argument rests upon premises that already assume that conclusion. Internalists disagree on account of the idea that we have particular foundational bits of knowledge that cannot be broken down any further. For example, if I believe that $1 + 1 = 2$, this may be considered to be a foundation of knowledge. Shawn also has such knowledge. Because he notices details in such a clear way, he can reliably deduce from those details what is going on. It's as simple as addition. Where Shawn's account falls apart is in his testimony; thus, he has to motivate the detectives on the case to come to their own conclusions by demonstrating concrete evidence. While Shawn's methods are unorthodox—he's playing the role of a psychic—the evidence he points to is concrete and reliable.

With the concrete evidence—and the various threads the police detectives have been fed by Shawn—the police themselves are able to piece together what happened in the crime. While they appear to be relying upon the testimony of a psychic, in truth, they are able to follow the logic that would have led them to the same conclusion Shawn presents them with – he just serves as a short cut in that he puts the dots on the map. While Detective Lassiter approaches Shawn with great skepticism, he finds that Shawn is remarkably accurate. Even though he can't explain why Shawn is right or how Shawn draws the conclusions he draws, he can't possibly argue with such evidence as questionable chicken ("Spellingg Bee"), or a woman who runs once she is accused of stealing a five million dollar wedding ring ("Speak Now or Forever Hold Your Piece").

While this line of reasoning might seem external, keep in mind it's only the evidence that is external to the officer. What's important is that the reasoning that leads to the conclusion is occurring *internally*. Through reflection on the various pieces of the puzzle that have been presented, Detective Lassiter and

Chief Vick are able to put together the puzzle through reflecting upon the pieces they have been given. Once this happens, they're able to confirm that the information they receive through testimony from Shawn is justified true belief. This also helps to serve as a defeater so that it builds their trust in Shawn's testimony in the future. Though the statement "Shawn isn't psychic" may still hold, the probability of that statement, for them, continues to fall. Naturally, there's the potential that someone will catch on to his game—and that creates tension in the show. Shawn has to be careful to maintain the psychic act and the mystery of him coming into the clues he finds in order to maintain his job as a consulting psychic detective. As time passes, and Shawn proves himself to be more reliable, externalists may have more of a foothold on the justification process happening.

As it stands, the fact that there's an incongruity between the justification experience Shawn has (and those who are wise to what is going on with Shawn) and the SBPD creates a tension that causes us to question whether the arrests made on the show are based on knowledge of the guilt of the suspects.

Even though it appears at first glance that the SBPD detectives aren't justified in their beliefs, an examination of the various theories of justification shows that the officers are themselves *internally* justified. That means that while Shawn presents the criminal, motive, and method, the SBPD detectives come to the same conclusion using their own logical reasoning process.

16
Shawn the Perfect Pragmatist

AMANDA K. LUSKY

Shawn Spencer is playfully adaptive, open to alternative perspectives, and updates methods through experience. His apparent, but not real, psychic abilities also popularize unconventional approaches to experience. Shawn also displays tough-mindedness by privileging facts above theories and countering dogmatic beliefs with skepticism. He highlights the significance of being tolerant and experimental with additive knowledge from other non-traditional views.

In Shawn's own quirky way, what he does is useful, it works, and still meaningfully provides knowledge for his community of detectives. Shawn actually makes for a perfect *pragmatist*.

Experiences

Shawn and Gus are constantly engaged in co-operative inquiry together with the Santa Barbara Police Department and other community members. They creatively use their experiences to solve cases with what ends up as a mix of conventional and innovative methods. Pragmatists prize certain behaviors, like openness and risk taking. These characteristics continually work for us in an unpredictable world. Pragmatism allows us to solve problems together for a more vibrant democratic community.

Shawn has the betterment of himself and Santa Barbara in mind when he's working at Psych. The surrounding community is safer. Characteristics of Shawn's pragmatic attitude also spread to whoever is connected to Psych. People start to believe new ideas, even weird ones, if they fit the circumstances. This open tolerance for alternative perspectives is a significant cornerstone for both pragmatism and democracy. So a pragmatically operated psychic detective agency is astonishingly indispensible for a lively and democratic Santa Barbara.

The police need Shawn's pragmatic techniques with cases that could be better handled beyond protocol. The Santa Barbara Police Department knows that they face unyielding red tape when trying to stop criminals and curb unlawful reactions from citizens. Shawn's eccentric antics are the only match for The Mantis's superhero-like vigilante actions ("The Amazing Psych Man and Tap Man"). Detective O'Hara's admiration for the Mantis inadvertently describes what Shawn and Gus have in common with the superhero figure. She remarks that most vigilantes are good people trying to help the community.

The Mantis uses his natural abilities to solve crimes. Detective O'Hara means this as a contrast to Shawn's supposed supernatural psychic gift. Yet, Gus's sarcastic reaction shows just how on the mark O'Hara's comparison with the Mantis actually is: "She's right, Shawn. I mean, if you were a regular guy solving these crimes that would really be impressive. But everyone knows that you're a psychic. I mean, it is a real unfair advantage." Shawn really doesn't have an unfair psychic advantage over fake superheroes like the Mantis though. Both have great pragmatic potential. They can go outside the Santa Barbara Police Department restrictions and make a difference in the world.

Daddy Issues

We can investigate Shawn's and Henry's relationship for insight into Shawn's success as a pragmatic detective. Shawn is a good detective mostly because he's hyperaware of his surroundings. He gained this psychic-like expertise through a somewhat traumatic childhood ("Pilot"). Henry Spencer, Shawn's dad, relentlessly trained his son to be a police detective. Shawn ends up disappointing his father by initially choosing a transient lifestyle after high school to cope with his parent's divorce.

Everything changes when Shawn later opens Psych as a psychic detective. Henry secretly approves of Shawn's new accomplishments and this fact is not lost on his son. It is an optimistic turn to their previously tense relationship. Shawn's disdain of his strict upbringing largely overshadows other happier moments with his dad. Not all of their shared experiences are terrible. It's just that there's an ever widening disconnect between what Henry wants for his son and Shawn's feelings.

Henry's positive reinforcement of his son's behavior was also too infrequent. Shawn once commented to his best friend, Burton "Gus" Guster, that he wasn't sure his dad loved him ("Weekend Warriors" in Season One). The hiding of familial affection persists until Henry and Shawn spend more time working together. Henry becomes visibly upset whenever Shawn is in danger in later seasons, like when he's shot and kidnapped ("Shawn Takes a Shot in the Dark"). The Yin and Yang cases, in particular, are turning points in their relationship where Henry and Shawn grow noticeably closer ("An Evening with Mr. Yang"; "Mr. Yin Presents"; and "Yang 3 in 2D"). They even gradually develop a mutual respect for their chosen careers. Shawn's and Henry's heartfelt interactions in "Santabarbaratown" in Season Six are a far cry from Season One when Henry won't help with Shawn's first case until he proves that he's still a keen detective.

This changing father and son relationship also highlights their philosophical conceptions. Both share similar values about fighting crime. Ultimately, it doesn't matter that Shawn and Henry have slightly conflicting detective techniques because they still help out the community. The distinctions between their personalities also start to blur when looking at their comparable abilities. Henry wanted to guide his excitable son into an honest and disciplined lifestyle. He admonishes young Shawn for gambling in "Poker? I Barely Know Her" (Season One). We may infer Henry's notions about respecting authority from his discussion of Shawn's "poker philosophy"— if I can do something then I should do it. His point is that Shawn should listen to him and not abuse his talent.

It seems easy enough to make money by taking advantage of your hyperawareness. Everyone eventually loses, as Shawn later discovers at the roulette table. Henry gave his son good advice but Shawn won't blindly follow his dad's lead. It is clear that Shawn never fully accepts Henry's values. He lacks Henry's respect for official procedures. Shawn would rather have fun and take advantage of whatever will get him out of trouble. Yet, he still reluctantly understands why his father taught him to use his detective skills for good results. Following a lead in the case sometimes requires adjusting rules for a desired outcome. Henry can appreciate his son's adaptability here to a certain degree.

Henry appears to be more dogmatic than Shawn about adhering to abstract principles but there are practical limits to this commitment. He does, after all, arrest Shawn to teach him a lesson about obeying the law ("Ghosts"). Henry is a complex character though. We shouldn't take his moral worldview as completely black and white. Even he allows surprising exceptions to what seems like a steadfast position, if that helps ensure positive consequences.

Henry sought out the coroner's report before the official briefing when he found out that Shawn broke into the British Ambassador's house ("Shawn Rescues Darth Vader"). He didn't inform the Santa Barbara Police Department about his son's crime. Instead, Henry warned Shawn about solving the case first before he's labeled the primary suspect. Shawn was apparently innocent enough to warrant his dad's protection from a police investigation. Here Henry understands that we may circumvent police procedures if needed without losing respect for their overall purpose. Regardless, Henry thinks that not all rules should be broken. Jerry Card, a corrupt ex-police officer, shoots him for that very character trait ("Santabarbaratown"). Jerry knew Henry would never become a bad cop. Henry, unlike his son, has too much principled respect for the uniform.

Meaningful Shared Experiences

Henry and Gus worry about Shawn's general lack of responsibility. Shawn's fun-loving character contrasts with his dad's and friend's seriousness. This also makes him seem unfit to run a private detective agency. Henry thinks that being a psychic detective is merely another job that Shawn will quit once it gets difficult. Shawn already defended himself against this charge earlier while convincing Gus to join him on a case.

Gus also doesn't think that Shawn can commit to a typical adult lifestyle. He questions Shawn about the fifty-seven jobs he has had since high school, from acupuncture to driving the Oscar Meyer Wiener Mobile. Shawn cites the considerable experience that he gained working those odd jobs as additional reasons for becoming a psychic detective. Now, all he needs is Gus's support. Shawn knows that he is more likely to stick with the job if Gus stays alongside him.

Shawn obviously cannot run Psych alone. For all of his independence and spunk, Shawn is startlingly dependent on encouragement. Gus consequently plays a complicated role in Shawn's life that Henry could never fill. Gus, in many ways, is equally vital as Shawn's detective skills for Psych's success. Sometimes his input is subtle, like when Detective Lassiter admitted that he didn't understand what Gus contributes to cases ("Shawn and Gus in Drag [Racing]"). Elsewhere, Shawn and Gus realize that they're an inseparable team with distinct talents ("Feet Don't Kill Me Now"). Shawn's supposed psychic methods won't work without co-operative inquiry with his friend. Both have tolerance of each other's quirks and unique knowledge. Together, Shawn and Gus are capable of achieving things that would otherwise prove quite challenging. Such cohesion is rooted in years of meaningfully shared experiences.

How to Make Our Psychic Visions Clear

There are numerous instances where Shawn—as well as other characters—employ the pragmatic method to achieve the results they want. The pilot episode is a great introduction to Shawn as a pragmatist. Shawn uses his hyperawareness and detective skills to good use even before setting up Psych. Shawn randomly calls in tips about solving cases to the Santa Barbara Police Department. He has some level of genuine concern for his community and knows that he's doing good deeds. Understandably, he's surprised when Detective Lassiter names him as the key suspect in the stereo robbery. Lassiter assumes that Shawn's information could only come from a guilty suspect, since it's too good. Detective Lassiter cites Shawn's criminal record, his lack of a steady job, and his overly specific tips as further evidence of guilt.

Shawn's creative solution to this problem sets him up as both a psychic and pragmatist. He uses his detective knowledge to inform his supposed psychic episode. He also does more than save himself from arrest. Shawn simultaneously solves another case by mentioning the taillight shards he saw in the other man's boot. Psychic abilities are simply a pragmatic tool to help resolve problems, personal and otherwise.

Pragmatism is a home-grown American school of philosophy begun in the late nineteenth century by thinkers such as Charles Sanders Peirce (1839–1914), William James (1842–1910), and John Dewey (1859–1952). William James saw pragmatism as a fluid method that emphasizes experiences as against abstract theory. We update our views to meet new challenges by pooling experiences together through democratic engagement. This way, our collective ideas remain viable.

John Dewey sees pragmatism as a means for a democratic community to solve its own problems together. We don't have to accept pragmatism as part of our personal conceptions for the community to benefit from our experiences. Instead, it is vital for a thriving democracy that people hold alternative views as well. Creative and co-operative problem solving are thus essential pragmatic skills. We need to work together, which means that we must tolerantly navigate our public environment. Variety of experiences lets us explore options that traditional approaches would otherwise neglect or misunderstand. Openness to new possibilities is also an important feature of pragmatism. Ideas should be updated as needed. It's an on-going process since experience always continues. This is why we must draw from public experiences when faced with complex situations, such as strange police cases.

Shawn would never think of himself as a pragmatist, mostly because he's probably unaware of the term's philosophical background. Yet his psychic-like approach to solving cases still employs numerous pragmatic techniques. Pragmatism also fits with Shawn's playful personality. William James associates a person's personal temperament with his or her chosen philosophical convictions. Tender-minded individuals treat abstract speculation as superior to practical consequences. Shawn, instead, exhibits tough-mindedness because he values experience over conventional theory.

Shawn is also not dogmatic in his views. Shawn pragmatically adjusts his conclusions to match the circumstances and isn't afraid of making wild accusations. Gus sums up Shawn's haphazard process of solving cases, "Lemme guess, you have a loosely formed idea that shouldn't work on paper but ultimately proves reasonably successful?" ("He Dead"). This nicely illustrates Shawn's pragmatic attitude. He doesn't get bogged down with privileging theory over experience. Shawn acts upon his odd ideas, regardless of conventional assumptions.

The Pragmatic Maxim

William James credits Charles Sanders Peirce with formulating the pragmatic maxim, which is a practical way to determine what ideas are presently useful. The pragmatic method requires us to look at what consequences stem from our philosophical notions. Our ideas are tools that can make a beneficial difference in the world if the pick the ones that do work for us. As a quick illustration of why we need the pragmatic maxim in philosophy, imagine that a squirrel steals Gus's candy bar and runs up a tree. Gus gives chase but merely ends up going around the tree trunk opposite the squirrel. He'll never catch the squirrel at this rate! One could ask what is philosophically happening here. Is Gus going around the squirrel or is the squirrel going around Gus? The pragmatic maxim can settle this philosophical dispute. James thinks that it all depends on what we want to accomplish, so we should explore the practical meaning of the term 'around'. We cannot only engage in abstraction if we want to focus adequately on tangible results. Pragmatists consider that we should avoid idle philosophical inquiry if there are no foreseeable practical consequences. We wouldn't bother Gus with metaphysics when he's trying to retrieve a candy bar unless that was a tactic to lure the thieving squirrel to sleep. Philosophical reflection cannot take priority over affairs in the world. The pragmatic maxim is about finding what works for us now until we must alter our course in light of future experiences.

Psych is a long-running television series so it's difficult to cover every pragmatism example with significant detail. Rather, I'll go through brief explanations of four events with key pragmatic themes. First off, Shawn isn't worried about being wrong. We catch this in the Season Three episode "Disco Didn't Die. It was Murdered!" when Shawn has to coax Henry back onto the case. Henry was paralyzed by being wrong in his biggest bust as a police officer. He points out that Shawn is more comfortable with making mistakes. Mistakes have pragmatic value though, sometimes more so than a desired outcome. We learn from both good and bad experiences. They inform our future actions.

Secondly, Shawn often takes unorthodox risks when solving cases. He accepts Detective Lassiter's wild accusation that the victim was murdered prior to the shark attack ("The Head, the Tail, and the Whole Damn Episode"). Despite this seemingly irrational claim, Detective Lassiter and Shawn are actually on the right track.

Third, Shawn is constantly seeking co-operative help from others' experiences. Shawn needed Gus's knowledge of safes to open the lock on the paleontologist's shed ("Sixty Five Million Years Off"). Gus has more proficiency with safes because he subscribes to an online safecracking magazine ("Speak Now or Forever Hold Your Piece").

Lastly, Shawn is not afraid to challenge rules if he's following the available evidence. He passes Detective Lassiter's lie detector test with his dad's undercover police techniques to avoid suspicion as a murder suspect ("Shawn Rescues Darth Vader"). Shawn believed the lies that he was psychic and not involved with the break-in at the British Ambassador's house. Physiologically, these beliefs cash out as true on the machine.

Such examples suffice to show the extent that Psych's characters, especially Shawn, behave pragmatically.

What the Psych Agency Has Accomplished

Unconventional investigations have significantly contributed to solving certain cases. Some conventional police procedures are limited here. This is how the Psych agency is more adaptable than the Santa Barbara Police Department. Shawn's pragmatic attitude fuels Psych's overall success. It's the most consistent and gainful employment that Shawn has ever had.

Psych stays in business because its services extend beyond intuitional conventions. Shawn and Gus don't always follow police procedures and the law. While we may frown and laugh at Shawn's methods, they work. We don't have to imitate their behavior. This is why pragmatism pairs well with democracy. The democratic community still benefits from Psych even though no one else has to act exactly like Shawn.

We almost expect bizarre cases dealing with pseudoscience at a psychic detective agency. Surprisingly, the more paranormal cases make up a relatively small percentage of Psych's overall caseload. None of these cases actually involves paranormal phenomena. The evidence sometimes began to point to that sort of conclusion. Shawn is surprisingly a bit more skeptical of pseudoscience though, unless it's sightings of Bigfoot. "Not Even Close . . . Encounters" from Season Five is a good example of when Shawn briefly accepts the paranormal lead. Shawn and Gus originally accept the lawyer's story about the UFO abduction. They have believed in the existence of UFOs ever since childhood. However, all of the available paranormal evidence was planted to discredit the lawyer, Roy Kessler. The culprit is a bad guy in this case, which also happens in every similar situation. Shawn and Gus still have to follow the spooky evidence at hand until it points toward the real suspects.

The Santa Barbara Police Department is even more constrained than Shawn on pseudoscientific issues. Detective Lassiter asks Stewart Gimbley to leave the police station after he claimed to be a werewolf, because "jail is for criminals, not delusional whackadoos" ("Let's Get Hairy"). Shawn is willing to consider alternative explanations until they fail to describe the evidence at hand. In Season Five, Shawn lets Gus follow the devil possession theory until it doesn't work for the situation ("The Devil's in the Details and the Upstairs Bedroom"). He's somewhat taking Henry's advice in this episode about keeping an open mind with your partner's ideas, "You get your partner's back, Shawn, even if it means putting your doubts aside for a minute." Like mistakes, doubts are also significant pragmatic tools to guide experience into preferred outcomes. Despite Shawn's misgivings, they follow on what Gus calls a "hunch based off of unverifiable information."

The overall pragmatic method still works even though Gus ends up being wrong with the case details. No one knows what the future will hold for Psych. There could be future cases that involve real pseudoscientific phenomena. At least Gus will have another opportunity to use his Ghostbuster uniform from "Heeeeere's Lassie!"!

Shawn doesn't believe in psychics ("Psy vs Psy"). He still does a good job with fooling everyone else around him. His playful demeanor strangely supports his perceived psychic abilities. He acts ridiculous mostly because he can. It also surprisingly helps with solving cases. The Santa Barbara Police

Department doesn't approve of Shawn's methods but they tolerate him for the results. Calling Shawn a "psychic," from the police's point of view, is an excuse for his eccentric behavior.

We can learn a few things about how people commonly view psychics by their reactions to Shawn. People sometimes regard psychics as strange individuals and possibly delusional. It's unfortunate how this unfair stereotype colors judgment of those engaged in pseudoscience, such as psychics and ghost hunters. Shawn's silliness plays into these preconceptions quite well. By being a successful version of a ridiculous character, Shawn is changing what it means to be a psychic. Psychics don't have to be real for beliefs in psychics to be useful for us. People in Santa Barbara are more open to the possibility of functioning psychics after Psych's success. Such tolerance will eventually extend to other alternative approaches that fit our experiences better. We can credit Shawn's pragmatic attitude for this enriched democratic community.

17
A Little Bit of This, a Little Bit of That, and a Whole Lotta Knowledge

COURTLAND LEWIS

If you're like me, you find Shawn's perceptual skills thoroughly impressive. He looks at photos, files, people, and crime scenes, and almost instantly catalogues every bit of information available. He then uses what seem to be random bits of information gathered from these perceptions in order to solve some of Santa Barbara's toughest—and sometimes silliest—crimes.

Shawn knows that he's right, and so do Gus and Henry, because they know his conclusions are based on years of training and practice. Everyone else, however, remains skeptical about Shawn's psychic abilities and the "knowledge" he claims to have concerning criminals and cases. The interplay between the characters of *Psych* and the audience's knowledge of Shawn's true abilities give *Psych* the rare virtue of shedding light on some of the complexities of classical and contemporary accounts of human knowledge. Let's start this episode.

Flashback . . . Ancient Greece

It's only fitting that we begin with a flashback. Imagine a young Shawn having a talk with his fully haired father in fifth-century B.C.E. Greece. As Shawn runs from the agora (the Greek marketplace) to the back door of the house, Henry stops him and asks, "Shawn, what counts as knowledge?" The first answer Shawn might offer is that knowledge is whatever he sees or perceives. This seems like a good answer, but Henry would quickly point out that such an answer leads to an absurdity. If knowledge is seeing, then not seeing must be ignorance, and as a result, every time Shawn blinks he would become ignorant.

What's more, Shawn's observation might be mistaken. He might have a belief that he sees someone off in the distance who resembles Gus, and conclude that it's actually Gus coming for a visit. However, when the figure gets closer it becomes apparent to Shawn that it's some other kid. Since knowledge doesn't cease when we close our eyes, and our perceptions can be mistaken, knowledge must be something else.

Because we're dealing with Shawn Spencer, we know he won't let his father dupe him this easily. With all the certainty he can muster, Shawn confidently tells his dad, "Knowledge is having a true judgment about something." "Excellent," Henry exclaims, "But how can you be certain that your judgment is true?" Take, for instance, the case above where Shawn claims he knows that he can see Gus approaching the house. Shawn's claim is based on his belief that Gus always comes by at this time of day, and that he sees what appears to be Gus heading towards the house. Unfortunately there's no guarantee that Shawn is correct. For all Shawn knows, Gus is walking behind the approaching stranger. If this is the case, then Shawn's judgment that Gus is coming for a visit is true, but his belief that Gus is the boy he sees coming to visit is false. Therefore, a true judgment about something can't count as knowledge. We need something stronger.

With a sense of exasperation, Shawn asks, "What if I have proof that my true judgment is correct? If I believe that Gus is coming to visit, and have proof that the person coming is in fact Gus, then will I not *know* it's Gus?" Shawn's final answer seems to do the trick. It suggests knowledge exists when we have a belief that's both true and that we have proof for believing. To state it differently, we have knowledge when we have a justified true belief.

The above flashback is inspired by a dialogue between Socrates and a young boy named Theaetetus, in Plato's dialogue *Theaetetus*. Here Socrates attempts to determine what knowledge is, and just as Shawn struggles to provide an answer good enough for his dad, so too does Theaetetus. In fact, by the end of the dialogue they fail to arrive at a satisfactory answer. Socrates thinks the idea of a justified true belief is circular—it's like saying that the knowledge we have is justified by the knowledge we have. Nevertheless, Plato's dialogue suggests that the strongest definition for what counts as knowledge is a justified true belief—a true belief with some sort of proof supporting the belief.

Is That All You Have, Spencer?

Knowledge as justified true belief remained the norm for epistemologists—those who study the nature of knowledge—until Edmund Gettier's 1963 essay, "Is Justified True Belief Knowledge?" Gettier uses two brilliant cases to illustrate that a person can have a justified true belief, yet not have knowledge. *Psych* illustrates both cases nicely.

During the first two seasons of *Psych*, Karen Vick served as the interim police chief. It's not until the end of Season Two, in the episode "Shawn (and Gus) of the Dead," that Vick becomes the full-time chief of police. Throughout the episode she's convinced that someone besides herself will get the job, and she would've been correct, if not for some help from Shawn.

But imagine a different scenario. Vick knows that someone will get the chief of police job. She also has strong evidence to believe that Raymond Sauter is the person who will get the job, and that he carries with him a picture of Shawn's character on *Telenovela*, Chad ("Lights, Camera, . . . Homicidio," from Season Two). A result of these two beliefs is that Vick knows that the person who will get the job has a picture of Chad. Her belief that Sauter will get the job and that he has a picture of Chad is the evidence for her belief that the person who'll get the job has a picture of Chad.

This is a simple logical deduction, similar to the ones we see Shawn make all of the time. However, there's a problem with Vick's deduction. Imagine further that unknown to Vick, she's the one who'll get the job, and that, she too, has a picture of Chad. Because she has a picture of Chad, Vick's belief about the person who'll be chief of police is true, and she's justified in believing it—it's a justified true belief. The problem is she lacks knowledge that the person who will get the job has a picture of Chad. The belief is falsely based on her knowledge of Sauter's possession of the picture, even though it's true that the person who'll get the job has a picture of Chad—muy impresionante! Therefore, Vick has a justified true belief, but fails to have knowledge.

The second case is illustrated with Juliet and Shawn. Suppose Juliet uses Shawn's status as Santa Barbara's lead psychic detective as proof that he's actually psychic. While arguing with Lassiter one day, she defends Shawn by saying, "Either Shawn is a Psychic or Gus is in Mazatlan, Mexico." Jules believes her statement to be true, and it's justified by Shawn's previous "psychic" actions. The problem is, Shawn is not a psychic, and as we know from the episode "There's Something About Mira," Gus sometimes visits Mazatlan. Assuming Gus is in Mazatlan, then Jules's belief is a justified true belief, but there's no way she knows such a belief to be true. Her belief is based on something she doesn't know— namely, Shawn isn't a psychic. So again, we see that a justified true belief doesn't count as knowledge.

If you're going, "Say, what?!" about now, that's perfectly normal. Gettier cases sound strange, but they're as logically sound as Despereaux is a master criminal. They sound strange because they're based on logical inference, which allows for statements like "Either Shawn is a psychic or Gus is in Mazatlan" to be true. According to logic, as long as one half of such a statement is true, the whole statement is true. Jules's belief is based on the left side of the statement being true, but because she combined it with a statement that is, in fact, true, her belief ends up being true. That's why she can have a justified true belief and yet not have knowledge. What's missing from Gettier-type cases is an explanation that more precisely captures how humans form beliefs—an account based on how we engage the world, not how we make logical inferences that might randomly be true.

I'm a Professional, Gathering Information

A key component of *Psych* is the training that Henry Spencer provides Shawn, both as a child and an adult. Henry's goal isn't simply to be mean to Shawn. He's trying to develop in Shawn a particular set of perceptual and reasoning skills he hopes will help Shawn become an accomplished detective. He wants Shawn to be capable of making *reliable* observations and deductions based on the limited amount of information available to a detective. The reliability that Shawn demonstrates with his finely honed skills offers a new way of understanding what knowledge is.

Since Gettier shows that justified true beliefs fail to count as knowledge, philosophers continue to search for new ways of justifying human knowledge. One of the most prominent ways is to show that it's the process of coming to know something that produces knowledge. If the *process* by which one perceives objects is reliable, then we can say it's the reliability of the process that causes one to have knowledge. This position is called *reliabilism*.

Reliabilism attempts to explain knowledge in a way that accepts the limitations of human knowledge. It maintains that humans do make mistakes and that our perceptions can be flawed. Because humans are fallible, knowledge that requires certainty should be rejected. Instead, we should focus on the degrees to which our beliefs count as knowledge. For reliabilism, we might have certain knowledge of stuff like mathematics, but our knowledge of everyday interactions with the world should be judged by how reliable our beliefs are produced.

Reliabilism suggests that knowledge is the result of the perceptual processes we use everyday—like seeing, hearing, touching, tasting, and smelling. You know, they're the five senses that we use every day in order to get to and from work, to not run into walls, and to not eat that rotten batch of "Fries Quatro Quesos dos Fritos." Knowledge comes in degrees, and people who have more developed perceptual skills are more reliable than those who typically ignore their surroundings. Also, there're times when your senses aren't reliable, especially if Mr. Yin poisons you, or if you eat that rotten batch of Fries Quatro Quesos dos Fritos. For the most part, however, our senses reliably transmit information from the outside world that becomes what most of us would count as a type of knowledge.

Unlike the logical examples offered by Gettier, reliabilism mirrors the method of natural science—physics and biology— that is based on reliability of gathering and testing evidence. A reliabilistic approach produces probability, not certainty, but that shouldn't deter us, for probabilistic reasoning comprises the majority of human experience. No one doubts whether there's a TV in front of them while watching *Psych*, even though it could all be a dream. By stressing probability over certainty, there's always the *possibility* that Shawn's conclusions will be wrong, but throughout the series he proves himself a reliable detective. He makes mistakes, but I won't bet my collection of *Tears for Fears* albums against him.

I Do Know What Uncertain Terms Are . . . I'm the One Who Had to Tell Gus

With reliabilism, we must be careful not to grant every reliable process the status of producing knowledge. Being causally connected to the external world through our reliable belief-forming processes—our senses—justifies something as knowledge, not simply being a reliable process.

Leonard Koppett reliably predicted the rise and fall of the stock market for eighteen out of nineteen years between 1979 and 1998. Using reliabilism, we might be tempted to say that his reliable ability to have predicted the future suggests he had some sort of knowledge about the future. The truth is, however, Koppett was a writer for *Sporting News*, and he based his predictions concerning the stock market on which league won the Super Bowl. He picked a random event and applied its outcome to an unconnected event, the stock market. Koppett's beliefs were in no way connected to the stock market, neither causally nor otherwise. So, reliabilism concludes that he didn't have knowledge.

From the point of view of reliabilism, knowledge results from being causally connected to the world through our reliable belief-forming senses. Predicting the future based on random sporting events is an impressive trick, but it's not a skill. So, even though Koppett's predictions were reliable they don't count as knowledge. The same is true with people like astrologers and palm readers. Astrology is based on the false assumption that the Earth is the center of the universe, and there's no evidence to support the claim that palms have any effect on the future. There's a difference between using our senses to experience things first-hand and using our understanding of people and events to make unrelated predictions about the future. Our senses give us reliable information about what is actually happening around us, like the blue Toyota Echo that is about to run us over, unlike random predictions that give us guess about what might happen in the future.

A more precise example of reliabilism comes from Keith Lehrer's critique of reliabilist theories. Lehrer proposes the case of Mr. Truetemp, which is supposed to show that reliabilist theories reduce human knowledge to the absurd level of automatic doors. Imagine a man, Mr. Truetemp, who unbeknownst to himself has a device implanted in his body that provides him with the exact temperature of the outside world. Mr. Truetemp "knows" the exact temperature, and he is causally connected to the world; but he can't explain how he knows what the temperature is. Lehrer thinks this is enough reason to reject reliabilism, but what he actually does is provide a succinct example of the complexity of reliabilism and human knowledge.

Consider Burton "Magic Head" Guster and his ability to discern any number of smells and fragrances with his "super sniffer." Although Gus's super sniffer appears to work almost instantly, it's more akin to Mr. Truetemp, at least at first. Think of how Gus's sniffer works. He first senses that there's a smell, and after this occurs, he uses his hand to waft more aromas into his nose, and then after analyzing the smell, he comes to a conclusion about what the smell is. What we see here is a process that begins with a lower-level physical recognition of something in the world and ends with a higher-level mental recognition of what the object is. Mr. Truetemp exemplifies the lower-level recognition of something in the world, and this supports the reliabilist's claim that there's a type of knowledge that results from reliably sensing things in the world.

Mr. Truetemp supports reliabilism's claim regarding how perceiving the world produces a type of knowledge, but what it doesn't illustrate is the human ability to shift into the higher level of mental recognition seen at the end of the process. So, if reliabilism is going to work as a theory of knowledge, then we need a further explanation of the higher level of knowledge seen in Gus's super sniffer.

Nailed It . . . Almost Nailed It!

Gus's super sniffer ("M.C. Clap Yo Handz") suggests there are two levels of human knowledge. There's a lower one based on our physical perceptions of the world, and there's a higher one based on our mental ability to reflect on the information gained from our physical perceptions. Gus's process of arriving at a higher level of knowledge isn't unique. Shawn does the same thing when solving crimes. He makes a series of observations, reflects on them, and arrives at a complex conclusion about whodunit. What separates Shawn from most other people is that he's trained his senses to retain everything he sees, just in case he needs to use it later. Shawn is so observant that he perceives much of the world at a much higher level than the rest of us who pay little or no attention to the details that make up everyday life.

A story from another famous detective exemplifies the difference between Shawn's abilities and others, while suggesting that we're all capable of developing similar skills. Sir Author Conan Doyle's character Sherlock Holmes has many of the same abilities as Shawn. In the story "A Scandal in Bohemia," Holmes has a conversation with Dr. Watson about the difference between seeing and observing. Here's how the story goes using Shawn and Gus. "Hey Shawn," Gus says inquisitively, "How are you able to solve crimes that others struggle with, while making them look so easy?" Shawn tauntingly responds, "Elementary, my dear Gus! I observe, while others merely see."

The difference between observing and seeing is the difference between higher and lower levels of knowledge. For instance, Gus knows there are steps leading up to the Santa Barbara Police Department—he's gone up and down them many times. But does he know how many steps there are? Even though Shawn has walked up and down the steps just as many times as Gus, it's a safe bet that Shawn knows how many steps there are. This is exactly what Sherlock Holmes points out to Watson—they both have the same lower-level perceptual experiences of seeing the world, but the difference is he, as well as Shawn, observes and remembers everything that he sees. Sherlock and Shawn see the world at a much higher level than most other people, but they've also trained themselves to gather data of a much lower level while going about their daily business.

The first philosopher to examine the idea that there are two levels of human knowledge fully is William Alston. In the essay "Two Types of Foundationalism," Alston argues that there's a level of knowledge based on our everyday engagement with the world, and that these perceptions are the foundation for the higher type of knowledge that results from reflection and introspection. He shows that if our lower-level perceptions of the world are reliable, then they can serve as justifiers for the higher-level knowledge we gain from combining these perceptions into a consistent narrative about the world.

Alston's account should sound very familiar. It's exactly what Shawn does in every episode. Such an account of human knowledge doesn't produce beliefs that are certain, but human life isn't always certain. So, we shouldn't get too upset if our account of human knowledge doesn't provide certainty. Sometimes Shawn makes mistakes because he wrongly puts together clues, but most of the time he's correct. If he just went around making conclusions willy-nilly, without any evidence, reliabilism and Alston's foundationalism would show that he doesn't have knowledge. Because Shawn uses a finely honed skill to arrive at well-reasoned conclusions, we can say he has knowledge.

You Must Be Out of Your Mind

Just as there are many who think Shawn is a charlatan, there are some epistemologists who think foundationalism is flawed. *Coherence theorists* are one such group. They argue that if justification requires giving reasons for why we believe something, then even foundational beliefs require reasons. Coherence theorists claim that foundational beliefs are unjustified and don't support any theory of knowledge.

Instead, coherence theorists argue that knowledge is justified by having a set of beliefs that cohere—in other words, that are consistent—with each other. In two ways coherence theorists are correct. First, we should hold consistent beliefs. This is exactly what Henry tries to teach Shawn, and it's the hallmark of good detective work. Second, if our knowledge is based on arbitrary beliefs that can't be justified, then we don't have knowledge.

The foundationalism that Shawn exemplifies, however, isn't based on arbitrary beliefs. Shawn's beliefs are founded upon his engagement with his surroundings. It's the reliability of his senses that are the foundation for his knowledge, and as a result, he can provide justifications for why he knows something by pointing to and testing his senses. So, the coherence theorist's criticism doesn't apply to the reliabilist-foundationalism seen in *Psych*.

Another group who thinks foundationalism misses the mark hold to what is known as *infinitism*. Infinitism maintains that knowledge only occurs when we have an infinite chain of non-repeating beliefs. The best way to understand infinitism is to see it as trying to avoid the shortcomings of both foundationalism and coherence theory. For infinitism, foundationalism is based on unjustified beliefs—the same criticism as above, and coherence theory is circular. Infinitism suggests that the only way to avoid these two conclusions is to require an infinite and non-repeating chain of justifications.

For the longest time serious epistemologists discounted infinitism, but Peter Klein's reformulation in "Human Knowledge and the Infinite Regress of Reasons" prompted a reconsideration of its viability. Klein's infinitism suggests that knowledge is achieved when we can provide reasons about a belief that don't rely on each other to justify our belief. To do this we must consider both what's possible and what's impossible. It's the comparison of these considerations that allows for an infinite set of reasons. Granted, we can't actually give an infinite set of reasons because we're finite creatures; however, the ability to engage in such an exercise exists, and Klein thinks this is enough.

As we just saw, infinitism's criticism of foundationalism doesn't hold weight against the reliabilist-foundationalism Shawn uses, and since we're not directly concerned with coherence theory, there's no point in investigating whether or not infinitism's criticism of it is correct. Instead, let's conclude by putting all of the pieces together, solving the riddle of human knowledge, and ending this episode.

Wait for It!

Shawn's crime-solving technique supports a reliabilist-foundationalist approach to justifying knowledge, but it also supports the inclusion of certain features of both coherence theory and infinitism—though the latter two might react to such an idea much like Lassiter does when he sees Shawn at his desk.

Think really hard about what Shawn, Henry, Lassiter, and Jules do when solving a crime. Part of performing an investigation is looking at all the evidence, considering every possibility and impossibility, and consistently putting everything together to arrive at the best conclusion. This process is exactly what Sherlock Holmes describes in his statement, "Once you eliminate the impossible, whatever remains, no matter how improbable, must be the truth," and it illustrates why human knowledge is—at least partially—comprised of features of all three structures of justification.

The gathering of evidence and data exemplifies reliabilist-foundationalism, the consideration of what is possible and impossible exemplifies the most important feature of Klein's infinitism, and consistently putting things together is the hallmark of coherence theory.

Shawn performs this process much better than anyone else on *Psych*. We see him reliably gathering data from his perception of the world. He then considers the evidence in relation to everything he's ever seen or known, including his favorite foods, 1980s songs, movie or TV quotes, and other pop culture references. Finally, he puts it all together, with a little flair, to solve crime and to get the girl—you know that's right!

Therefore, *Psych* and Shawn suggest a cutting-edge approach to justifying beliefs that combines the best parts of what are considered the most promising theories of what counts as knowledge. Gus ("Methuselah Honeysuckle") may never be the next Wittgenstein—or winner of *American Duos* . . . I've heard it both ways, and Shawn may never skip the WWE's Royal Rumble to write a philosophical essay, but luckily for us we can learn a lot about human knowledge by watching *Psych*.

VII

Some Dark
Juju-Magumbo

18
The Fool Who Fools Fools

DENA HURST

Remember this from the pilot episode?

> **GUS:** Psych? As in gotcha?
>
> **SHAWN:** Or as in psych-*ic*.
>
> **GUS:** You named your fake detective agency Psych? Why not just call it, "Hey, We're Fooling You and the Police Department. Hope We Don't Make a Mistake and Someone Dies because of It"?
>
> **SHAWN:** The best way to convince people you're not lying to them is to tell them you are.

And so it begins—Shawn, the fake psychic detective, the trickster.

We meet Shawn as a young boy with a somewhat stern father, Henry, sitting together in a diner. Henry refuses to allow Shawn to have a piece of pie until Shawn can describe the hats that people are wearing in the diner—without looking around. We get our first glimpse of the observational skills that he was taught as a young boy, skills that he honed into adulthood and which serve as the basis for every episode.

We visit young Shawn in the beginning of every episode, which allows us insight into the psyche of the adult Shawn. Shawn, we learn, has a history of being bright but bored, adventurous and impulsive, and charismatic enough to convince young Gus to go along with his schemes. Chaos seems to follow him as he fails to consider all possible consequences before he acts, or at least fails to see negative consequences as sufficient deterrents.

Much like the trickster in mythology, Shawn brings disorder to order. The function of the trickster is to break the rules and challenge hierarchies, a lesson he learned from his father in the season one episode "9 Lives":

HENRY: Where's the ring?

YOUNG SHAWN: At the bottom. Now I gotta eat the whole box.

HENRY: (flipping the box over): And where's the ring now?

YOUNG SHAWN: At the top.

HENRY: Right. See, sometimes, Shawn, you don't have to dig so deep. All you gotta do is turn something upside down to make it right-side up and then . . . you get your prize.

Shawn's challenges to hierarchy are also evident in his continual jousting with Lassiter, who represents law and order and all that is right with the world, or at least Santa Barbara.

Despite his finely tuned senses, Shawn is not infallible and often makes leaps of deduction that defy common sense. He usually tap dances his way out of his blunders by using his wit to cover them up or deflect attention elsewhere. Relying on psychic powers that conveniently come and go allows Shawn to surface clues when he finds them and remain silent when he doesn't. Well, perhaps not silent, but when the psychic signals are jammed, he has an excuse as to why he isn't able to provide a vital clue or why he fingers the wrong person as the perpetrator.

Fellatio del Toro

Tricksters play jokes and find amusement at the expense of others. In his exchanges with Lassiter, we see the sheer joy Shawn has in taunting him. In the Season Four episode "Bollywood Homicide," Shawn introduces Lassiter by saying, "This is Detective Carlton Lassiter. I do his job. And sometimes his hair. Though clearly not today." And Shawn never fails to provide an amusing introduction for Gus, as well, always much anticipated in each episode: Gus "Silly Pants" Jackson, Shutterfly Simmons, Ovaltine Jenkins, Nick Knack, Gus "Big Head" Burton, Fellatio del Toro, and the list goes on.

Tricksters remind us that life isn't predictable, that things don't always go as planned, and that we ought to lighten up. Sometimes tricksters teach us important lessons, particularly when we're feeling complacent or content, and sometimes they act on a whim, with no rhyme or reason to their mischief other than their own gratification. Tricksters work outside the bounds of society, and we see this with Shawn's routine mockery of both laws and social norms. His world is one giant playground and the people he encounters are toys (perhaps with the exception of Juliet).

The shenanigans of tricksters represent only one aspect of their nature. Tricksters can also be helpful. They can create good in the world as well as chaos, if it pleases them to do so. Despite playing the role of clown, tricksters are quite clever, often surprisingly so. This is part of Shawn's charm. He's very bright and wickedly witty, and yet prefers to hide behind humor both because it amuses him and because it protects him. Gus's imitation of Shawn in "Shawn (and Gus) of the Dead" is a fairly accurate portrayal of Shawn's approach to life: "Look at me, look at me. I love my hair. I can make obscure Eighties references that nobody understands. Laugh at me, ha-ha . . . ha."

By playing the clown, there are few consequences when he is wrong but much delight and praise when he's right. A significant lesson that Shawn learns from his interactions with his father is that life is easier when people expect less from you. By finding a creative outlet for his natural intelligence and restlessness, Shawn can do good when he's so inclined, be less accountable for being a screw-up, and amuse himself in the process by flouting authority in its many forms (mainly the Lassiter form).

It's . . . the Process

Thus part of Shawn's appeal is his trickster qualities—the lying, deceiving, joking, ridiculing, and general buffoonery. He thumbs his nose at convention, and we like that because we wish we could cut loose as well. And in a sense we can because we're in on the game. Thanks to fancy highlighting technology, we see what Shawn sees, and we are privy to his reasoning as he hatches crazy plots with Gus. But Shawn's version of the trickster is one that tries to set things right in the world, to save victims and punish criminals and generally nasty people. Characters like Shawn give us some measure of comfort that wrongs can be set right; that no matter how clever the wrong-doer is, he or she can be found out; that there are mysteries in life, but that ultimately there is an answer to those mysteries.

It doesn't always matter to us how those mysteries are resolved. What's most important is that we have understanding, which is why we sometimes buy into insubstantial or faulty reasoning. Some reasoning is better than none, and in our everyday lives, what matters to most of us is that our beliefs about the world make some kind of sense and not that they meet rigorous epistemic criteria (pardon the philosophy-speak). For Shawn as a trickster, though, the method is as important as the madness, and his claim of psychic powers is a fitting method, one that signifies his trickster nature. He is the fool who fools fools.

One reason we believe in the seemingly impossible, even when given a variety of alternative explanations, is that we want to find a pattern to events. Finding patterns and creating a narrative to explain the patterns is the way our brains make sense of the world. But we often see patterns based on our pre-existing biases, to borrow from the work of philosopher Alfred Mele. Just think of a time when you wanted an object quite badly. Once you decided upon that object, did you start noticing how many people have the object that you want? Or have you ever bought a new car and then noticed how many people suddenly seem to be driving the same car?

This notion of seeing patterns works with beliefs as well. If you want to believe something is true, you will find enough evidence in the world to support that belief because you will interpret events around you through the lens of your belief.

A Really Cool Premise

Let's look again at the Pilot episode of *Psych*. Shawn watches crime reports on the news and phones in tips based on his observation. After one particular tip about a murder, he goes to the police station to collect his reward, but is called back to an interrogation room by Detective Lassiter and his partner. Based upon the details of the crime that Shawn has given,

Lassiter has created one possible narrative, the one that makes the most sense based on his past experiences and beliefs— Shawn knows the details of the crime because he is the perpetrator, or at least knows who the perpetrator is.

This is a reasonable assumption, and one that's hard for Shawn to refute as he has no alibi. How do you prove a negative, after all? Trying to feebly explain that he has near superhuman powers of observation does not get him closer to freedom, so Shawn provides another explanation that would at first glance seem even more far-fetched than the truth—that he is psychic. The reactions that this announcement garners are broadly representative of how people generally feel about psychics. Lassiter scoffs, ever the skeptic. A gullible young officer immediately believes, based on things Shawn is able to reveal about him. And Lassiter's partner is somewhere in the middle, not a believer, but not willing to completely discount the idea, either.

In this scene we're faced with two scenarios—that Shawn is a killer because he has way too much information about the crime and can't prove that he isn't the killer, and that Shawn is psychic. That he is psychic is accepted as a viable explanation because it also fits the facts, namely that he has way too much information about the crime. And just as his innocence, in the absence of the evidence, can't be proven, his psychic abilities can't be disproven. How do you prove or disprove that for which there is no empirical evidence? That he is the killer is the more logical explanation from the perspective of the police. And yet, aside from Lassiter, the police are willing to go along with Shawn's claims. His explanation meets their need for a narrative connecting the facts as they know them.

But aside from this being a really cool premise for a TV show, we can rightly ask why anyone would go along with the idea of a psychic when another narrative, one more easily proven or disproven with good old-fashioned police work and perhaps involving an unpleasant stay in jail, is offered.

I Know Your Little Act

Google the term 'psychic' and you'll be amazed (or not, depending on your view of human nature) at the hits returned for people who are psychics, know psychics, rely on psychics, or aren't a psychic but have played one on TV. Mystics, seers, and sages have been with us since the earliest of societies and have traditionally been the ones who have provided counsel to the community, warned of danger, or interpreted signs foretelling a good harvest or the birth of a baby. Psychics today offer us some of these same services. People visit psychics to help them make sense of their lives, to have their futures told or their pasts interpreted, to discover the meaning of life and death. The idea of a person who can see beyond the physical world is as old as the trickster and just as prevalent across cultures.

Psychics help us fill in the narrative of our lives when we don't have all of the facts available to us, and our willingness to believe is based on our need for nice, neat explanations. This is partially the role that Shawn fills as a psychic detective. Because Shawn sees things that others don't, he's able to fill in the gaps in other people's knowledge with inferences that he draws based on his observations. In trickster fashion, rather than present his inferences or observations in the detached rational manner of a Sherlock Holmes or Hercule Poirot, Shawn prefers a theatrical approach, the fingertip-to-forehead method and sometimes even the flopping-on-the-floor method.

But we, the audience, know Shawn's psychic act is a ruse. Our thoughts are given voice by Lassiter, who alone through all of the seasons has remained skeptical about Shawn's psychic abilities: "I've known you for six years, Spencer. I know your little act. You do your little dance, you beat polygraph machines. You always manage to guess the right culprit after missing the first four or five times" ("Shawn Rescues Darth Vader"). Because we are in on the game, it isn't Shawn the psychic that we root for (unlike Patricia Arquette's character in *Medium*).

The Amazing Psych-Man

We're drawn to Shawn because he's a trickster; we laugh at his antics, at the way he bumbles his way through to a solution, at the way he ridicules the police while also being proud to help them. As the trickster in mythology is a demigod, so we might see Shawn as a demi-superhero. He's not a full-blown superhero, having weathered no radiation storms in space or suffered the ill-effects of a scientific experiment gone awry. He can't fly, he isn't super stretchy, and he doesn't have a skeleton made of steel; in fact, his best physical defense is to go "bone-less"—make his body completely limp—as seen in the Season Six episode "The Amazing Psych-Man & Tap-Man, Issue #2."

Shawn's rank of demi-superhero is awarded based on his sharpened observational powers, so finely tuned that they're vastly superior to those of the average person. His ability to draw inferences based on those details amazes those around him, until the "trick" is revealed. As Holmes would say to Watson, it appears extraordinary, until it's explained; but once explained, the solution is startlingly obvious.

We're also drawn to characters like Shawn because they represent something that we each feel we could become given the time and inclination. The more fantastic superheroes of comic books and movies have human abilities exaggerated exponentially so as to be in the realm of fantasy. They represent what we might wish to be even while we simultaneously know that can never develop such abilities. But the power of observation . . . now that's a power we can relate to.

On Your Mark

The trickster is a figure found in the mythology of every culture, and tricksters serve a vital purpose. But tricksters are only effective as long as there are people willing to believe them. Hence, the flipside of the trickster—for every liar, there must be a believer; for every con man, there must be a mark. We can, as spectators of Shawn's tomfoolery, delight at not being the mark and laugh gleefully at those who are. We know there is a sucker born every minute, but we never think we're the sucker.

But aside from providing us with cheap giggles at the expense of others, the trickster is a path to deeper understanding of ourselves and the world around us. Tricksters are ambiguity incarnate, creator and destroyer, deceiver and deceived. They challenge us to see the world differently because they live on the boundaries of society, ever pushing outward. They challenge socially accepted norms and live outside the rules that restrain others. In this fashion they both mark the boundaries for us while also showing us what lies beyond if only we could find the strength to join them.

From Shawn's outrageous nicknames for Gus to his back-talking Lassiter to his interfering in police investigations and other people's lives, Shawn pushes the limits of acceptable behavior. His life is built around a lie and all that he has gained—respect from his father, the satisfaction of helping people in trouble, a job that challenges him, love from Juliet—is a product of that lie. Though he has a sense of right and wrong, what's right and wrong at any given time is what is convenient for him.

Shawn also shows us the mirroring power of the trickster. Based on the notion of personal identity provided by philosopher David Hume and expanded upon by Daniel Dennett, we construct our sense of self through a kind of loose narrative in which we play the starring role. Shawn does this through his invention of himself as a psychic detective. We know that we do this as well, showing different faces to strangers, co-workers, and close friends and family members. But few of us can invent our lives in the way that Shawn has (without going to jail, I might add). We envy him in that not only is he able to invent the life he leads, but also that he's able to get away with it despite naysayers and skeptics.

So perhaps the best gift that tricksters give us is hope. Their pranks and tests and arbitrary interventions force us out of complacency. They expand the realm of possibility for us but not beyond the bounds of what is attainable. Even though they might show us the way and then pull the rug out from under us, it's through them that we learn to laugh at ourselves.

We need tricksters like Shawn because they offer us easy answers to tough problems, and even when we see the tricks of the charlatan revealed, we continue to believe because the hope that he offers continues. If not this one, we think, then surely the next one.

19
Too Good to Be True

COURTNEY NEAL

Shawn Spencer is anything but restrained. It's a rare outing to the police station or a crime scene that doesn't result in a showy and often loud psychic vision or reading that puts Shawn and Gus on the case.

Shawn often makes what appear to be wild accusations, whether it's declaring an accidental death a murder or that a T. Rex is the killer, but he never lacks confidence in his predictions. These psychic visions often provide the foundation for the case, and no matter the outlandishness, Shawn is proven right. Despite his wild claims and eccentric displays Shawn is not usually questioned as to whether he is actually psychic. The chief and others tire of his antics, but it's the showy displays, not his concrete information, they dislike.

Yet these outbursts of psychic ability are not out of the blue, but are based on Shawn's careful and extremely subtle observations. The vast majority of Shawn's deductions are done inside his head or are developed with Gus, while all elements and displays of 'psychic-ness' are saved for members of the public. Why then do the residents of Santa Barbara not only put up with, but genuinely believe Shawn is psychic? Because it's simply easier to believe.

A Plausible Explanation

Shawn's father carefully trained him in all elements of detective work, honing his observation and deduction skills which were evident at a young age and essentially perfected by the time Shawn was eighteen. Shawn uses these skills to solve crimes and relies on them with complete sincerity; he is serious about the importance of evidence, quite contrary to his public persona as a psychic. In order to receive information from his so called psychic juices, Shawn has his trademark psychic hands-to-the-head as well other outbursts or displays he feels will more strongly sell the belief that his information is super-natural rather than scientific.

These displays are essential because, as seen in the pilot episode, Shawn's information is a little too good. Certain aspects of Shawn's skills, like an eidetic memory or acing the detective exam as a teen, are understandable and acceptable to society. So why then does he have to feign psych ability to explain his crime solving ability?

Pseudoscience is a phenomenon in which untrue factual claims or false reports of events are viewed as legitimate, despite the inadequate quality of the evidence for these beliefs. Pseudoscience does not rely on observation or experiment as science does, but is often based on myths, opinions, or hearsay. Beliefs are then based not in reality, but in what people choose to believe either because of appealing stories or because of hasty conclusions from their own experience.

People often don't want scientific explanations, but something seemingly simple that accords with their own beliefs and experiences. This is how we explain widespread belief in ghosts and psychic ability, despite the lack of strong evidence for these phenomena. Certain observations, like noises in the basement, will be given ready explanations (Ghost!) over other plausible explanations (mice?) because the former explanation is more appealing. Many pseudoscientific claims are also worded or stated in such a way that they can't be disproved, further adding strength to illegitimate claims.

People turn to these beliefs not because they're stupid, but because these beliefs are somehow more appealing. Easy answers are favored, so if a complex or mysterious experience can be explained by a plausible explanation, regardless of whether it is truthful or not, people will often believe it. This explains why when something is not easily explained people are more likely to reach for a simple explanation, whether it fits proper evidence or not. Shawn quickly realizes this in the Pilot episode after Lassister and the other officers demand a simple explanation for how Shawn could have come up with all his tips, their disbelief that Shawn could solve crimes they could not, leading them to assume he must be in on the crimes.

Shawn realizes that his thought process is a dangerous idea to others and his explanation isn't believable even though it's true. After explaining some of the criminals' tells, like the manager's nervous tic, to give credit to his claims, Shawn is instead threatened with arrest and time in a holding cell. Since the truth isn't an option, Shawn picks the best excuse he can by using his natural abilities: he claims to be psychic.

Shawn knows that people will believe in psychics (especially the officer who has magical charms and other supernatural pieces in her workspace); so using his skills Shawn concludes this is the best option based on his understanding of pseudoscience and other people's beliefs. The ability to provide the truth though is not enough to complete the picture so Shawn uses two psychological principles to pull off his psychic cover: cold reading and social influence.

I'm Getting a Name that Starts with P . . .

Cold reading is a skill in which the reader or 'psychic' makes a series of vague statements that the subject recognizes and connects to his or her life. These statements do not have to be specific—the more general the better—because by casting a wider net of options, the reader is more likely to say something the client will recognize. For instance something vague, like "A name that begins with L", will be validated by the client's insistence that a dog Lulu is being referred to. This statement however is so vague it could refer to a grandfather named Lewis or that the client grew up in Louisiana.

The psychic can then hone in, based on these clues as well as defining features such as age and gender to create plausible connections the subject then solidifies, also sometimes using information the reader has privately gathered. These connections do not all have to be accurate because people will forget errors in favor of correct guesses. The psychic reader then has the ultimate advantage because his or her client is ready to have a psychic reading and will either consciously or unconsciously supply the reader with information that will validate anything the reader says.

Most of the time Shawn has at least some information before going into interviews, but he's successful in doing a cold reading completely, well, cold. In "Shawn vs. the Red Phantom" Shawn assumes the podium at a comic convention in order to find a clue to his missing client and in doing so conducts a text-book session of cold reading:

> SHAWN: I'm getting a reading right now, yes. You, ah, spend a great deal of time in front of your computer. And I see a girl, yes, you like her from afar. She doesn't really know you exist.
>
> MAN: Yes! Yes! Her name's Megan. Do I have a chance?
>
> SHAWN: Don't put too much work into it. I think she wants to be just friends. Wow boy! I am getting an R, I'm getting an R, does any-one here have a name that begins with R? Oh, up, wait a second, wow, hold, nobody, and a D! Yes, a D. An R and a D. An R name, Rolph, Rob, Rob and a D name, yes, Dan, Doodle, Duke, Don! Rob and a Don.
>
> ROB AND DON: Yes that's us!
>
> SHAWN: [*to Gus*] An actual Rob and Don together. Sometimes I scare myself.

In the first case Shawn uses the generalities he knows about the audience to make educated and vague guesses about the man's life that can suit many other people present as well. The man supplies information too, further crediting what we as the audience can see are assumptions based on Shawn's perception of comic book nerds. His reading is also filled with stereotypes and common phrases that increases the likelihood it would apply to many people, thereby increasing the odds it will fit the client.

The second example shows that people will view a reading as truthful because it was accurate for them personally, regardless of the probability that in a room of hundreds there would be a Rob and a Don present or at least connected. After this exercise, the entire convention believes that Shawn is psychic, even though he has only made vague statements and guesses, but because those ring true and are verified by the audience, Shawn's claim as a psychic grows stronger.

Shawn, like any good psychic reader, also modifies his guesses during each reading, changing his guesses when required and claiming any wrong guesses are due to cloudy interference or that his psychic juices were blocked. Shawn uses this technique over and over again in interviews to not only test out potential leads, but to gain the client's confidence as well. Sometimes Shawn's guesses are wrong, but these are quickly forgotten in favor of the times when he is correct, especially when those correct details are incredibly salient and accurate. It's not so much that a psychic must be correct all the time, but they must be correct about something.

Controlled Thinking

Although Shawn often grasps at plausible theories and explanations, his guesses aren't just shots in the dark but are often based on observations and deductions, filtered through a process known as controlled thinking: thought that is conscious, intentional, voluntary, and effortful. Everyone has the ability to use controlled thinking and it is often related to subjects that are important to us, whether it is deciding who to date or marry or what to make for dinner. The key to using controlled thinking is to evaluate information and go through deliberate thought processes, rather than using the quicker version of automatic thinking that is based on heuristics, or mental shortcuts.

Shawn, though seemingly carefree and always ready with a joke, misses nothing and is carefully analyzing all the information he gathers, as the climax of each show depends on his synthesis of clues gathered during each episode. Controlled thinking increases Shawn's cold reading because he can hone in on accurate information more quickly, while at the same time making it appear it was gained via psychic visions. This process often serves as a jumping off point in interviews as Shawn uses one solid lead to gain others until he has solved the puzzle.

The clues Shawn gathers and his subsequent deductions are unique, not because the other detectives do not use controlled thinking, but because Shawn alone can make these connections in a way that has led him to claim psychic ability. Lassister, always the skeptic, vocalizes the inconceivable nature of Shawn's abilities in the Pilot episode, unable to believe that Shawn can read a criminal's guilt from TV interviews because

Lassister himself can't do this. Shawn has access to the same, if not less information than the police when he calls in tips he has solved by watching the news, yet this information is processed in a different way through a combination of Shawn's natural talents and his training. Simply knowing things then isn't enough to be psychic because other explanations, like being an accomplice, are available; Shawn then has to act the part of a psychic too.

Being Psychic

Psychologist Robert Cialdini has studied and identified different types of social influence principles, basic heuristics or thought patterns that unconsciously affect our behavior and perception of people and events. The social influence principles Shawn is a master of are *liking*, *social proof*, and *commitment and consistency*. Liking is pretty straight forward and can be based on physical attractiveness, similarity to the person being influenced, or compliments, things Shawn has used to gain the trust and affections of those connected to a case. When people grow to like Shawn, they are more disposed to believe his claims and tips, even if these are unfounded (another reason why Lassie is resistant to Shawn's claims).

Social proof is the shortcut we use when we determine what is correct by finding out what others believe is true. If other people believe Shawn's psychic, then it stands to reason we should too! Shawn introduces himself at crime scenes and to other people as the head or lead psychic with the Santa Barbara Police Department and if someone in a position of authority believes it, we are far more likely to believe it as well. The residents (and police) of Santa Barbara have been given certain examples of Shawn's ability as a psychic, and the more people who believe this, the stronger Shawn's claim becomes. It's more difficult to hold contrary ideas and it is reassuring to believe what others do as well. This also traps Shawn in his own lie, one that becomes a hindrance in his growing relationship with Juliet in the later seasons, the side effect of commitment and consistency.

Human beings love consistency; we often buy the same brand items, take the same route home, and act the same way as we did before. Yet this familiar ways of doing things can become a trap. Shawn committed, in a moment of haste, to being a psychic and although he can maintain it and use it to fulfill his childhood dream of a detective agency, he must also stay committed. Shawn on occasion has even pulled the psychic card with Gus and Henry who clearly know Shawn is not a psychic.

In Season Five's "Feet Don't Kill Me Now" Shawn uses his psychic front on Gus, momentarily forgetting that Gus knows he isn't psychic. Shawn brushes this off, claiming it's hard to remember who knows he's not really psychic, but it implies that Shawn himself feels the weight of maintaining appearances. Shawn's psychic act has grown to be a crutch, something that allows him to use his observations and deductions, but is also something he must always have 'on' in order to maintain his deception. Commitment and consistency also strengthen Shawn's reliance on acting out the part of a psychic because if people have seen Shawn in action before and believed him, they will be more likely to believe him a second and a third time. People have come to expect Shawn's psychic reliability, and by doing so, they believe his claims more fully

They Tell Me You're a Psychic

The self-fulfilling prophecy is a phenomenon in which we expect a certain behavior or outcome, and this belief leads us to act in a way that makes that behavior or outcome come about. This is not just related to ourselves, but can affect how we interact with other people, unconsciously acting in a way that will mesh with our original expectations. Through this principle our schemas or thought patterns about the world come true.

Once Shawn is introduced as a psychic, people treat him as such, whether it's requesting medium services or hiring him to solve crimes for the police department. In expecting a certain behavior, Shawn can then, through the use of cold reading and social influence principles, act in a way that people think psychics should act, thereby solidifying his false claim as a psychic. People view Shawn's actions as evidence of psychic phenomenoa, disregarding or choosing to ignore evidence of observation or controlled thinking. These things compound to not only create but also maintain Shawn's psychic identity. Pseudoscience comes full circle as people choose to believe the simple and visible explanation that Shawn is psychic, rather than look for a more logical and scientific explanation, that he is in reality a modern day Sherlock Holmes.

Shawn Spencer, Lead Psychic

Shawn's deception and cover as a psychic is still going strong after multiple seasons and is often unquestioned, precisely because he's so successful at playing the part. Even characters who don't believe in psychics trust Shawn's outcomes, primarily because of these psychological factors. The explanation that Shawn is psychic is not only readily available, but seems reliable as well as Shawn not only acts the part, but has the skills to back up his claims.

The human mind is already susceptible to believing things that are not very well corroborated by evidence, and will even forget or ignore examples that go against its belief, provided there are some striking examples that support it. Shawn is then the perfect embodiment of pseudoscience, capitalizing on people's misconceptions and tendency to believe in the spectacular over the scientific.

20
Exploiting the Supernatural

Jeff Ewing

Shawn Spencer doesn't really have any supernatural psychic abilities; rather he has a practical ability to read a situation combined with above-normal—not paranormal—crime-solving insights.

We're introduced to Shawn in the Pilot episode, when we see him calling in the solutions to unsolved crimes based on their coverage on televised news. His insights into these crimes are so accurate that the police assume he must have inside knowledge. To avoid being arrested and possibly charged with crimes, Shawn claims he gets his knowledge of the crimes because he's a psychic. He reveals the hoax only to his father and to Gus, who joins him in the Psych detective agency.

Shawn exploits the Santa Barbara Police Department's willingness to believe in his psychic ability, to get away with odd behavior and to be places he shouldn't be as a civilian. Although Shawn achieves some good results for the community with his deception, he also uses acceptance of his psychic ability to his own advantage. The only consistently critical member of the SBPD, Carlton "Lassie" Lassiter, is nonetheless amazed by Shawn's practical success, and his doubts are generally over-ruled by everybody else's acceptance of Shawn's psychic talents—precisely because of that very success.

Bottom line: Shawn is able to get what he wants, and achieve certain of his chosen ends, because folks at the SBPD are willing to accept this supernatural, paranormal, metaphysical juju-magumbo.

Supernatural Smack

The most famous critic of the use of the supernatural to provide a cover for exploitation and oppression was Karl Marx
(1818–1883), who famously proclaimed that religion is "the
opium of the people." Marx was a materialist—someone who
thinks that only physical things and events exist—but he went
beyond mere materialism to show how, throughout human history, people in power have employed anything paranormal,
supernatural, or religious—like ghosts, gods, and psychic influences—to control the poor and the oppressed at the bottom of
the social order.

Marx held that the basis of every society is economic,
because "the mode of production of material life conditions the
general process of social, political, and intellectual life." In addition to economics, Marx divvies up society into family, the state
(government, law, police, and the like), and what he refers to as
the "ideological realm." The ideological realm consists of institutions like cultural groups and religion, as well as beliefs about
the world such as those of the social sciences and morality.

Marx claims that, as long as there is a ruling class, the ideas
of the ruling class will be the ruling ideas, and these ideas dominate and stifle those who are ruled, the subject classes. Ruling
class ideologies also preserve the status quo through a combination of alienating individuals from their true selves, hiding
oppression in class society, while idealizing and universalizing
the status quo, and making it appear as though only the status
quo is possible.

Religion Controls and Degrades

Of all the ideological institutions, Marx criticized religion most
extensively for its alienating and oppressive influence. Think
about how Christianity, for example, has been such a dominat-
ing force in the West for some two thousand years, causing the
deaths of numerous innocent people through religious wars
and inquisitions. Or think of Islam, or even early Judaism with
their accounts of genocide against others or even at times
against the wayward among their own adherents.

Supernatural beliefs do have some factors that make them
unique among ideologies and institutions. For Marx, such
beliefs are not only empirically false, but are human-created

and maintained—Marx is famous for having said that "Man makes religion; religion does not make man." Such beliefs represent an "inverted world consciousness," ultimately attributing the products of human activity and the traits of humankind to a being outside of humanity itself, in effect perpetrating the most obscene alienation by externalizing the goodness and agency of the human species itself.

But most importantly, supernatural beliefs use that alienation and externalization as a mechanism of degradation and control. Concerning Christianity—the dominant religion of the West—Marx maintains that Christ is the "intermediary to whom man attributes all his own divinity." People essentially empty themselves of all power, goodness, and other noble traits by projecting these qualities onto Christ.

The ruling class has always maintained that supernatural beings and processes are beyond everybody else's comprehension, and that the rulers or their private *consiglieri* are the only ones privy to real knowledge of the supernatural. This way, the rulers can control the hoi polloi. Consider all of the shamans, witch doctors, priests, ministers, gurus, rabbis, imams, and other holy persons throughout human history and consider the always close connection between these holy persons and the King, or the Holy Roman Emperor, or the Chief, or the Emir— they are the ones qualified to translate the supernatural and the Divine to the public, and coincidentally their translations frequently support the power of these rulers. Religion's function for the ruling class, like all ruling class ideologies, is to hide and obfuscate the status quo, or to make it look inevitable.

This isn't to say that Marx thought all ideologies and spiritual beliefs are inherently oppressive (though he did think them false). Marx sees religion as a comfort and as something that might even be used against the status quo. But religion offers comfort through illusion.

> Religious suffering is, at one and the same time, the expression of real suffering and a protest against real suffering. *Religion is the sigh of the oppressed creature, the heart of a heartless world, and the soul of soulless conditions. It is the opium of the people.*

For Marx, religion doesn't reflect some real, transcendent reality; rather, the cloak of religion and the supernatural often hides the real goings on in the world. And further, religious beliefs and other supernatural beliefs are often used to achieve wholly secular, practical ends.

The Psychic, the Material, the Whole Damn Series . . .

Shawn uses others' absolute or contingent acceptance of supernatural beliefs as a cover for his own real-world capacity for observation. Despite the charade, he solves many crimes, achieving his own goals as well as the goals of the SBPD. Shawn does good things with his talents (even if he lies about their source), but also hides his true (and very material) powers, treating them as products of some supernatural capacity that only he has.

Shawn gains many real-world privileges from attributing his insights to psychic ability—starting with avoiding being arrested from the get-go, and under this guise Shawn is able to start a well functioning detective agency and be involved in police investigations without being an official police officer. Marx would likely relate Shawn's ability to hide his material powers behind a psychic veil to the ability of priests and shamans to hide material processes and knowledge behind the veil of supernatural connection.

Shawn himself would agree with this interpretation— though he would probably defend it, while Marx would be quite cross about it. Shawn, like Marx, denies the possibility of a real supernatural reality. In the Season One episode "9 Lives," Shawn defends having a séance to his friend Gus, explaining "Gus, there are no rules against having a séance. Anyone can have one. It's like a garage sale or plastic surgery." He expresses related sentiment in the Season Two episode "Psy vs. Psy," when bested at the time by a rival. Gus suggests to Shawn "Maybe she's just more psychic-y than you," to which Shawn responds, "Gus, don't be ridiculous, there's no such thing as psychics." Shawn is well aware that his 'powers' are an act, and denies (in private) that similar supernatural 'skills' are even possible, while he uses others' beliefs in their possibility for his own ends.

Shawn benefits from the privileges and diversity of experiences his aptitude for metaphysical fakery enjoys. He explains to Gus: "Look Gus, all those jobs I took because I wanted the experience. But then I mastered it and I moved on. But this job has a little bit of everything!" ("Pilot"). Shawn gets to live perhaps the only life with enough diversity to keep his boredom at bay, and while deception is involved, he can appease his own conscience because he brings criminals to justice.

So Shawn, like priests and mystics in Marx's analysis of religion, uses people's belief in the supernatural to hide real material processes under cover of spiritual phenomena, from which he benefits. But for Marx, the role of religion tends to be to secure the power of the ruling class over the ruled. While Shawn is deceptive and enjoys particular privileges and income from that deception, we could argue that his fakery serves a good purpose—without it, he would never be able to use his talents to solve crimes. Is there a difference between Shawn's use and those of Marx's priests?

Psychic Detecting Is Alienated Labor

While Marx generally thinks of religion as false and serving the interests of the rulers, and despises its use as a way to control and degrade people, Marx also argues that people cling to religion as a consequence of real-world suffering, so in a sense religion is an expression of and protest against real-world problems. Marx's objection to religion is that it's a false solution to suffering, and he advocated throwing away the false solution in favor of changing the causes of suffering—overthrowing class society. Marx has sympathy for spiritual believers but little sympathy for religion itself.

But what about those times when the spiritual isn't employed to dehumanize or to justify systems of oppression? Shawn may reap benefits from his supposed psychic ability, but he's certainly not gaining employment through direct exploitation or through money extorted from parishioners. And while his psychic gifts do aid the police—in Marx's view, agents of a repressive state that protects the ruling class—Shawn is almost exclusively employed to help in ways that benefit actual people (instead of merely defending property or the interests of the rich). Marx would still point out that it is Shawn's observational and deductive abilities that get the job done, not the 'psychic ability' he pretends to have. Shawn has an easy response, however—his career began with him calling in tips to the police based on his observational capacities alone. His insight could only be 'understood' by the police under the guise of psychic ability. . . ironically, the police find Shawn's insights more believable as psychic ability than as observational and deductive aptitude (and thus, without the psychic ruse, Shawn would have looked like a suspect, not an asset to the police force). Shawn's case is a unique one—feigning supernatural abilities was the only way for Shawn to avoid the repressive powers of the state being wrongfully turned on him (while he was in the process of doing good).

Ironically, this puts Shawn in a rather strange position—faced with the very material threat of the coercive powers of the state being turned on him, Shawn hides his true abilities. True, he reaps material rewards, and enjoys the work he does. He also seems to enjoy quite well playing the psychic—sometimes a little too much. But instead of receiving credit for his actual skill, he has to hide it, taking credit for something he does not do and losing credit for what he actually accomplishes. Feigning psychic ability is his constrained choice against the watchful eye of the police force—if he chooses to deny his claims to psychic ability and attribute his successes to his own material skill, his detective agency is over and criminal charges are quite possible.

In a certain sense, pretending to get detective insights from the supernatural almost resembles the conditions of an alienated worker more than the priest whose so-called spiritual authority justifies hierarchy. So how, exactly, would Marx ultimately weigh in on Shawn's use of the psychic?

Psychic Benefits?

Marx and Shawn both have a problematic relationship with the supernatural. Both believe that there is no truth behind claims to supernatural, psychic, or otherwise mystical or magical knowledge. Marx recognizes that individuals find solace in religion and its explanations of suffering and reality, but sees religion as offering false explanations and solutions for very real social ills. Marx also sees religion as supporting hierarchical class structures and state authority, and degrading human beings in favor of a Divine realm that, Marx believes, doesn't exist.

Shawn, like the priests and shamans Marx dismisses, hides his very real and very material observational and deductive skills behind the mask of psychic ability. In doing so, Shawn makes a career built on deception that provides him unique access to police cases, income, and a career far more interesting than he might otherwise find.

While Shawn does in effect peddle false supernatural revelations, misleading many people in the process (and in this sense, Marx would cast a critical eye on his work), in another sense, Shawn is a victim of his own success. Shawn may aid police, who are analytically integrated within the structures of the state, often identified by many Marxian thinkers as primarily serving the interests of the ruling class. These functions of the state and the police (protecting private property and corporations, criminalizing dissent, and the like) are not the functions of the police that Shawn helps. Shawn investigates cases where individuals are threatened or harmed—such as kidnappings and murder—and uses his pseudo-psychic prowess for the benefit of others. Unlike the priests in Marx's analysis, then, Shawn's career as a psychic detective serves not to dominate or degrade individuals, but to benefit them.

While Shawn does enjoy his work and reap benefits from it, in some ways it remains an alienated form of work. Shawn has his first psychic "insight" to get out of being suspected in criminal activity—and Shawn has to continue that ruse for the very same reason. As a consequence, Shawn builds a fake career, in which his true skills will never be really seen or recognized by anyone he helps, and all the credit he receives will be based on his false supernatural abilities.

Shawn has to define himself by something he is not—in effect living a double life, and produce a product (psychic insight) if he is to avoid losing his career (and, worse, his liberty). Ironically, instead of peddling the supernatural to hide the real nature of other people for the benefit of hierarchical structures (as in Marx's critique of the role of priests), Shawn is forced by those hierarchical structures to peddle the supernatural in a manner that hides his own real nature (not to himself, but to most of the people who know him or interact with him through his detective work).

Fake Fakir

So how would Marx process the detective career of Shawn the mistaken mystic, the fake fakir, the pseudo-psychic? I think Marx might be somewhat conflicted. On the one hand, Shawn makes a career out of aiding the state via intentional metaphysical trickery. On the other hand, Shawn is in effect forced by the state into that career, and uses his very real talents in a manner that helps people on a day-to-day basis.

Having been forced into the psychic detective business, Shawn gets a lot of enjoyment out of his work, but is nonetheless alienated in a very Marxian way—for which Marx would have a lot of sympathy. Ultimately, I'd bet that Marx would grudgingly classify Shawn as yet another complicated victim of a hierarchical system—he may have to 'sell' metaphysical falsehoods, but it is in the context of an economic system too stifling for him to be otherwise happy, and a state that would question his real talents more than his fake psychic ability.

This, indeed, might be the true point that unifies Karl Marx and Shawn Spencer—that Shawn's predicament comes as a result of a world where recognizing true human excellence is somehow harder than attributing that human excellence to an external supernatural realm. Marx may use Shawn's predicament to point us to the real culprit—not to Shawn, hiding behind a psychic sham, but to a hierarchical system that forces Shawn to choose between living a lie and going to jail for helping others.

VIII

Learn How
to Bend

21
From a Death to a Blooper

The heart of *Psych* is the relationship between Shawn
Spencer and Burton "Gus" Guster, and their bizarre antics
that strongly contrast with "normal" deportment. This contrast is most obvious in Shawn and Gus's dealing with death—
hysteria typically giving way to joking that leads to them
solving the case. Such a response to death suggests a sensibil-
ity much in keeping with Daoism, that most mystifying
Chinese philosophical tradition.

The Way (*Dao*) of Shawn and Gus illustrates the working of
Dao, a natural movement of reversal that invariably upsets
and overturns our expectations. Dao, the Way of All Things, is
always "reversing," ever elusive and playful. Adapting to such
twists and turns requires abandoning common sense, and
embracing paradox and parody—exactly what we need to
"make sense" of *Psych*.

Dao!

Daoism is probably the most misunderstood Asian tradition.
The Western label "Daoism" derives from the Chinese term
Dao 道 (way, path, speech), which the *Daodejing* 道德經 ("Classic
of the Way and Its Power"), Daoism's best known text, declares
cannot be put into words but only indirectly hinted at.

Dao cannot be clearly seen or known, but can be evoked
through images: water, Mother, an uncarved block of wood, a
vaporous cloud, a baby or child, a quiet and mysterious
woman. From such images we can infer that Dao is the cre-

ative source of all things, vague and impersonal, shy and ever elusive, seemingly weak but surprisingly powerful; the way of Nature itself. As such, Dao contrasts with the hard and assertive, the artificial ways of humanity and civilization.

To thrive in Dao is to discard artificiality, turn to nature and merge with its rhythms. Daoist texts speak of this as *wuwei* 無為 ("non-acting"), an effortless and spontaneous "going with the flow" in harmony with Dao that transcends the petty views and goals of humanity. Ironically, there are many Daoist texts ("scriptures" is probably too strong), including the *Daodejing* (mentioned above, attributed to the legendary Laozi, "Old Master"), the *Zhuangzi*, a compilation of weird stories, sayings and poems attributed to a mysterious "Master Zhuang" from the third century B.C.E., and the *Yijing* ("Book of Changes"), an ancient book of divination that provides concrete guidance for living in synch with Dao.

Dao, the Way, is a natural flowing movement referred to in Chinese by various terms—*fan* 反 ; *fu* 復; *gui* 歸 —all of which we can translate as reversal, the closest we can get to a "description" of Dao's workings. Reversal is constantly unsettled, marked by seemingly chaotic changes in course, yet one who attends to Dao can intuit a vague pattern, an oscillation between the cosmic poles of *yin* 隱 (dark, cold, female) and *yang* 陽 (light, hot, male).

Dao perpetually moves from *yin* to *yang*, never fixed, continually upsetting and undermining. Its Way inevitably disrupts plans and attempts at control. Dao is paradox, an ultimate contradiction between two opposite and irreconcilable truths. The opening line from the old TV show *Tales of the Unexpected* hints at how to live in a Daoist vein: "A wise man trusts only in lies, believes only in the absurd, and learns to expect the unexpected."

The Way of Dao, the Way of Reversal, doesn't conform to our wishes and resists attempts to force things to our views. Dao undermines our assumptions, and pokes fun at our artificial striving to "fix" things or even fully understand them. Dao is cosmic humor. Dao laughs at us, and helps us laugh at ourselves. The *Daodejing* says, "If they did not laugh at it, it would not be Dao."

A major way Dao disrupts is through death. Like Dao, death just is, neither good nor bad; death is but part of Dao, and rather than deny it, we should accept and go along, just as we flow with Dao. Death really is not opposed to life. Indeed, *true* life only comes from realizing this, opening naturally to the fullness of the here-and-now. As Laozi says, "Setting out to live is entering into Death." Shawn and Gus in their quirky fashion show us how to do this, making us face death as natural and inevitable, while demonstrating how silly and artificial we usually are in dealing with it. In so doing, Shawn and Gus exemplify an uncannily Daoist Way.

Reversal and the Dao of Shawn and Gus

As we've seen, the key to Dao's reversal is death. In *Psych*, death is the catalyst for everything. Already we have here a major reversal of our normal expectations, especially for an alleged comedy. Ironically, death, the "end of life," marks the beginning of the show. Almost every one of the many episodes of *Psych* begins with and revolves around a mysterious death—a horrific but all-too-common event in everyday life.

Ordinarily we might say "This should not happen!" but the fact of the matter is that it *does* happen, and in the show it *has* to happen for Shawn and Gus to go to work, even if they don't like it ("Why does it always have to be a dead guy?"). Similarly, death (and other "bad things") happen yet we, too, should carry on. Shawn and Gus's first Daoist lesson: death happens, yikes! but let's move along. Moreover, Shawn and Gus must "reverse," tracing things backwards to arrive at the truth, suggesting that the quest for truth has a certain Daoist dimension

Psych also exudes a Daoist air in its light-hearted way of treating serious events. Much Daoist humor, in fact, arises form the collision between reality and our expectations. *Psych* is a very funny show, overflowing with jokes and parody, and death is central to this. Unlike their colleagues who are trained law enforcement professionals, Shawn and Gus are rank amateurs who time and again stumble over dead bodies, attend autopsies, interject comments during official police briefings, even face threats of death from suspects on a regular basis. They're very aware of what's going on, but they remain singularly themselves in the direst of situations, unlike most of the show's characters.

We see this light-hearted attitude best in the funeral parodies in several of the shows most humorous episodes. In "Six Feet Under the Sea," from Season Three, Gus gets Shawn to accompany him for emotional support to a funeral that turns out to be, not for a friend or family member, but for Shabby the Sea Lion. On the way in, Shawn explains why he hates funerals: "Depressing organ music, and six time out of ten there's a snake in the casket." Towards the end of the service, Gus prays aloud, "Shabby, be free, swimming in the Ocean of Heaven, where there are no natural predators." In "He Dead," (Season Four), Shawn attends the funeral of a dead millionaire. As he enters, he nods to the assembled press, saying "Probably only here for the photo ops." As the scene unfolds, Shawn gets up to deliver a eulogy and quotes the lyrics from "Dust in the Wind," and at the end thanks the attendees for their apparent applause. He then turns to Gus, clearing his throat and saying he "breathed in some dead guy."

So Psych-Like

In the *Zhuangzi* we encounter a remarkably similar *Psych*-like scene, in which Zhuangzi himself is at the funeral of his wife, happily singing and banging on a pot rather than weeping and wailing as we would expect.

He explains to his puzzled friend:

> When she first died, I certainly mourned just like everyone else! However, I then thought back to her birth and to the very roots of her being, before she was born. . . . Her life's breath wrought a transformation and she had a body. Her body wrought a transformation and she was born. Now there is yet another transformation and she is dead. She is like the four seasons. . . . She is now at peace, lying in her chamber, but if I were to sob and cry it would appear that I could not comprehend the ways of destiny.

The message is clear: when we follow the reversal of Dao we see that Death is a natural movement of Dao, and as such, funerals are pointless responses that run counter to Dao. Once we "get" this, we will be fine. In fact, rather than rail and wail, we can even find a paradoxical joy in it. At the very least, our solemn rites of mourning reveal how shockingly little we know of Dao, and most certainly don't help the deceased or us.

This latter point is especially important. Shawn and Gus refuse to follow convention—be it at a funeral, crime scene, or in the midst of a busy police station—and actually seem to do the *reverse* of what's expected. Just like Dao. They *can* be serious at times, may even have initial bouts of fear and terror, screaming and wailing as they sprint for the nearest exit, but they don't get hung up, and instead *return* to pick up where they left off. Emotional shocks pass, and they continue on. A passage in Chapter 5 of the *Zhuangzi* explains that the Daoist sage is like this, having all the normal emotions but not fixating on them: "He lets all things be and allows life to continue on its way."

Shawn and Gus also evince a Daoist Way in their playful "methods." Shawn has knack, possibly an eidetic memory, but it is not the product of analytic thought. He was trained informally by his Father but never cultivated it in a formal, step-by-step fashion. Shawn's "gift" is inexplicable, it emerges spontaneously, seemingly as his whim but it is unerringly "right." As such, it exemplifies the Daoist notion of *wuwei*, much the way Cook Ding in the *Zhuangzi* amazes his lord by perfectly carving up an ox without thinking and without ever needing to even sharpen his knife: he merely follows Dao, sensing the natural gaps within the carcass, pausing only at the occasional difficult part.

Gus, too, has a few of these natural but mysterious abilities. His "supersniffing," safe-cracking expertise, and ability to gauge a woman's measurements with unerring accuracy may seem even sillier than Shawn's antics but they prove surprisingly helpful at the most opportune moments. All in all, their ways aren't meticulously planned out but respond to the immediate situation at hand. We might say that this is the Way of "Anti-Method," not the product of intentional training or conscious thought, yet in the end it is *this* Way that succeeds.

Psych also promotes the importance of being like a kid rather than an adult, one of the more prominent Daoist images. We see this especially with Shawn and his refusal to "grow up" despite the continual haranguing of his father, Lassiter, Juliet, even Gus on rare occasions. Shawn's Way of the Child resonates deeply with Laozi's valorizing of the infant (weak but strong in a Daoist fashion) and Zhuangzi's description of the legendary "immortals" who epitomize Dao and who have "flesh like young girls."

Shawn's child quality is deeply paradoxical, as he is both *childish* and *child-like*. Shawn is *childish* when he impetuously jumps into situations without thinking, stubbornly insists on his own way as correct, as well as his obsessions with sugary snacks and cartoons. And yet Shaw is childlike—imaginative, sweet and charming, loyal to Gus and his other colleagues. He also constantly plays with various toys, yet is often quite kind and thoughtful; for example, helping Chief Vick gets a permanent position and saving "Woody" the coroner from possible jail.

The Way of the child is to be both *childish* and *childlike*; there cannot be one without the other, just like *yin* and *yang*, the twin poles of Dao's reversals. Similarly, Shawn wouldn't be Shawn without being both childish and childlike, and both dimensions of his character are what allow him to succeed.

And the Reversals Keep on Coming

Once we take this Daoist view, more and more things in *Psych* fall into place. Indeed, it appears that *Psych*'s Daoist reversals return again and again. Furthermore, these reversals are not just examples of Daoistically defying "normal" expectations surrounding death. Another Daoist aspect of *Psych* is the dialectical relationship between Shawn and Gus. Although great friends, they consistently bicker back and forth in a weird yet playful tug-of-war. Just like the constant back-and-forth between those polar opposites, the *yin* and *yang*, so Shawn and Gus are never static and often at odds, yet they need to be this way to function. Their very relationship is reversal, something underscored by the rare occasions, as in "An Evening with Mr. Yang," the finale of Season Three, when Gus (rather than Shawn) takes the lead in joking and general silliness.

Another reversal regarding Shawn and Gus is that despite being our main characters, they are anything but heroic in the usual sense. Traditionally, death in all societies is the ultimate disruption and horror; coming to terms with mortality is a focus of most religions and the central theme of the archetypal "hero myth." Like a shaman, the detective must respond to this threat, learn how it can be neutralized, defeat it, and return the world to normalcy. The stereotypical detective (Philip Marlowe or "Dirty Harry") must be a true hero. Since Shawn and Gus are "detectives," we would assume they would also be heroes. Yet, they are decidedly antiheroic; they can be quite fearful and have no training in weapons, self-defense, or standard law enforcement procedures. Even worse, Shawn and Gus have difficulty staying on topic, and are constantly making fun of each other and the situations in which they find themselves. You could not find as unlikely a pair of heroes as these two, and yet as fans of the show know, Shawn and Gus almost always succeed.

Daoist reversal also manifests in the many occult references we find in the show. Daoism has long included an assortment of ghosts and wizards, exorcists, mediums, shamans and what not. This makes a certain sense, as these are figures associated with the mysterious and uncanny aspects of reality, and they often appear in the *Zhuangzi* and other Daoist writings. The occult and paranormal are constant themes in *Psych*, and much of the show involves the characters playing with, playing off, and parodying these ideas: inventing the urban legend of "Scary Sherry," dressing up as Vampire Lestat and Blackula, and joining with the dummies staging a murder in a carnival "Haunted House" ride.

Once more, Shawn and Gus make us face death, albeit with humor instead of fear or grief, and once more these more "spooky" aspects of death underscore the Daoist philosophical point: the dividing line between life and death, so often assumed as clear and distinct, is actually quite permeable. Yet the reversal goes further here, since the show actually parodies and pokes fun at these popular conventions; much as in *Scooby Doo* (one of Shawn's favorite cartoons), there are no "real" ghosts, just a bunch of silly crooks who get caught by those "meddling kids."

Here, Lassie . . . Here, Boy

Yet another reversal shows in the striking contrast between our "antiheroes" and Carlton Lassiter ("Lassie"), the overly serious, gun-happy chief detective. Lassie is definitely *not* Daoist, apparently following a more Legalist way that is direct, forceful, harsh, and meticulously planned. There is nothing spontaneous or playful in Lassie's Way and he *does* get results but rarely to the extent Shawn and Gus do. At times, he has succumbed to the Way of Shawn and Gus, as in the final scene of "Scary Sherry: Bianca's Toast," where he connects with Shawn, Gus, and Juliet during lunch, getting a cheerful "Hey Lassie!" and a fortune cookie which he smilingly eats as the scene fades.

Even more interesting, Lassie actually becomes more successful when he adopts a more Daoist *wuwei* approach, as in "Feet Don't Kill Me Now," when he takes up tap-dancing under Gus's tutelage, and as a result, taps into more a intuitive, Shawn-like way of thinking that enables him to wrap up a number of unresolved cases. Once more, the Dao of Shawn and Gus slyly wins out over the more serious and forceful Dao of Carlton, much the way the *Daodejing* reminds us that "Softness overcomes what is hard / Weakness overcomes what is unyielding." A similar lesson emerges from "Bounty Hunters," in Season Two, where Shawn and Gus show up a mightily-muscled childhood hero and bounty hunter.

Daoist reversal also manifests in the very structure of a typical *Psych* episode. The show begins in the past with young Shawn and some incident. As the show unfolds, the theme from the opening scene ends up being crucial—a straightforward example of Daoist reversal and return. "Young Shawn," the child, sets the tone for the show's Way. Moreover, as we have noted, Shawn's child-like or childish qualities are always crucial to the case's resolution. The examples of this are too numerous to cite but one of the best is in "Not even Close . . . Encounters" in Season Five, where Shawn and Gus reconnect with their nerdy childhood friend Dennis and once more immerse themselves in various toys, cartoon, and sci-fi memorabilia. And since this is *Psych*, the nerdy gadgets and memorabilia turn out to be instrumental in solving the case.

Like Ca-Razy

Once we take on a Daoist perspective, the reversals proliferate like ca-razy. To give just two more examples: *Psych* subtly evinces a Daoistic "way of the female" (contrary to most police shows), with women (Juliet, Chief Vick, Shawn's mother) far more accepting of Shawn and Gus's work and clearly being on better terms with them than the stereotypically 'male' figures such as Lassiter and Shawn's dad, who are held up for ridicule.

As a cult show, *Psych* effectively blurs the line between television and reality. Like all TV shows *Psych* mirrors reality while also creating it. *Psych* is woven into fans' lives, they spend hard-earned cash to acquire *Psych* merchandise (T-shirts, coffee mugs, posters, box sets), travel to various fan conventions, log on to various fan websites (official and otherwise), even writing book chapters exploring the show's philosophical dimensions. It's *more* than "just TV" and in many respects exemplifies today's media-saturated culture where such lines are blurred. There is something of a Daoist point here, perhaps best expressed, in Zhuangzi's famous "butterfly dream," where the laughing sage ponders upon awakening whether he was Zhuang dreaming he was a butterfly, or is now a butterfly dreaming he is Zhuang. Is this a dream or is this real? Is *Psych* just a show, or is it something more?

Defying a Definition of the Dao

By now you can see where I'm going. These allusive, playful, and suggestive Daoist aspects of *Psych* would seem to be building to an obvious assertion: it's a "Daoist show." And certainly we would have a point here. In fact, there are some interesting more or less explicit Daoist references in show itself: the Yin and Yang trilogy (Season Three's "An Evening with Mr. Yang," Season Four's "Mr. Yin Presents," and Season Five's "Yang 3 in 2D") and even Season Six's "The Tao of Gus." We can also trace a subtle Daoist aspect in the show's mysterious, indefinite roots.

Psych is its own unique show yet it also harks back to numerous sources: serious (Sherlock Holmes and Dr. Watson), comedic (Marx Brothers, Laurel and Hardy, Abbott and Costello), and even the in-between (*I Spy*, *Scrubs*). *Psych*'s innumerably nostalgic allusions to various pop culture icons of Shawn's (and the target audience's) youth are all instances of reversal, a turning back to earlier times. Perhaps most obviously, the show is on-going parody of the entire television genre of police procedurals, exhibiting the playful approach that informs much of the *Zhuangzi*.

Still, Dao evades definition. We can't figure it out or sew it up neatly—reversal by its nature cannot permit final settling down or resolution. And it's difficult to define *Psych* neatly. Is it a comedy or a mystery? We could dub it a "dramedy," a word allegedly coined in the late 1970s by the entertainment industry for productions that do not fit neatly into the categories of either comedy or drama. However, even *this* word doesn't quite fit *Psych*. The show itself remains vague and indefinable. Similarly Laozi admits in the *Daodejing* that he does not know the Way's name and so just calls it Dao. In the end, of course, such insistence on linguistic pigeonholing is *not* in keeping with Dao and its "reversals." Pinning the Daoist label on *Psych* won't work because Dao defies words and the impulse to categorize is itself a *human* endeavor, an artificial striving that is the very antithesis of (reversal of?) *wuwei*.

It would seem best, then, to say that *Psych* is *not* "Daoist" (just as neither Winnie the Pooh nor Piglet are Daoists, fans of Bernard Hoff's *The Tao of Pooh* to the contrary). But we might say that the show (certainly Shawn and Gus) provide an intriguing and inviting "taste of Dao," uncannily like the various exemplars of Dao in the *Daodejing* and the *Zhuangzi*.

Ending with a Blooper

It seems appropriate to draw these Daoist meditations on *Psych* to a close by touching on the tendency for each episode to close with a blooper tagged on at the end, something customary since Season Three. The case is solved, the show has (seemingly) ended yet as the credits role, we revert to an earlier scene that didn't make the final cut—yet another type of reversal. These bloopers are often funnier than scenes that made the cut, and, ironically often center on antics of Lassie, who by all evidence is quite the cut-up on set. Yet the inclusion of these scenes suggests they aren't real bloopers. We sometimes get the sense that these post-script scenes are actually set from the very beginning. These bloopers upset expectations the show itself has instilled within us, call into question the hard and fast distinction we often make between the serious and the comedic, mistake versus success, and scripted TV versus reality TV.

So is all this Daoist analysis of *Psych* right? Is it wrong? Do such Daoist comparisons and suggestions regarding *Psych* make any sense? Zhuangzi and Laozi would probably say "No." What would Shawn and Gus say? Does it make a difference in the end? It's a *fricking* TV show, after all! By this time I know the editor (Rob, are you reading?) wants me to shut my pie-hole. So let me close with this reminder: the only thing that shuts *my* pie-hole is pie.

22
What Friends Are For

PATRICIA BRACE

> And those who are in their prime need friendship to do fine actions; for when two go together . . . they are more capable of understanding and acting.
>
> —ARISTOTLE, *Nicomachean Ethics,* line 1155a10

Over the course of the show, the characters on *Psych* have developed relationships and friendships of different types. Since age five, Shawn and Gus have been almost constant companions and are present-day business partners in their unusual detective agency. Although Shawn is friendly with other people in Santa Barbara, it's really his relationship with Gus that seems to be the deepest friendship that is central to the show.

In his *Nicomachean Ethics*, Aristotle (384–322 B.C.E.) argues that the best kind of friendship between two people is all about an appreciation of the beautiful, virtuous, and other good qualities of the other person as well as a mutual awareness of each other's good. Aristotle describes several types of friends:

- **friends of utility**
- **friends of pleasure**
- **erotic friendships**
- **parent-child friendships**
- **and complete or "perfect" friends whose relationship is based on virtue and goodwill.**

Probably none of the relationships at the Santa Barbara Police Department (SBPD) can be considered perfect friendships, but some may come close.

Use Me, but Don't Abuse Me

According to Aristotle, *friendships of utility* are those relationships where mutual benefit is to be gained from each other's services, as in a business relationship. For example, you may have a mechanic you go to on a regular basis, and you may have established the kind of relationship where you're friendly toward him, no doubt, and "care about" him insofar as he serves the purpose of fixing your car. You may chat about his interests, his vacations, and even his family. You may feel the same way toward your dentist, because she's useful for keeping your teeth in good shape; your doctor, because she gets paid to keep you healthy; your gutter-cleaner guy, because he keeps your gutters clean.

Friendships between co-workers may be seen primarily as ones of utility, too, as each person has usefulness to the other in terms of a task or series of tasks which they are required to complete. This is the basis in Season One for Shawn's relationships with members of the SBPD. Their interactions aren't necessarily based on liking each other—in fact Shawn starts off on the wrong foot by outing Lassiter's illicit affair with his first female partner ("Pilot"), earning the detective's hatred. However, each stands to gain something good for themselves through their professional association, in this case, the ability to solve crimes more successfully.

The Buddy System

Aristotle also talks about *friendships of pleasure*, which are those relationships where satisfaction is gained from mutually enjoyable experiences. This could be bowling, tennis, chess, stamp collecting, sex, drugs, rock'n'roll, or all of the above. It could also be finding satisfaction in fixing problems, working on a project, or solving crimes together, as the folks at the SBPD do. For example, the friendship between Detective Lassiter and Detective Juliet O'Hara is one of both utility and pleasure. An attractive, slender young blonde, Juliet's sunny personality is almost the total opposite of Lassiter's sour, wooden, and socially inept one. They both, however, are dedicated to their work and actually enjoy solving crimes together.

The longer they work together, the closer Lassiter, Juliet, Shawn, and Gus get to each other, until by Season Six, they have saved each other's lives during several cases and even regularly socialize outside of work. This doesn't always go well, as when Juliet decides to give Lassiter a surprise birthday party and mistakenly invites all of the people he arrested to the event ("Poker? I Barely Know Her"). When he's accused of murder in Season Three's "Lassie Did a Bad, Bad Thing" Lassiter turns to Shawn and Gus to exonerate him. In Season Six's "Last Night Gus" when Gus, Shawn, and Lassiter have a crazy night out and wake up not remembering anything, but worry they may be responsible for a dead body, they work together to rediscover the night's events and unmask the real killer.

The buddies at the SBPD also share pleasurable hobbies. For example, in "Feet Don't Kill Me Now," Gus and Lassiter enjoy taking a tap dancing class and even performing together, with the unexpected utility benefit of helping Lassiter get out of his head and make connections in clues that help solve a case. In the Season Six episode, "Neil Simon's Lover's Retreat," when Shawn and Juliet go away for a couples weekend, Gus, Lassiter, and Henry all find themselves at a grocery store on a Saturday night, with no real plans, so they go out to a bar together. Socializing outside of work moves beyond utility and fits Aristotle's definition of friendship of pleasure.

Romeo Shawn and Juliet

Aristotle notes that intensity, desire, familiarity, enjoyment of each other's appearance, longing for the other in his or her absence, and an "appetite" for the other's presence are often associated with friendships of pleasure, which he dubs as the subtype, *erotic friendship*. In Seasons Three and Four, Shawn has a serious love relationship with his high school crush, Abigail Lytar, which is reflective of an erotic relationship. But there's also erotic tension present in the relations between Juliet and Shawn, who've always had an attraction to each other: Juliet digs Shawn's kind nature and smart-alecky ways, while Shawn is intellectually, emotionally, and physically attracted to her. As Shawn's romantic feelings for Juliet grow over the course of the show, he has the typical worry that if they become romantic he'll lose her as a friend, which will also be problematic for their working relationship.

Though Shawn and Juliet are attracted to one another, they both date other people over the course of the show, and initially set boundaries defining their friendship as a utilitarian one, related only to work, (see their restaurant conversation in the Season One episode, "He Loves Me, He Loves Me Not . . . Oops, He's Dead"). Juliet had a serious boyfriend before she came to work in Santa Barbara, but he had to enter the Witness Protection Program ("A Very Juliet Episode"). Shawn also had a problematic fling with Gus's sister, Joy, which causes problems in his friendship with Gus for a short time ("Christmas Joy").

Over the course of the third and fourth seasons, we see manifestations of Juliet's jealousy of Abigail's place in Shawn's life, such as when Jules and Gus search Shawn's apartment and she notices two toothbrushes in the bathroom ("Shawn Takes a Shot in the Dark") and pointedly asks Gus if Shawn and Abigail are living together. Circumstances conspire to keep Juliet and Shawn's relationship on a strictly work basis—for example on the night Juliet finally decided to take the bull by the horns and ask Shawn out, he has his first real date with Abigail and so had to refuse Juliet's request ("An Evening with Mr. Yang").

In the Season Five episode, "Extradition II, the Actual Extradition Part," Shawn and Juliet are finally alone together standing at the edge of a gorge. Juliet at first tells him she wants to just stay friends in Aristotle's utilitarian or pleasurable senses: "We missed the moment . . . The way things are— they're okay . . ." Shawn does his usual inane banter, this time comparing Legos and Duplo blocks as a metaphor for why some people don't fit together, then finally admitting to Jules that since he met her he's seriously considered trading in his beloved motorcycle, symbolic of his independence, for a car.

By the end of Season Six, in "Santababaratown," Shawn tells Juliet that he used to worry about himself first and Gus second, but now all that's changed, implying that now she's first on the list. They're at last ready to begin an erotic friendship based on their long-standing utilitarian and social friendship.

Complete Friendship

That such friendships are rare is natural, because men of this kind are few. And in addition they need time and intimacy; for as the saying goes, you cannot get to know each other until you have eaten the proverbial quantity of salt together.

—ARISTOTLE, *Nicomachean Ethics,* line 1156b30

Aristotle tells us that when friends of utility or pleasure no longer find each other useful or pleasurable, these types of "incomplete" friendships will dissolve. This makes sense since there's nothing *else* holding those kinds of friendships together. Aristotle argues that the most complete kind of friendship between two people is all about an appreciation of the beautiful, virtuous, and other good qualities of the other person as well as a mutual awareness of each other's good.

Concerning the awareness of each other's good, being concerned for the very well being of your friend is of fundamental importance. A sweet—yet vaguely creepy—example of this can be found in the first episode of Season Six, "Shawn saves Darth Vader."

When he finds out Shawn and Juliet are dating, we see how Lassiter has grown to care about his young detective partner, Juliet, as more than just a utilitarian or social friend. We get a call back to the pilot episode, as a protective Lassiter hooks *himself* up to the lie detector and reminds Shawn how his last partner, whom Lassiter "really liked," was transferred when their illicit relationship was outed. Lassiter tells Shawn that he knows that Shawn can beat a lie detector test, which had also revealed no lie when Shawn claimed psychic powers. He then promises Shawn that if he "doesn't treat O'Hara with the respect she deserves, or if you hurt her in any way," he'll shoot Shawn "repeatedly." Shawn looks down, with great concern, at the perfectly straight line on the lie detector paper. A complete friend wishes good to their friend for the friend's own sake, and so even though he has doubts about Shawn's veracity, Lassiter supports Juliet's decision to be with Shawn even while he protects her honor.

Actually, it's the relationship between Shawn and Gus that seems more like a complete friendship. The long-standing, close relationship between the two men began when they were five, and although Shawn didn't attend college, as Gus did, the two remain friends to the present. Gus's parents even turned down a chance for him to go to an advanced elementary school program because they were worried that he couldn't handle being separated from Shawn. In almost all of the flashbacks that open the shows, the two boys are featured engaged in some activity that has bearing on the present, and those that only feature Shawn usually have his father imparting some life lesson, such as when Henry—sounding much like Aristotle, actually—tells Shawn: "Trust is the most important thing in a partnership and friendship" ("Game, Set . . . Muuurder?").

Shawn shows time and time again that he is concerned for Gus's well being, as in "Gus Walks into a Bank." While Shawn waits in the car, a man inside the bank pulls a gun and traps Gus along with several other people. Shawn risks his life by posing as a pizza deliveryman when the gunman demands food. His motivation is not selfishly heroic; he knows he can figure out a way to save Gus and the other hostages. In the end he is also able to save the gunman, who was actually an innocent dupe, forced into the situation when his wife was kidnapped by the real bank robbers.

Virtue and Complete Friendship

Besides mutual awareness of each other's good, according to Aristotle complete friendship encourages virtue and abhors vice: "good people's life together allows the cultivation of virtue." Virtue is all about seeking the mean between two extremes—the not *too much* and the not *too little*, but the *just right*—in your actions, reactions, and emotions while living your life.

On the one hand you could be too reckless in battle, going berserk, while on the other hand, you could be too afraid, running away from the fight. Those options would both be "vicious" extremes, while courageously standing your ground would be the mean between those extremes. The same goes for anything we do, like eating or drinking too much (the vice of self-indulgence), eating or drinking too little (the vice of self-denial), and eating or drinking a sensible amount (the virtue of self-control).

Being virtuous, however, is something Shawn has always had trouble doing. We see that as a child Shawn didn't always seek the mean. Although brilliant, he had the tendency to take the easy way out, such as in the Season One episode "Game, Set . . . Muuurder?" when he was caught by Henry cheating at a game of *Battleship* with Gus by neglecting to place any of his ships on the board. He also prefers flash over substance, as in his loss to young Gus, on his simple banana bike, in a race refereed by his father during the Season Two episode "Zero to Murder in Sixty Seconds." Shawn refused to see that the many hours of practice Gus put in were a better choice than the time Shawn spent on outlandishly decorating his bike and choosing just the right race music, the Rocky themed "Eye of the Tiger."

He'll often look for the quick and easy route, such as making money as a kid by learning poker at the station house behind his father's back (and soundly beating a room full of cops) in Season One's "Poker? I Barely Know Her." But, having said this, Shawn's resilience, perseverance, and courage certainly are noteworthy, virtuous qualities. Episode after episode we see these virtues.

My Father, My Friend?

Besides friendships of utility, pleasure, and virtue, in the *Nicomachean Ethics* Aristotle talks about paternal friendship: "For a parent is fond of his children because he regards them as something of himself." Compounded by his parents' divorce, for which he (unfairly) completely blamed his dad, the relationship between Shawn and his father was always a difficult one. This is a big part of the problem in Shawn and Henry's relationship.

Henry sees Shawn as a chip off the old block, and in many ways he is. Both men are handsome, physically fit, extremely intelligent, and capable of great loyalty. However, Shawn's rebellion against the intense training forced on him by his father coupled with his resentment over the divorce makes him turn his back on the family legacy of police service. When Shawn refused to go to the police academy (and when he does get a chance later in life, as seen in the Season Five episode "We'd Like to Thank the Academy" we should be glad he didn't), he was turning his back on Henry. This rift between the two men is apparent from the first episode, in Shawn's reluctance to ask his father for any help, and Henry's constant disparagement of the Psych agency.

Aristotle recognizes that a child must achieve some level of maturity before he is able to understand the importance of the connection to the parent. While the parent becomes "fond" of the child as soon as it's born, the child may only become fond when enough time has passed so that he has some "comprehension or perception" of the parent. Over the whole course of the show so far, Shawn proves that his abilities, learned at Henry's knee, are the basis for his success as a detective, so finely honed that they allow him to don the guise of a psychic. He finally learns to give credit where it is due by thanking his father for his teachings, and conversely Henry periodically admits that Shawn is good at what he does, for example, in "Poker? I Barely Know Her," grudgingly recommending Shawn to go undercover to enter a high-stakes poker tournament to uncover a cheating scam.

Henry worries that Shawn will never become a responsible adult and so he continues to be a strong parental presence in his son's life, demanding quid pro quo for any favors he grants him. Whenever Shawn needs his dad to lend him a specialized piece of equipment, intervene with Chief Vick, or otherwise help him on a case, Shawn must make a deal. Henry drives a hard bargain and Shawn ends up painting Henry's house, attempting to build a doghouse and complete various other household tasks. Part of this attitude may be based on Henry's experiences with his own ne'er-do-well treasure-hunter brother, Jack, (Steven Webber) who has the same personality type as Shawn ("The Greatest Adventure in the History of Basic Cable").

Friendship within the family, especially between brothers, has a special place, according to Aristotle, because they are raised together and have the same paternity. However both are estranged from their father, Henry Sr. (Brian Doyle Murray) and their disparate personality types make friendship difficult.

In Season Four Henry eventually rejoins the force, at Captain Vick's request, and helps capture a serial killer known as Mr. Yin, threatening Shawn, and Henry again becomes an important presence in the SBPD. This job allows him more time to oversee and interact with Shawn, which helps them grow much closer. By Season Six, they have come to appreciate each other and have a much stronger, closer to complete friendship than ever before. Shawn understands the reasons for his parents' divorce, how hard the police life was on them both, and has embarked on his own adult love relationship in complete friendship with Juliet.

As the episode draws to a close, Henry announces his retirement and the two men plan to meet later for a beer, (something they have never done before) after Henry meets with an old friend from the SBPD to give him the sad news of a mutual friend's betrayal death. Unfortunately Henry has been deceived in his trust and loyalty, for, like the dead man, the man he meets with is neither an honorable nor a virtuous friend. Years ago he and the dead man committed a crime for which they received $50,000, and when the figure is stated, Henry realizes that the man was in on it. Henry, an honest cop to the end, asks him to turn himself in, but as we watch, stunned, he is instead shot down.

Vicious People

For Aristotle there is a certain class of people who are incapable of ever forming complete friendships. Mercenary people, he says, form friendships primarily for utility, even erotic ones, from which they probably don't even derive pleasure. In effect they are users, taking what they can get with no thought to the good or evil they do to others. He differentiates decent people, who are virtuous and seek the good, from the vicious, who are unscrupulous and poor decision makers.

This kind of person is at odds with himself, wanting one thing but never satisfied even if he acquires it, and always wishing for something else. The ex-cop who shoots Henry fits this mold. They always choose the easy path of vice and any pleasure through their cowardice or laziness which will eventually destroy them. They often surround themselves with others because they cannot stand to be alone and are usually full of self-loathing and regret. Their relationships are often short-term, based on enjoying each other's vices as they fulfill both utility and pleasure.

Prime examples of this type are the *Psych* villains Mr. Yang and Mr. Yin, featured in a through-story arc that ends three seasons of the show. First appearing in the Season Three finale, "An Evening with Mr. Yang," the serial killer is obsessed with Shawn and his family and kidnaps his mother, Maddie. In "Mr.

Yin Presents . . ." which ends Season Four, it's revealed that Yang had a partner, whom she says is even sicker than she is. This time the murder scenarios are based on Hitchcock movies, and after two people in contact with Shawn are killed, Yin summons him and his friends, Gus, Juliet, Lassiter, and Henry to a "deadly casting call" in which they must act out death scenes in various Hitchcock films. In fact this is a ruse, meant to distract them while Yin kidnaps Juliet and Abigail. With help from his friends, Shawn is able to save both women.

"Yang 3 in 2-D," the finale of Season Five, is where we find out the true nature of the relationship between Yin and Yang, who are father and daughter. This is the twisted reflection of the relationship between Henry and Shawn, as Yin trained her from an early age in the arts of crime. They were partners in vice, but Yin feels betrayed by Yang, who failed him when she was captured by Shawn, her obsession since she met him as a little boy, wanting his life. That she saves both Gus and Shawn from Yin by killing him instead shouldn't surprise us. It is revealed that Yin actually committed all of the murders attributed to her, yet she still feels tremendous guilt because she helped him. As Aristotle claims "base people are full of regret" and "have no friendly feelings about themselves." Only through her association with Shawn has Yang been able to see how wrong her life with her father had been, allowing her the virtuous act of rescuing our heroes.

Friends Are the Greatest External Good

These examples of the friendships of selected characters in *Psych* illustrate the range from simple utility and pleasure to the richer, more complex ones. For Aristotle friendship is the most important of the external goods necessary for your life to be declared, at its end, truly happy. Complete friendship encourages virtue and abhors vice: "good people's life together allows the cultivation of virtue." It's only through his on-going friendships with others that Shawn begins to understand the value of virtuous practice.

23
Shawn Reborn

C. Scott Sevier

From the beginning of each episode of *Psych*, we're exposed to the influence of authorities of various kinds. Many of these authorities form the backdrop for the episode's storyline, and many of them will also attempt to insert themselves into (or thwart) Shawn's investigative process: the detectives and police chief, his girlfriends, and even at times his best friend and investigative partner, Gus. Shawn is generally reluctant to accept advice from any of these sources, though he is often willing to employ their aid when it suits him.

Shawn's simply a modern-day Sherlock Holmes, whose keen powers of observation and deduction allow him to "read" clues that go unnoticed or unappreciated by others, including trained law-enforcement professionals. His incredible memory allows him unrestricted access to the lessons of his childhood. He is, therefore, able to benefit from these lessons from the past as though they were immediately present to his perception. Given his very specialized and unorthodox training coupled with his present occupation and its attending hazards, Shawn is able to outwit a variety of antagonists, solving roughly a case a week, and usually one around Christmas. In effect, Shawn relies heavily upon the authority of his childhood father, whose lessons are regularly employed to good effect.

Shawn's other authority is the present-day Henry Spencer, to whom Shawn constantly returns for advice. This incarnation of Henry is absent or appears only rarely in the earliest episodes, but the frequency of his appearances, along with Shawn's reliance on him, increases with each season. Indeed, by the end of Season Four, Henry has returned to the police force, and is acting as liaison between the police department and its consultants, notably, psychic detectives. Given Shawn's seeming disdain for the input of others in general, and from his father in particular on many other issues, it's perhaps surprising the frequency with which Shawn turns to Henry for assistance with his investigations. Henry's is the only voice Shawn consistently admits into his counsel. When it comes to police work, however, Henry's voice is, for Shawn, authoritative.

Daddy Issues

In *Nicomachean Ethics*, Book IX, Aristotle suggests that a true friend is "another self." *Psych* takes this insight to a rare extreme. In one episode, in fact, this is explicitly stated. When Shawn is kidnapped by would-be armored vehicle robbers, Henry teams up with Head Detective Carleton Lassiter to find him. Several times throughout the episode, Lassiter comments on the similarity, and even identity, of Shawn and Henry. When Lassiter issue a command to "Spencer," without any qualification, both the elder and younger Spencer asks "which one?" Lassiter responds by saying that they are the same person.

Certainly we could understand this as simple hyperbole. We often compare offspring to their parents. Indeed, some measure of similarity is inescapable. Nevertheless, the amount of repetition of that theme in the particular episode caused me to consider whether show creator Steve Franks intended to make a stronger statement. There is a real sense in which Henry can be said to have deliberately recreated Shawn in his own image. Consider the rigorous training regimen through which he put the younger Shawn. Henry has taken Shawn's education very seriously, and has both started at a young age and been intentional about his training. In this, he has followed the advice not only of Aristotle but also of Plato. Both thinkers stressed the importance of intentionality in education as well as the importance of beginning early, indeed, from infancy.

Add to this what Plato has to say in his *Symposium* about the nature of love. There, Plato, in the guise of Diotima, a woman who instructs Socrates on true love and beauty, asserts that all humans desire immortality, though there is more than one way to go about achieving it. There is a fairly rich backstory to this, and it requires some knowledge of Plato's doctrine of ideas or forms. According to Plato, the world is composed of things more and less real. The material world is, for him, less real than the intelligible and immaterial world of ideas, which are the forms.

There are levels within reality: real trees are more real than statues, paintings, reflections or shadows of trees; some of the forms are more real than others. The form of the good is the highest of them all, the form of the forms, as it were. We perceive material objects with our physical senses, but we understand them, and so grasp their underlying forms (their "essence," "nature," or "concept"), with our immaterial intellect, our rational soul. Human beings are hopelessly enamored with the material world of sensation, however, and so we have difficulty grasping the forms, especially the higher and better forms like justice or goodness. One form, however, outshines all the rest, and so is most accessible to human perceivers: beauty.

Another, Better Self

When we perceive beauty, we naturally love it, and develop a desire to reproduce it. Those whose love of beauty never rises above the lowest level related to the senses will fixate on the physical beauty of an individual, and desire to reproduce bodily with that person. These lovers attain a kind of immortality through their physical offspring. However, the more reflective among us may consider that all bodies share in the same beauty, and will be encouraged to reproduce beauty through magnificent poems or speeches. Such attain a higher sort of immortality, through their lyrics.

Plato points out that the literary offspring of Homer or Hesiod far outlive any physical offspring. And so on it goes. There are several rungs in the ladder of beauty, and reproduction of beauty at each ascending level results in a higher sort of immortality, by grasping onto a higher level of beauty. The one whose love for beauty has led him beyond physical bodies to the souls underlying them will be inflamed with the desire to reproduce learning in the objects of his affection. This is the response of the philosopher and teacher, whose offspring are at one and the same time his students and ideas.

Using Plato's framework as a guide, we can say that Henry has recreated Shawn not only physically, but also educationally. He was not content to stop at mere procreation, but he has sought to improve Shawn's soul, populating it with beautiful ideas, equipping it to best grasp and function within reality, attempting to make Shawn into another Henry—into another self, a better self. This, according to Aristotle, is a mark of true friendship.

Henry has, therefore, replicated himself both physically and psychologically, that is to say thoroughly. Shawn is another Henry. Thus, when we see Henry week after week provide Shawn with valuable advice related to his cases, we have a very interesting dynamic: an old Shawn (Henry) giving the young Shawn advice. Young Shawn's main authority is, in a sense, himself. It is in this way that Shawn can be both defiantly independent while, at the same time, persistently dependent upon the advice of his father. His father's voice has become, through memory and training, the voice of his own internal compass or conscience; but Shawn is also nourished by his father's voice in the present as well, as Shawn continues to seek him out for ongoing advice. We all carry around the voices of the authorities of our youth. They become, for us, a kind of ingrained, inner dialogue—the accumulated wisdom of our experiences. Perhaps because of Shawn's unique training and its profound effects upon his memory, the voices are not simply the internalized experience of a long-gone past; rather, he constantly draws upon those experiences directly, through recollection (another Platonic educational theme).

Where Medieval Meets Modern

We have then, in the character of Shawn Spencer, a combination of competing visions. There is, first of all, the medieval vision, which is always looking backwards towards the sages of the past, relying upon those authorities who have stood the test of time. The medievals avoided innovation except where necessary, and they were always particularly cautious when it came to the matters of greatest importance. In philosophy and theology, especially, the authorities had always to be consulted and addressed before moving in a new direction, and then judiciously. In the Middle Ages, Aristotle, Cicero, Boethius, and especially Augustine were held in highest esteem. One could not posit a theory at odds with any of them without substantial justification, and special caution was required in theology, where the specter of heresy was always looming. This reliance upon authorities was an especial aid to lesser minds, to keep them from going astray.

Contrast this with the modern ideal of autonomy, which was grounded in the individual's powers of reason and freedom, appearing notably in René Descartes (1596–1650), the designated "father of Modern philosophy," and coming to full maturity in the thought of Immanuel Kant (1742–1804). For these thinkers, there is no authority higher than reason itself, and each person must trust to his own judgments of reason. Anyone can in principle fall into error about anything at all.

Why trust to wise men of the past who, their wisdom notwithstanding, were also subject to the foibles not only of their age but of their humanity? We must forge ahead by the dual lights of reason and empirical observation, though not always in equal measure. The one who relies solely on the wisdom of past thinkers is their slave—not free, not autonomous. To be truly free, truly morally responsible, truly rational, you must have no final authority but that which is found in the self, in reason, or in the deliverances of the senses. This perspective is perhaps one of the most characteristic of Shawn. He is fiercely independent, regularly refusing to hear the (often sensible) voices of dissenting opinion, relying on his keen powers of observation and rational deduction, with rare exception.

We find in Shawn Spencer a combination of the intuitions of both the medieval and the modern age. At one and the same time, he relies on his own wits, eschewing the conventional wisdom of the day, particularly when it comes to investigation, and yet relying on the wisdom of his father, who is inevitably a product of that same conventional system, whose own skills in observation and deduction have been learned through his police training and subsequent experience on the force.

Perhaps the reason why Shawn can so easily disregard the conventional rules is because they serve only as a guide to those who have not yet internalized their wisdom, which he has already done. What these rules codify, for those who lack a deep understanding of the subject, Shawn has an intuitive knowledge of. It has become, for him, what Aristotle calls "second nature," the product of many years of habituation.

Shawn's refusal to rely upon the testimony of authorities is at times, however, more vicious than it is virtuous, and represents more of a rejection of competition than any legitimate reflection on their unreliability or unverifiability. In Season Five's "Shawn 2.0," when challenged by his nemesis Declan Rand, Shawn denies the accuracy of Rand's profile of Shawn (which was, in fact, prompted by Shawn's goading), even though he confesses to Gus immediately afterwards that the profile was accurate.

Shawn's refusal to admit an accurate pronouncement, in this case at least, is due not to any principled commitment to an independent standard of evaluation of evidence, but rather to simple pride. He will simply not be outdone, nor admit defeat. I wonder whether this same spirit does not underlie much of the modern rejection of authorities. For though it would be inaccurate to say that, philosophically, we are still living in the modern period, we are the descendants and inheritors of these same modern sensibilities, and this is especially true when it comes to the subject of authorities.

We favor the iconoclast. And yet, at the same time, our cultural reliance on the figure of the scientific expert is so pervasive as to be nearly invisible. We haven't so much abandoned the practice of relying upon authorities as we have simply exchanged one sort of authority for another, while congratulating ourselves for having done away with authorities altogether. The truth is that the modern revolution in philosophy did not significantly renovate the methods of philosophical thought, but merely rearranged the furniture a bit.

Renaissance Man?

In any case, it is simply untrue that the modern age has done away with authorities. Even during the birth pangs of rebellion against the medieval reliance on authorities, in the Renaissance, there was no wholesale rejection. Instead, the authorities were very conspicuously and consciously changed. "Renaissance" means "rebirth," and the moniker was intended to characterize a movement seeking to recapture the glory of the ancient Western traditions of Greece and Rome.

Very little of ancient thought survived into the Middle Ages, and since writing materials were expensive, and due to the incredible investment of time (often months or years) required to hand-copy a single manuscript, texts were judiciously selected for preservation. There were many reasons for the separation of the Latin-speaking West from the Greek-speaking East, but the result was that, by the sixth century, few in the West could read Greek, and very few significant philosophical works had been translated into Latin. The status would not improve until the thirteenth century, when interest in classical language and literature began to blossom in the West. The vast number of Greek, Arabic, or Hebrew texts that were to be translated into Latin were translated during the period we call the Renaissance.

You Kant Put Descartes Before the Horse

Even into the modern period, for all of the talk of rejection of authorities, the reliance upon them still persevered. Descartes is often thought to have made a solid break with the medieval methods, including the reliance upon the ancient authorities, such as Aristotle and Augustine. Nevertheless, he frequently makes profound metaphysical assumptions in his writings that were innovations of the very Middle Ages he is supposed to have rejected. A famous example of this is his proof for God's existence. Descartes insists that the only way he, a finite being, could conceive the idea of an infinite God is if that idea had been caused by something adequate to cause such a concept. In other words, something actually infinite was required to produce the idea of an infinite. This view, that like produces like, and that a cause must have as much reality as the effect, has come to be known as the "causal adequacy principle." It was very popular among medieval philosophers.

Moreover, Descartes very often draws inspiration directly from Augustine. Similarly, Kant's dependence upon the will, and even his conception of the good will, finds its analog in Augustine's claim that the good will is "a will by which we desire to live upright and honorable lives," that "when we will these things, we have a good will," and that "to have a good will is to have something far more valuable than all earthly kingdoms and pleasures." With Descartes and Kant, we have two thinkers who have voiced their independence from past authorities while simultaneously, and (to be charitable) perhaps unconsciously, appropriating their insights.

Shawn, at least, does periodically acknowledge the wisdom of others as well as his own limitations. Nevertheless, even when we see the most profound growth in Shawn, in the moments when he comes to realize just how interconnected he is, how dependent, when at his most deferential—as he is in Season Five's "The Polarizing Express"—the insight and the deference are brought about through the machinations of his own superego (incarnated by, and as, Tony Cox).

Even here, when Shawn seems suddenly to mature before our eyes, that growth is orchestrated and overseen by the supreme authority of self, albeit the subconscious self. We're on the heels of a vicious cycle here. If the superego is the subconscious embodiment of his father's wisdom, it is difficult to see where Henry's authority ends and Shawn's begins. But then, this is a problem inherent in any theory of absolute autonomy, since in the end there seems to be no final distinction between your own authority and the authority of your teachers.

The Fruit Doesn't Fall Too Far from the Tree

Shawn embodies competing ideologies found in the medieval and the modern period, respectively, that of reliance on external authorities and on autonomous reason. This tension was more pronounced during the Renaissance period, during which authorities weren't overtly rejected so much as replaced, with the more recent voices giving way to the older voices of a bygone golden age, of classical origins, characterized by an increased interest in studying the literature of the ancients in their own language, especially Greek.

Shawn likewise doesn't reject all authorities, but attends to the insight of his own father, a complex figure who functions for Shawn as his embodied superego, which is itself the internalized insight of his father. Autonomous individuals don't emerge from a vacuum, but are produced, through a combination of genetics, environment, nurture, and training. Shawn's very independence as a thinker and investigator is ultimately, and perhaps ironically, dependent upon the authority and training provided by his father.

24

The Amazing Psych-Man Versus the Sexist Mentalist

Mona Rocha

JULIET O'HARA: Okay, can I stop you there? First off, in your portrayal of me, I sound like I'm in eighth grade.

SHAWN SPENCER: Well, in my portrayal of you, you only have an eighth-grade education.

JULIET: Ah.

—"Spellingg Bee," Season One

Remember when Shawn meets Juliet for the very first time in the coffee shop? Remember she's sitting in his seat when he comes back? Yeah, that time.

Shawn doesn't know that Juliet is part of a sting operation. Even if he knew, Shawn probably wouldn't care since it's breakfast time and he's already ordered his juice. Besides, Juliet is pretty and that's a lot more interesting to Shawn. But she keeps rebuffing him, so in typical Shawn fashion, he rambles off the information he's gathered about her using his gift of observation, in a high pitched voice designed to impersonate Juliet, who's trying to ignore him . . . since you know, she's on the job and is a professional.

But the stereotypically high-pitched voice that Shawn uses—a thin, high, shrill voice usually associated with a young girl—gets to Juliet, and she intervenes. Shawn defends himself, but only digs himself in deeper as he paints a picture of Juliet in a highly stereotypical and somewhat sexist fashion as an empty-headed woman, with two cats, and with only an eighth-grade education.

Now, mind you, I love Shawn. But I'm also a feminist. So this scene got me thinking: is *Psych* a sexist show? After all, not everyone around Shawn knows that he's a fake psychic. Gus and Henry know. Carlton was never tricked: Lassie consistently refuses to acknowledge that Shawn is a real psychic. But the women of the show, the Chief and Juliet, have a less clear relationship to Shawn's abilities. They *may* believe he's psychic.

Feminists have long criticized fiction that leaves women in inferior epistemic positions ("epistemic position" is just a fancy philosophical way of referring to how much they are able to know) since these types of stories make it look like women have to prove their worthiness to share in knowledge. Fiction promotes the myth that knowledge resides in, and flows from, men, and that men can justify keeping this knowledge secret until women prove themselves capable of understanding and being responsible with the knowledge.

Psych seems to fit this format: Shawn has special access to knowledge, which was passed down to him from his father, and most of the men understand how he gets it, but the women are kept in the dark. Does this mean *Psych* is sexist? I don't think so, but perhaps the best way to prove my position is to compare it to a show that is sexist in this exact way. Fortunately, there is a show that is fairly similar to *Psych* that we can use for comparison. In fact, it's pretty similar because *The Mentalist* probably ripped off its main idea from *Psych*.

Although both shows appear to represent this sexist myth about male access to knowledge, only *The Mentalist* is a sexist show. In *The Mentalist*, Patrick Jane consistently revels in keeping knowledge secret from his boss, Teresa Lisbon, and there is often very little justification for his doing so other than that he believes she cannot handle knowing the right answers since she will do the wrong thing with the facts.

In *Psych*, on the other hand, Shawn implicitly trusts the women around him, Juliet O'Hara and the Chief, Karen Vick. Shawn holds onto his secret only because it's necessary for him to be allowed to solve crimes. While Patrick's relationship to Lisbon is one of misogynist paternalism, Shawn's relationship to Juliet and the Chief embodies feminist values. Through collective, non-hierarchical, collaborative problem solving and through his respect for women, Shawn and *Psych* emerge not only as the more entertaining—by far—but also as the more feminist—also by far.

Myopic Chihuahua

So what do feminists stand for anyways? Almost everyone knows that feminists support equality and self-determination for women, but there are a few other things that are at stake, too. For example, feminists worry over how the conception of the self is constructed and valued in our society. Feminists argue that how we view a person—including how we view ourselves—is based on social constructions, including social determinations of what it means to be a man, a woman, white, black, homosexual, heterosexual, and so on. Different qualities are associated with being a man or a woman, and the qualities associated with being a man (rational, intelligent, brave, strong, responsible, leadership) are regarded more highly than the ones associated with being a woman (emotional, caring, passive, unpredictable).

The qualities gendered as male are recognized as being integral to creating and running a well-organized society. On the other hand, the qualities that are associated with women are less valued. Feminist philosophers point out that these characterizations are unfair since they place women in the weaker position, as needing protection and as unable to take care of themselves. These gendered notions of characterizing women not only belittle feminine attributes—ignoring that there is a good deal of value in our emotions and intuition—but they also fail to give an accurate representation of women's full personalities, interests, and abilities.

So, when Shawn reduces Juliet to a high-pitched voice with two cats and not even a high-school education, it could be worrisome and sexist. However, we can't be myopic here. It's important to keep that whole interaction in context. Shawn was purposefully making up an outrageous scenario so as to grab Jules's attention. He was goofing off in an attempt to flirt with her. I am not saying that it's excusable for a man to say something outrageous or sexist. I am simply saying that Shawn, in his usual fun-loving and playful manner, chose a ridiculous approach to attract Juliet's attention.

Besides, there is no bone in Shawn's body that is imbued with patriarchy or misogyny. Perhaps due to his contentious relationship with his authoritarian father while growing up, Shawn realizes that there are alternative ways of doing things. Shawn does not perceive himself as an all-knowing authority when it comes to women and their lives. Sure, he is not afraid to express how superior he is when it comes to collecting clues and solving cases. But he exhibits decidedly feminist values in his approach to crime solving. He works collaboratively and non-hierarchically with Gus, Jules, the Chief, Henry, and even Lassiter.

Remember all those ridiculous introductions that Shawn has for Gus that we're so fond of? They all come about because Shawn does not work by himself, as the stereotypical lone male hero. He works with his best friend, Gus, whom he introduces as "Magic Head," "Gus T. T. Showbiz (The Extra T is for Extra Talent)," "Spell Master," or "Die Harder." Shawn has nicknames for the other people he works with, too. Lassiter is "Slim" or "The Penguin," Juliet (whom we all think of as "Jules," which is a nickname) is "Cagney," and the Chief is "Chiefie." Shawn changes his name, too—"Shawn Gthorndal" (It's pronounced Thorndal, it's a silent G) and "Emilio Estevez Esteeevez" are some of my favorites—indicating that he does not belittle any of his partners' worth through his unorthodox naming practices. In fact, the nicknames function as a way to equalize rank in the Shawnverse. Hierarchical relationships are wholly negated through the use of nicknames.

Shawn's irreverent working style also includes relying on women. In "Talk Derby to Me," Shawn suggests that Jules go undercover as a roller skater to infiltrate a robbery ring. With the knowledge gained first-hand from her, he eventually breaks the case. Again, in "Bollywood Homicide," it's Jules's undercover work as part of a fake relationship that makes it possible for Shawn to uncover the identity of the jealous, homicidal lover at the heart of the case. Once again, it's Juliet who comes to the rescue by providing invaluable support in getting Shawn and Gus onto an army base, so they can investigate a mysterious death in "You Can't Handle This Episode," in Season Four. And it's Juliet whom Shawn calls to save him from the madman running loose around Camp Tikihana (she finds him hiding in a closet, not doing push ups) in "Tuesday the 17th."

Shawn relies unabashedly on Jules. Not only does Shawn value her contributions, but he is also not afraid to ask for her help. This collaborative outlook, combined with a healthy appreciation for the contributions women can make, is clearly feminist in nature.

Unlike stereotypical male heroes, Shawn is willing to share the glory of solving a case with the women he works with. When he's called in to investigate a homicide on an oilrig, Shawn tells Gus, "Gus, don't be a myopic chihuahua. I have a foolproof plan that not only solves the case, but gives the Chief all the credit" ("There Might Be Blood"). This kind of selfless sharing of credit is characteristic of collaborative, feminist problem solving.

Yes, Shawn loves that the Santa Barbara Museum has a plaque referring to him as a Paleo-Sleuth, noting his solving of the dinosaur case, but he does not solve cases for the glory, prestige, or revenge like say, Patrick Jane in *The Mentalist*. Shawn does it for fun. And the snacks. Pineapple smoothie, anyone?

Hey Man, We All Get Help Sometimes

Shawn is always willing to share the credit, even giving some credit on occasion to quarrelsome Lassiter. For example, in "From the Earth to Starbucks," Shawn works to convince Lassiter that Lassiter's detecting activities are up to par, even downplaying his own contribution to Lassiter's biggest case:

LASSITER: I caught the Back Bay Killer.

SHAWN: I remember it well.

LASSITER: Although I had a tip . . .

SHAWN: The blue sedan.

LASSITER: Yeah. That was you?

SHAWN: It might have been.

LASSITER: See what I mean?

SHAWN: Come on, you still had to put it all together, right?

LASSITER: Look Spencer, the blue sedan was the key to the whole thing. It was the murderer's car.

SHAWN: Yeah, but who had to run the plates? (Season One, "From the Earth to Starbucks")

Shawn dedicates the rest of the investigation to building up Lassiter's self-confidence by solving the case that puzzles Lassiter. This interest in the wellness of each group member is decidedly feminist. When Gus asks for clarification on the case, Shawn says,

SHAWN: We gotta solve that case.

GUS: What case?

SHAWN: The one Lassiter can't solve.

GUS: He's gonna hire us for a case?

SHAWN: Oh, god, no. He'd never do that.

GUS: So, we won't get paid.

SHAWN: Exactly.

GUS: And we're just doing it for the glory?

SHAWN: Nope. We give Lassiter all the credit. In fact, I don't even think he can know we're helping him. ("From the Earth to the Starbucks")

Even though Gus objects to the plan since the two won't get paid, this act goes on to prove that a truly selfless attitude, one oriented toward the good of the collective group, permeates the Shawnverse. With Juliet jumping in to help Shawn, and indirectly to help Lassiter, it becomes even clearer that this is a show where individual strengths blend together and where individual ability is not celebrated in itself: problem solving, the sharing of knowledge, and collective workmanship are valued over the individual.

We all love *Psych*. One of the reasons we do is because all the characters seem to like and respect each other. There's good-natured banter and ribbing going around, but we don't doubt even for a minute that all the members of the team are all there for each other. They work smoothly together, too, without egos getting in the way.

Chief Vick and her Coast Guard sister put aside their bickering to help Shawn and Gus in the sea lion case in "Six Feet Under the Sea." Even doubting Lassiter asks Shawn to go undercover to aid in solving a murder at a secret society in Santa Barbara ("Dis-Lodged"). This kind of effort, foundationally collaborative and team-oriented, is feminist in nature. That's what makes it stronger than your lone male hero approach: working with great people with multiple abilities, multiple skill sets, and multiple ways of approaching a problem is inherently better than a singular effort.

You Know That's Right

So not only is Shawn a feminist hero who works collaboratively and non-hierarchically and asks for help from women, but he also respects women. This respect goes deep, and Shawn expresses it even when it might be contrary to his own interests. In "There Might Be Blood" Shawn and Gus are undercover on an oilrig. When introduced to the owner of the operation, it turns out that he's a male chauvinist as he introduces his daughter as a Yale graduate, but notes, "Apparently, Yale University didn't teach her any manners—or how to get a husband." As her dad dismisses her and sends her to fetch "cocktails while the men talk," Shawn and Gus exchange disgusted glances. Shawn protests this treatment, even though it might make more sense to just go along with the owner and therefore smooth the way for the investigation. But Shawn doesn't go along with this sexist treatment, breaking in to say "Not to be rude, Billy Joe, but it's the twenty-first century, and women have earned the right to be treated equally." It doesn't work, and it actually blows their cover, but Shawn stands up for feminist goals.

Shawn also does not use his powers of observations against women, for his own interests. In "From the Earth to Starbucks," we see Shawn on a date with a new girl. As the two converse over drinks, Shawn realizes that the girl he's on a date with is on the rebound. She just broke up with her boyfriend the night before, thinking he was cheating on her, but her boyfriend wasn't cheating on her at all.

SHAWN: Look, he took your jewelry because he's trying to figure out your ring size. He took you to Tiffany's to buy you that fancy necklace because he's really trying to scout out what kind of stones and settings you like.

DATE: What about last Friday?

SHAWN: Oh, come on, the Eastland Center? There's no clubs there, he wasn't there with a chick. He was probably in the north side of the parking lot at Robbins Brothers picking out the ring. (Season One, "From the Earth to Starbucks")

Telling her all this hurts Shawn's chances of developing a relationship with her or of scoring, but he does it anyways. Even though he could clearly tell that the girl was ready to move on, he does not take advantage of her vulnerable position. He respects her and uses his talent to help her straighten out her love life.

If Shawn so clearly respects women, why does he keep secret knowledge from the women in his life? Because if he were to let on that he's not a psychic, then he could no longer work with the Santa Barbara Police Department. The fun of detecting would end. Shawn's not keeping his secret because he thinks he's superior to the women in the show, but rather because he wants to be able to continue working with them.

Red Shawn

Now, where *Psych* is feminist and shows respect for women, *The Mentalist* comes up wanting. Patrick Jane, the expert consultant for the California Bureau of Investigation (CBI) and former fake psychic, has a difficult and contentious relationship with the women on his team. Often times, he doesn't let his boss, Teresa Lisbon, in on his thoughts, process, or deductions . . . purposefully. As Patrick tells Lisbon, "If I told you about every hunch, you would get very irritated" (Season One, "Red Handed"). Shawn, on the other hand, delights in imparting every little bit of knowledge, accompanying it with interesting mimes, ticks, and leg twitches.

Patrick believes he needs to keep facts back from Lisbon, for her own good or protection. This attitude—that he knows what's best for Lisbon—is characteristic of patriarchal paternalism.

To treat Lisbon as a fully capable and mature individual who is capable of making decisions and expressing choices, Patrick needs to discuss work-related matters with her, especially since she's in charge. The fact that Patrick regularly refuses to discuss the case he's "consulting on" with Lisbon shows he does not respect her as an adult or as an officer of the law.

In *Psych*, Shawn, Gus, and Lassiter all respect Juliet and her insights. For example, in Season Five's "Romeo and Juliet and Juliet" they respect her ideas so much that when she transfers after Yin had kidnapped her, they invade her new city hall office to seek out her opinion on the Chinese Triad case. Awkwardly meeting in Juliet's office, Shawn exclaims to Lassiter: "Oh my God, we're on the same page. You're trying to lure her out of this dungeon with details of the case!" This visit underscores the fact that they all value Juliet's expertise.

On *The Mentalist*, collaboration is harder to come by. Even when Lisbon asks Patrick point blank what's going on, Lisbon can't get a straight answer:

LISBON: Who do you think did it?

PATRICK: Jabba the Hut.

LISBON: Seriously.

PATRICK: Ming the Merciless?

LISBON: Okay.

PATRICK: Alf? (Season Three, "Red Mile")

Instead of confiding to Lisbon, Patrick guards his deductions assiduously. He doesn't have to do this, since, unlike Shawn, Patrick isn't trying to pretend he is a psychic. He could share his reasons and observations, but almost never does until the end of the episode. He believes his ways of doing things are better than hers, even complaining when she sticks to the rules ("Red Handed"). Yet we really can't judge his ways since the show often leaves Patrick's methods as mysterious as if he really were psychic.

Patrick's abrupt manner and refusal to work collaboratively usually causes problems for Lisbon, so much so that her own leadership is undermined or questioned by her superiors. For example, in "Red Hair and Silver Tape" (Season One), Patrick goes behind Lisbon's back to solve a kidnapping case. He convinces another team member not to follow orders and go undercover to trap the suspect, without informing Lisbon of what he's orchestrating.

In "Blood Money" (Season Two), Patrick breaks into a suspect's home without a warrant and without informing Lisbon, endangering the investigation and getting key evidence thrown out of court when the judge deems it tainted as "fruits of the poisonous tree." Because of the high cost of this stunt, Lisbon is disciplined for not controlling Patrick, and is therefore suspended for several days.

Other times, such as in "Blood Hounds" (Season Three), Patrick's actions leave Lisbon stranded, as he hurries off to solve a crime by himself. Patrick, calling Lisbon on his cellphone: "Lisbon, yes. I ditched you. Uh, I must confess. Look at the bright side, I left you with a car this time. . . . There's no need to be so grumpy, it's okay." Patrick's attitude—a lone crime solver who does not co-operate or work well with others—undermines both police cases and female leadership. Clearly Patrick is not a collaborative, feminist crime stopper. He is more of a misogynist, stubborn crime solver.

In many episodes, Patrick antagonizes witnesses or dismisses interviews without clearly communicating with Lisbon or sharing his deductions with her. In "So Long and Thanks for all the Red Snapper" (Season Four), Lisbon and Patrick are conducting an informal interview at a shipyard. Patrick starts the interview by mocking the female suspect under his breath (repeating her answer under his breath derisively), follows that up by insulting her outright when it is discovered she has three kids (he calls her a "breeder" to her and her husband's face), and then terminates the interview without giving Lisbon the courtesy to ask any final questions she might have. He leaves, informing all involved that they are finished with the questioning.

This kind of behavior is typical for Patrick, and is very far from the collaborative, joint feminist venture of solving problems that's present in *Psych*. In "Blood for Blood" (Season Three), people complain to Lisbon: "What is he doing? Could you please control your man?" with Patrick responding, "Oh trust me, she's tried." This kind of interaction reduces Lisbon professionally—she becomes not an investigator, but a babysitter for an eccentric and rude man. In "Bloodstream" (Season Three) Patrick sums this relationship by saying "She does the detecting and I do the insulting."

Making the woman in charge appear to be weak and incapable of controlling a subordinate is not only non-collaborative, but it makes it seem as if it is a mistake to place women in leadership roles. It goes against the feminist project of celebrating women's abilities and feeds into the stereotype that women are just not as capable as men. Shawn might be irreverent in professional situations, like sitting in the Chief's comfy chair or requisitioning a Segway to complete a case, but he would never dream of even implying the Chief or Juliet were anything less than very capable and accomplished at their jobs.

Your Story, Much Like Your Lunchbox, Smells a Little Fishy

Don't get me wrong. *The Mentalist* is an entertaining show. I record it almost every week. But I prefer my entertainment to be fun and feminist. That's why I love *Psych*. *Psych* celebrates strong women and doesn't undermine women's leadership roles. Juliet and Chief Vick are respected throughout the series, with their skills and contributions being highlighted in countless episodes. Shawn and Gus work co-operatively with all of the folks connected to the Santa Barbara Police Department, even bringing Henry into many of their investigations. In *Psych*, knowledge is shared for the common good.

Most importantly, if Shawn keeps up the ruse of being a psychic, that doesn't mean he falls within the men-use-secret-knowledge-sexism-trap. Rather, the secret knowledge is simply a non-sexist tool that allows Shawn to keep playing the game he loves best: detecting. The same cannot be said of Patrick Jane. Patrick keeps knowledge to himself purposefully, and he does not trust the women around him with it.

Regardless of his motives, Patrick comes across as steeped in patriarchy since he refuses to engage the women around him in rational communication. Yes, Patrick is quirky and suave in his own way (with his love of tea and penchant for wearing suits), but he's no feminist. Shawn is. An irreverent karma chameleon steeped in 1980s references, Shawn completely blows our minds with his unconventional feminist approach. I mean, he even bakes in an Easy Bake oven! Really, who could ask for more? We fans of delicious flavor certainly couldn't.

Psycho Psychics

A *psychic* is someone who claims to have paranormal (outside or above the norm) abilities. Most of these abilities are extrasensory perception (ESP).

So psychics can supposedly do things like "see" events in the future or past, communicate with others mentally, make things move with their minds, or even talk to the dead. The pseudoscience of *parapsychology* is the "study" of such nonsense. You can probably tell from the preceding sentences that I think this is all a bunch of BS, as there has never been even one, legitimate, repeatable instance of ESP recorded in any respectable, peer-reviewed journal or book throughout the established scientific community.

At best, peer-reviewed (and anecdotal) evidence suggests that people who claim to be psychic are simply lucky guessers, very good at remembering details or their dreams, or they become conscious of the non-conscious, automatic cognitive processing that occurs in humans all the time. And a lot of them are simply bullshitters trying to take your money, or gain power and prestige, or any combination thereof. There's nothing supernatural about psychic "abilities"—it's all squarely within the purview of nature and natural abilities, much like magic tricks only with *verbal* and *mental* sleight of hand, smoke and mirrors, and a whole lot of gullibility.

When the journals *Annual Review of Psychology*, *Psychological Bulletin*, *Science*, or *Nature* comes out with a paper titled, "The Human Ability to Predict Future Circumstances" or "Locating Persons through Physical Contact with Their

Personal Items" *then* I'll start to believe. Even then, I'd be utterly flabbergasted and dumbfounded. Psychic abilities are the stuff of science fiction, rather than science, and make for great entertainment—that's one of the many reasons why *Psych* is so much fun. Below, I lay out a few examples of real-life psychics and their circumstances, primarily for entertainment purposes, too, as you'll see.

Okay . . . it's not all for entertainment. I want to do a bit of educating here. Seventy-three percent of Americans actually believe in paranormal activity, according to a Gallup poll conducted in 2005, with ESP being the belief most cited at forty-one percent. I'm ashamed of this. No wonder we're ranked seventeenth in the world in science (as well as twenty-fifth in math and fourteenth in reading). A whole bunch of us need to wake the F up, learn the scientific method so that it seeps into our bones, become card-carrying members of The Skeptics Society, and start taking more critical thinking and logic classes! There, . . . I said it.

Hey, guess what? I'm a psychic and can see the future. Not only do I predict that you'll keep reading, but also that you'll enjoy at least half of what you read below. Pretty amazing, huh?

Babylonian Astrologists (around 2000 B.C.E.)

What's your sign? I'm a Pisces, which according to Western astrologists means I'm adaptive, intuitive, introspective, generous, sensitive, artistic, and even a bit psychic. (I told you I was psychic!) Now, ask me if I actually exhibit any of these traits. Well, maybe two or three—all kidding aside, definitely not the psychic part!

Apparently, when the moon is at a certain stage, I'm supposed to prefer standing rather than sitting, and when the Earth is at a certain point in its orbit around the Sun, you'll find me in water or craving to be in water. Now, ask me if any of this BS is true for me. Astrologists attempt to link astronomical bodies (planets, stars, moons, meteorites, basically anything non-terrestrial) or the perceived movements of those bodies with human personalities, human behaviors, world events, or other earthly phenomena.

The Babylonians were among the first to systematize this pseudoscience, but astrology can be found interspersed with ancient Sumerian, Chinese, and Hindu beliefs, too. The stars fascinate us, no doubt, and we want to make sense of astronomical bodies in relation to our own third rock from the Sun, so it's understandable that people would have bought astrological beliefs up until about a hundred years ago. However, we're now living in an age where we know that the Earth isn't the center of the universe, and a full moon doesn't directly cause people to lose their inhibitions. Yet, we can read a horoscope in almost any daily newspaper which features supposedly clairvoyant predictions related to my water sign, Pisces, as well as the other eleven signs of the Western, tropical zodiac: Aries, Taurus, Gemini, Cancer, Leo, Virgo, Libra, Scorpio, Sagittarius, Capricornus, and Aquarius.

I just did an Internet search for my Pisces horoscope for today, and one "seer" said something like this: "You can't quite get a handle on your emotions right now, so don't bother trying to understand them precisely." And another seer on a site said this: "A moment of clarity today will help you to understand those feelings that have been bothering you." I think these two seers need to pow-wow and get their story straight! BTW, my wife's a Scorpio, so you know we were made for each other—after all, it's written in the stars. . . .

The Pythia or the Oracle at Delphi (around 800-400 B.C.E.)

Located on the slopes of Mount Parnassus in Greece, Delphi was a place where people would travel to meet with the Pythia, a priestess who supposedly had the ability to see the future, known in ESP circles as *precognition*. Now, almost every Intro to Philosophy student reads some Plato and his dialogue *Apology* is an account of the trial of Socrates, who was charged with atheism and corrupting the youth of Athens. We all know how it ends, with Socrates being found guilty and drinking hemlock. (Incidentally, do you know what Socrates's immortal last words were? "I just drank *what?!?*" Not really, just kidding.) Socrates apparently was pretty annoying to lots of folks in Athens—kind of like a pestering fly—going around challenging people who thought they were wise. In the *Apology* Socrates says that the main reason why he buzzed around Athens is that the oracle at Delphi claimed he was the wisest person in that city, and he wanted to test this claim to see if it was true or not. I wonder if he would've died a natural death—or been such a great mentor to Plato—if he *hadn't* taken the Pythia seriously.

The Pythia and Oedipus Rex (around 429 B.C.E.)

It's the age-old story: king hears from oracle that son will kill him; king asks servant to kill son; servant decides to abandon son instead; son gets found and raised by others; son grows up to kill king (his own father) unknowingly, marry queen (his own mother) to become king, have sex with and father two daughters with his own mother, find out about all of this eventually, and poke his own eyes out.

Oedipus Rex is an Athenian tragedy by Sophocles that still causes us to think, "That's some F-ed up sh@t" by the end of it. We also want to shower immediately afterward to wash the incest off. Eeeewwweee! As in Plato's dialogue, the Pythia figures into Sophocles's play, along with a couple of other oracles. This story has worked wonders throughout the years in getting people to believe in fate as well as psychic "seers" who claim to predict future events. Unfortunately, while no doubt one of the cleverest stories ever penned and an absolute must-see or must-read, I predict that lots of people will continue to believe (foolishly) in fate and charlatans who claim to "see" that fate.

Michel de Nostredame or Nostradamus (1503–1566)

"You will not find me alive at sunrise." This is what Nostradamus told his secretary while lying on his deathbed the night before he died. Some prediction, huh? He was *on his deathbed*, people!!!

This "prediction," along with several others Nostradamus penned throughout his lifetime, has not only helped to gain this sixteenth-century French pharmacist international fame, but also helped fetch an immense following who credit him with predicting numerous major world events that have occurred since his death in 1566.

He was pretty famous during his lifetime for his prognostications, with Catherine de Medici (wife of King Henry II of

France) making him the royal counselor and physician. There was a great show in the late 1970s hosted by Leonard Nimoy (Mr. Spock) called *In Search Of*, and I recall the episode where Nostradamus was featured and everyone was making a hubbub about how he "foresaw" Hitler and the Nazis with the following lines from his 1555 work, *Les Propheties* (*The Prophecies*):

> Beasts wild with hunger shall cross the rivers:
> Most of the fighting shall be close by the Hister,
> It shall result in the great one being dragged in an iron cage,
> While the German shall be watching over the infant Rhine.

People today continue to make so much of how 'Hister' looks awfully close to 'Hitler'. Unbeknownst to the wackos who still think Nostradamus was psychic, Nostradamus himself explains in one of the almanacs he wrote in 1554 that 'Hister' is the Latin name for the Danube River. And beasts were and still are constantly crossing rivers, and people were and still are dragged in iron cages, and Germans were and still are constantly "watching over" the Rhine River! In fact, when you read *The Prophecies*, Nostradamus claims all kinds of things that really aren't out of the ordinary about wars and all kinds of other horrible things (and happy, positive things, too) that regularly occur throughout human history. So, when seen in the grand scheme of things, Nostradamus wrote about the future, making well informed guesses and inferences, just like any educated person. And, of course, he played on superstitious fears and started believing his own hype since people couldn't get enough of his apocalyptic writings.

Helena Blavatsky (1831–1891)

It's funny that Gus doesn't believe in psychic abilities, but he does believe in UFO abductions ("Not Even Close . . . Encounters"), werewolves ("Let's Get Hairy"), demonic possessions ("The Devil's in the Details, and in the Upstairs Bedroom"), ghosts ("Who Ya Gonna Call?"), and probably other supernatural-ish stuff. Gus has much in common with Helena Blavatsky, a self-professed medium and the founder of the Theosophical Society in 1875, a "research" institute where

Hinduism meets Buddhism meets Daoism meets Jainism meets Judaism meets Islam meets Christianity meets extraterrestrials meets the occult. The tenets of the Theosophical Society are claimed to be *esoteric*, meaning that they're so bizarre, confusing, and outlandishly false that only weirdos can understand them.

Sometimes the ability to communicate with the dead is considered a psychic ability, referred to as the *sixth sense*. Blavatsky apparently made a living before her theosophical pursuits as a circus bareback rider as well as séance medium, complete with a levitating table and crystal ball. Speaking of séances, I always find it fascinating that people will play with a Ouija board and claim that the heart-shaped planchette that they place their hands on "moves by itself," indicating that someone from the "other side" is supposedly moving it. Now, I'm not the sharpest tool in the shed, but your fingers *are* on the planchette when it's moving, right, or did I miss something?

Edgar Cayce (1877–1945)

Known as the Sleeping Prophet because he would make predictions while in some kind of self-hypnotic trance, Cayce was at the forefront of the New Age Movement of the early twentieth century, which combined a shallow understanding of quantum physics with astrology, dream interpretation, karma, reincarnated souls, dietary restrictions, holistic medicine, and, of course, ESP.

Like Nostradamus, Cayce remained a Christian his entire life, and he thought that while humans talk to God in prayer, God talks back to humans in meditation. This idea was not all that new to Christianity given the tradition of meditation found in Christian mysticism dating back to early medieval Europe. (I was actually in the seminary studying to be a Catholic Priest for the Archdiocese of Chicago from 1984 to 1993—can you believe that!?—and seminarians would often go on retreats to meditate so as to "discern God's will" for their lives.)

Near the end of his life, Cayce claimed he could travel outside of his own body, something called *astral projection* or an *out-of-body experience*. (I hear *The Twilight Zone* theme playing in my mind for some reason.) He also thought that Atlantis was a real place and that after it was destroyed by a big crystal power overload, killing all on the island, most people on the Earth today contain the reincarnated souls of these folks from Atlantis. No wonder I have such an affinity for the beach and the ocean! And I thought it was just because I'm a Pisces.

Harry Houdini, the Original Ghostbuster (1874–1926)

This guy actually fought against psycho psychics. Months before he died in October of 1926, Houdini went to hearings in Washington, DC, to testify before the House of Representatives that he was a showman, he knew he was performing stage magic (nothing but tricks), and that he also went around challenging others who claimed to be psychic and were charging money for such services. At the hearings he even performed a few magic tricks and explained how they were done.

Houdini was well-known and hated by many psychics, mediums, and other occultists in his day, being a card-carrying member of the *Scientific American* committee and offering big cash rewards to anyone who could truly demonstrate a psychic ability. No one ever collected. At the end of several days of testimony, one of the congressmen from New York put forward a bill which included the following:

> Any person pretending to tell fortunes for reward or compensation where lost or stolen goods may be found; any person who, by game or device, sleight of hand, pretending, fortune-telling, or by any trick or other means, by the use of cards or other implements or instruments, fraudulently obtains from another person money or property or reward, property of any description; any person pretending to remove spells, or to sell charms for protection, or to unite the separated, shall be considered a disorderly person . . . and shall be punished by a fine not to exceed $250 or by imprisonment not to exceed six months, or by both such fine and imprisonment.

$250 was a lot of cashola back then, and I'm encouraged that the leaders of our country recognized that this stuff is all mumbo jumbo (or juju-magumbo, as Shawn might say) and the work of charlatans. Houdini died of a ruptured appendix, poor guy; although, it would've been more glamorous, I bet, if he had died while doing one of his neato trapped-under-water-in-a-straightjacket stunts.

Stefan Ossowiecki (1877-1944)

This is one of those guys who hated Houdini, and he likely would've had to pay the $250, if he'd lived in New York City and tried swindling folks with his claimed abilities. Seeing objects inside of sealed containers, talking to the dead, transporting his mind to the other side of the planet, and moving things with his mind are all abilities Ossowiecki claimed to have while living most of his life in Moscow. He was a big influence on Hans Bender (1907–1991), who was one of the biggest figures in parapsychology and founder of the Institut für Grenzgebiete der Psychologie und Psychohygiene in Freiburg.

In their 2005 book, *A World In A Grain Of Sand: The Clairvoyance Of Stefan Ossowiecki*, Mary Rose Barrington, Ian Stevenson, and Zofia Weaver claim that Ossowiecki was the real deal, "the most gifted psychic ever to come under the scrutiny of researchers." In May of 1939 Ossowiecki made the predictions that, in the near future, Poland and Italy would remain allies and Poland would not go to war. However, as we all know, the Germans invaded Poland just a few months later on September 1st, World War II began, and Italy remained an ally of Germany along with other Axis powers. Given the geopolitical moves of Mussolini and especially Hitler in the late 1930s, a friggin' high schooler living anywhere in a civilized society in May of 1939 who had access to a newspaper could have predicted that Poland was headed for war and that the already strained relationship between Poland and Italy would collapse—especially Polish high schoolers! The "most gifted psychic ever" my ass!

Peter Hurkos (1911-1988)

"I see pictures in my mind like a television screen. When I touch something, I can then tell what I see." So claimed Hurkos of his clairvoyant abilities. But when you think about it, every person with a normal-functioning nervous system can do the exact same thing.

Hurkos made a name for himself in two ways. First, as a cold reader, where he would use high-probability guesses and inferences about a person based upon body language, mannerisms, and other features to make it look as if he could read their thoughts or memories. Like any gifted cold reader, Hurkos quickly picked up on signals from people as to whether his guesses were in the right direction or not, and then highlighted any lucky-guess connections that the person acknowledged while glossing over missed guesses. The result: cha-ching! He made lots of dough this way. Hurkos also was a psychic detective in some thirty cases throughout his life, but he apparently lied several times about being successful at solving a case.

His "talents" were used famously and unsuccessfully by police in the early 1960s for the Boston Strangler serial killings. Why do the police use a psychic detective in the first place? Usually because they're at a dead end. And it's not that police actually believe in someone's psychic abilities; it's more that a person can offer a fresh set of eyes on the case. Or, as in real-world cases that are similar to that of Shawn Spencer, someone has a sharp mind and a decent eye for detail, making for a good detective and an even better liar.

Uri Geller (born 1946)

The other day I was in a restaurant with my family that featured a magician, and he came up to the table, picked up the spoon I had just used to stir my tea, and I watched as he apparently made it bend right before my eyes. Of course, he showed me how it worked, having already bent another spoon and cleverly replaced that spoon with my teaspoon with his sleight of hand; however, there are other ways to perform the trick, including using spoons made of a substance that bends due to heat from one's fingers.

Uri Geller made headlines starting in the 1970s with supposed telekinetic abilities—which he claims to have received from extraterrestrials—to include bending spoons. When appearing on *The Tonight Show* with Johnny Carson in 1973, he didn't feel "strong" and was unable to bend any spoons since they weren't his own props and had been selected for him. Talk about a guy who wants to capitalize on his own hype: Geller has sued or attempted to sue numerous people and organizations throughout the years for libel, slander, and inappropriate use of his name.

You'd think that someone with such an impressive teleki-netic ability could cause pens to sign documents, or gavels in courtrooms to pound, or even lips to move, ruling in his favor. In the late 1990s, the furniture store Ikea featured something called a Uri Stool, which had bent wooden legs, and apparently Geller was considering suing that company. Why couldn't he have just *unbent* the wooden legs and be done with it?

Sylvia Browne (born 1936)

I recall seeing Browne on *The Montel Williams Show* in the 1990s as she would appear in a segment called "Sylvia Wednesdays" where she'd take questions from the audience, do some cold reading, and make predictions about world events. One time I recall her saying something along the lines of, "People will never be convinced unless they open their minds and are willing to believe." Speaking of predictions, it's absolutely fasci-nating that Browne has acquired such fame and fortune as a psychic since basically every single one of her predictions has not even been close to being on target. Maybe it's because she's so adamant about her abilities and she makes for easy pickin's. When I was a graduate student in philosophy at Saint Louis University, Browne made national news in 2003 with a local case featuring missing eleven-year-old Shawn Hornbeck, who had been missing since 2002. Browne claimed that Hornbeck was dead, had been abducted by a tall guy with long black dreadlocks in a blue sedan, and that his body was located near two large rocks in the woods some twenty miles southwest of Richwoods, Missouri. Of course, this caused a flurry of tips being called in, along with massive man-hours spent combing the wooded areas looking for the rocks. In 2007, Hornbeck was found very much alive, he had been abducted by Michael J. Devlin, an average-sized man with short brown hair in a small white pickup truck who's now serving seventy-four life sentences. She once claimed, "Psychics can never be one hundred percent. I think that would be scary to be one hundred percent." Yes, that would be scary.

John Edward (born 1969)

If you'd like a fairly accurate demonstration of how almost all cold readings work, you've got to watch Will Farrell's skit on

Saturday Night Live where he parodies *Crossing Over with John Edward.*

Playing Edward, Farrell begins by focusing on one area of the studio audience claiming, "I'm getting a woman's name starting with a J." When everyone looks around confused, he moves on to the letter K, then R, then F, and finally a woman says, "I know someone whose name begins with F." It's actually not the woman's dead mom, grandmother, or aunt, but the lady sitting next to her who came with her to the taping of the show! And the SNL audience, as well as all of us watching at home, laughs.

Edward combines cold reading with mediumship, and, like so many other psychics, he claims that his ability to communicate with the dead is a gift from God. On the one hand, I think that if Edward pretends to talk to someone's dead relative or friend and can give that gullible person a sense of emotional closure and peace, then let him do it. On the other hand, well, it's a lie that often comes with a price tag. However, according to Michael Shermer, Edward kind of stinks at cold reading, being correct between ten and twenty percent of the time, as opposed to the 1990s psychic phenom, James Van Praagh (born 1958), whose track record is twenty to thirty percent.

James Randi (born 1928)

This guy's not a psycho psychic but instead has devoted his life's efforts since retiring as a stage magician to debunking psychics and other dishonest tricksters. He started the James Randi Educational Foundation in 1996 to "promote critical thinking by reaching out to the public and media with reliable information about paranormal and supernatural ideas so widespread in our society today."

Since 2003, Randi's foundation has put on The Amaz!ng Meeting, a conference featuring scientists, atheists, skeptics, and other rational folks (if you don't see my bias by now, you're obviously not reading this section). Through the One Million Dollar Paranormal Challenge, Randi will give a million dollars to anyone who can demonstrate paranormal abilities under conditions agreed upon by Randi and the person taking the challenge. Of course, no one has ever claimed the cash, though over a thousand folks have applied to be tested. Magicians

Penn Jilette and Raymond Joseph Teller are big supporters of Randi, and also had a great show on Showtime from 2003 to 2010 called *Penn & Teller: Bullshit*, that everyone should watch. It's refreshing to see magicians such as Randi and Penn and Teller following in the footsteps of Houdini by debunking psycho psychics and other scammers who take advantage of the not-so-smart people on this planet.

We've all probably heard the phrase, "There's a sucker born every minute." My advice is to try to act like a person who was born in the fifty-nine seconds in between.

The (I Know You) Know-It-Alls

ROBERT ARP, PhD, is a data analyst and modeler working for the US Army. He has authored and edited numerous works in the philosophy and pop culture realm, and in other areas of philosophy, too. See robertarp.webs.com.

Rob's Psychic Prediction: Honey Boo Boo becomes the 56th President of the US.

GREGORY L. BOCK, PhD, is an associate professor of philosophy at Walters State Community College in Morristown, Tennessee. He has authored several journal articles in the areas of ethics and the philosophy of religion, and he co-authored a chapter in *The Big Bang Theory and Philosophy* with his brother Jeff.

Greg's Psychic Prediction: Some people will buy this book thinking it has something to do with psychology and will inevitably feel lied to.

JEFFREY L. BOCK is an operations manager in a small web marketing company in Longview, Texas. His master's degree is in history from the University of Texas at Tyler, and he regularly pretends to be a philosopher and fiction writer in his spare time.

Jeff's Psychic Prediction: No matter who writes and directs the next *Star Wars* movies, fans will be disappointed.

PATRICIA BRACE, PhD, is Professor of Art History at Southwest Minnesota State University, in Marshall, Minnesota. She has contributed chapters to *Dexter and Philosophy: Mind Over Spatter*, *The Philosophy of Joss Whedon* and several other pop culture volumes with co-writer Rob Arp.

Pat's Psychic Prediction: By the year 2025, Facebook will rule the planet. A cadre of resistance fighters, led by the neo-Luddite faction, will disrupt the Net, de-friending billions. In the world-wide panic, the zombie apocalypse begins, as the feedback loop to the implants destroys the brains of those who refused to heed warnings and disconnect in time . . .

CRISTINA CEBALLOS is a Physics and Philosophy student at Yale University. She focuses on normative ethics, especially the ethics of lying, and has been published in the SUNY Oneonta 2012 Conference Review.

Cristina's Psychic Prediction: In twenty years, we will no longer need driver's licenses because cars will drive themselves.

JEFF EWING is a graduate student in sociology at the University of Oregon. He has written a number of chapters connecting popular culture to philosophy, including chapters in *Terminator and Philosophy* and *Arrested Development and Philosophy*.

Jeff's Psychic Prediction: In the year 2123 we will learn that the whole universe is really a computer simulation when one night, all of a sudden, all visible space turns to a Blue Screen of Death.

LAURA GUIDRY-GRIMES, MA, is a philosophy PhD candidate at Georgetown University. She has co-authored articles on research ethics and vulnerability in medical contexts. In her dissertation, she plans on exploring issues at the intersection of psychiatric ethics and social justice.

Laura's Psychic Prediction: James Roday and Dulé Hill will invite all of the contributors to this book to a fancy Hollywood party . . . or at least send each of us an autographed pineapple.

DENA HURST, PhD, is an instructor, researcher, and leadership consultant for the Florida Institute of Government at Florida State University. She has authored and edited numerous works on leadership and public policy issues including diversity, gender, and class theory. She co-authored a leadership guidebook, *Oracle of the Obvious: Secrets to Leadership*, and more enjoyably has written articles and chapters on philosophy and popular culture. See www.denahurst.com.

Dena's Psychic Predictions: Godot will return and wonder what all the hoopla was about. There will be a momentary glitch in the Matrix during which we will all be able to see that Mitt Romney is Agent Smith. There will be another superstorm after which New Yorkers will awaken to see the head of Lady Liberty protruding from a sandy beach, and ape-like cries will echo in the distance. (too soon, perhaps?) Geneticists will discover that there is a ninety percent similarity between human and cat genes. Oh, wait . . . and, of course, Hobbits will be discovered living in the New York sewer system.

CYNTHIA JONES, PhD is an associate professor of philosophy and Director of the Coalition Against Violence and Exploitation (CAVE) Program, the Gelman Constitutional Scholars Program, and the Pan American Collaboration for Ethics (PACE) at the University of Texas Pan American. She publishes and researches in bioethics, ethics and technology, intelligence ethics, and pop culture. Some of her recent publications appear in the *American Journal of Public Health*, *Teaching Ethics*, and *The Onion and Philosophy: Fake News Story True, Alleges Indignant Area Professor*.

Cynthia's Psychic Prediction: Gus definitely will or will not find a real girlfriend soon.

SKYLER KING is studying English and philosophy at the University of Missouri-Kansas City. Besides writing for this volume and others, he is working on a novel that will hopefully be published upon completion. If you are interested in reading more of his philosophical writings, visit **unmitigatedreasoning.wordpress.com**.

Skyler's Psychic Prediction: CERN will discover the graviton within the next ten years, which will lead to the mass production of elite Spartan soldiers and Gravity-Hammers.

COURTLAND LEWIS, PhD, is a visiting assistant professor at the University of Alabama at Birmingham. He co-edited *Doctor Who and Philosophy: Bigger on the Inside* with Paula Smithka and is currently co-editing *Futurama and Philosophy* with Shaun Young. His main area of research deals with ethics, justice, and issues of forgiveness.

Courtland's Psychic Prediction: 2014 will be the year aliens make first contact with Earth, and philosophers will broker a deal with them that leads to the eradication of poverty, hunger, and war.

AMANDA LUSKY, MA, is a philosophy graduate student at the University of Kentucky. Her areas of research include pragmatism, philosophy of mind, and cognitive science.

Amanda's Psychic Predictions: Email and texting service sent by thoughts debuts in 2017 and instantly yields disastrous consequences. Cats try to take over the world in 2021 but are quickly sidetracked by the sound of a can opener. Gus finally becomes a player.

JAMES EDWIN MAHON, PHD, is Professor of Philosophy and Chair of the Department of Philosophy at Washington and Lee University. He's the author of "The Truth About Kant On Lies" in *The Philosophy of Deception* (2009) and "Lying for the Sake of the Truth: The Ethics of Deceptive Journalism" in *Contemporary Media Ethics* (forthcoming), as well as "The Definition of Lying and Deception" for the *Stanford Encyclopedia of Philosophy.*

James's Psychic Prediction: The late 1980s and early 1990s will eventually be known as the apex of human civilization.

DANIEL P. MALLOY, PHD, is a lecturer in philosophy at Appalachian State University. His research focuses on issues in ethics. He has published numerous chapters on the intersection of popular culture and philosophy, particularly dealing with the illustration of moral questions in movies, comic books, and television shows.

Daniel's Psychic Prediction: After the coming apocalypse, philosopher-kings will be given free rein to rule the world according to the principles of reason and justice. This will lead to a second apocalypse almost immediately.

BENJAMIN MCCRAW, PHD, teaches philosophy at the University of South Carolina Upstate. His research focuses on issues in epistemology and philosophy of religion; especially in their intersection in religious epistemology.

Benjamin's Psychic Prediction: The world will end on December 21st, 2022 (the Mayans forgot to carry the one).

NICOLAS MICHAUD is a philosophy teacher at Florida State College Jacksonville and Jacksonville University. He regularly writes chapters for the philosophy and popular culture genre, co-edited *The Hunger Games and Philosophy*, and is editing *Frankenstein and Philosophy*. He often is a guest speaker and lecturer on topics in philosophy, leadership, and education. See www.amazon/author/nicolasmichaud.

Nick's Psychic Prediction: Tapioca pudding is the next evolutionary stage of intelligent life and will shortly take over the world.

MICHAEL J. MUNIZ, MA, is currently pursuing a PhD in philosophy. He has written several short stories and a novelette, though this is his first major contribution to "serious" philosophy. He was a high school teacher in Miami before moving on to the higher paying job of Grad Assistant.

Michael's Psychic Prediction: The iPhone 6 will bring about the Apocalypse.

COURTNEY NEAL is a graduate student at DePaul University and has studied death and resurrection in sci-fi and fantasy TV.

Courtney's Psychic Prediction: The moon will be colonized in 2052 and christened "New Florida" in 2055, becoming the galaxy's biggest tourist trap.

RONDA (BOWEN) ROBERTS owns WRE Consulting Services, an editorial consulting business, and is an independent scholar. She has written numerous articles on philosophy, business, education, current events, wine, and computer technology. See writingresearchediting .com and winingwife.com.

Ronda's Psychic Prediction: Through the creation of a new genetically engineered crop—the applange—things will no longer be as different as apples and oranges.

JAMES ROCHA, PhD, is a fake, psychic assistant professor of philosophy at Louisiana State University, who makes "predictions" in Kantian ethics (you will have to do your duty and you won't like it), feminist philosophy (the sexes will one day learn to live together), and philosophy of race (Gus will be confused with a black actor you've never heard of).

James's Psychic Prediction: By the middle of the twenty-first century, (fake) psychic philosophers will be the rock stars of America, touring the country predicting that there will be people confusing the Morning Star with the Evening Star, people drinking twater who think they are drinking water, and even more violations of the categorical imperative.

MONA ROCHA is completing her dissertation in Women's History at Louisiana State University. She specializes in militant feminism, concentrating on the feminist message of women in militant groups such as the Weather Underground and the Black Panther Party. She has written papers in history as well as feminist philosophy and philosophy and pop culture.

Mona's Psychic Prediction: *Psych* will outlast all of the TV shows that copy it, and eventually *The Mentalist* will have an episode where someone accidentally calls Jane, "Shawn."

ROBERTO RUIZ is lecturer in philosophy and ethics at Bergen and LaGuardia community colleges. He has previously contributed to *The Onion and Philosophy: Fake News Story True, Alleges Indignant Area Professor*, and runs the science and philosophy blog, Philosophy Monkey (http://berto-meister.blogspot.com). His interests include the philosophy of science, evolutionary psychology, female anatomy, and burritos (not necessarily in that order).

Roberto's Psychic Prediction: He's got some news for you: "I don't want to burst your bubble, but Chairman Meow is Chair*woman* Meow."

THOMAS D. SENOR, PHD, is Professor of Philosophy at the University of Arkansas. He works in philosophy of religion and epistemology; his papers are available at philpapers.org.
GRAHAM D. SENOR is a philosophy major at Hendrix College.

The Senors' Psychic Predication: The GOP will nominate Jesus Christ for President of the United States at their 2016 convention; He will decline the nomination.

C. SCOTT SEVIER, PHD, is Visiting Assistant Professor of Philosophy at California State University, Fullerton. He specializes in Medieval Philosophy, Renaissance Fairs, and cinnamon festivals—not necessarily in that order.

Scott's Psychic Prediction: By 2020, cinnamon will have become the world's most popular condiment. Most popular item to dip in cinnamon? Fries Quatro Queso Dos Fritos—it's fresh to death!

JEFFREY E. STEPHENSON, PHD, is a visiting assistant professor of philosophy at Montana State University, Bozeman. He has published in character and morality, social justice and healthcare, and human subjects research ethics.

Jeff's Psychic Prediction: None of the predictions offered by the authors in this volume will come true.

JOHN M. THOMPSON, PHD, teaches religion and philosophy at Christopher Newport University in Southeast Virginia. He specializes in East Asian traditions and Buddhism but has very eclectic interests—mainly cartoons, rock'n'roll, taekwondo, and spending time with his beautiful wife and two daughters.

John's Psychic Prediction: "Squirrelassassins.com" will soon become the world's most popular website; all those who visit will be given a free pineapple.

DAN YIM, PHD, teaches philosophy at Bethel University in St. Paul, Minnesota. He researches race and gender and metaphysics, and has published some articles in early modern philosophy, contributed a chapter to *Fashion: Philosophy for Everyone*, and written on friendship in *30 Rock and Philosophy*.

Dan's Psychic Prediction: As marijuana continues to be legalized across the US, demand for snack products will outpace production capacity. The munchies will result in a vast, well-funded underground criminal network stealing and trading in snack products. Armored car companies will add Doritos to their list of clients.

Index